THE
MASTER
MARKETER

**HOW TO COMBINE TRIED AND TESTED TECHNIQUES
WITH THE LATEST IDEAS TO ACHIEVE
SPECTACULAR MARKETING SUCCESS**

CHRISTOPHER RYAN

**KOGAN
PAGE**

First published in the USA in 1993 by IdealWorks Publishing Inc.
UK edition published in 1994 by Kogan Page Ltd.

Kogan Page Limited
120 Pentonville Road
London N1 9JN

British Library Cataloguing in Publication Data
A CIP record for this book is available from the British Library.

ISBN 0 7494 1233 X

Typeset by BookEns Ltd., Baldock, Herts.
Printed and bound in Great Britain by Biddles Ltd, Guildford and Kings Lynn

TABLE OF CONTENTS

FOREWORD

Throughout my career, I've read and reviewed literally hundreds of books on the subject of marketing. Many of them are superb. Several remain in my office library. I keep a special few near my desk for reference. This book is one of those special few.

This book does not delve deeply into any one area of marketing. It does, however, offer a detailed overview that can point you in the right direction. Different situations demand different tactics. It can help you discover the specific marketing tool needed to solve a particular marketing problem.

By itself, one piece of advice, a Core Master Marketing Principle outline in the first chapter – "*If you can't measure it, don't do it*" – is worth more than the price of the book. However, there are 11 others of equal, or greater, value.

Level the Playing Field for Your Clients

Consultants and agency executives may want to keep a few copies on hand for clients. There's hardly a business on either side of the Atlantic (perhaps some small retailers) that doesn't use some form of direct marketing.

Yet, many executives will actually deny doing so when asked . . . and, they aren't lying. It's a matter of semantics. They know what they do. They just don't call what they do direct marketing.

Personally, I find it much easier to work with people who speak the same "language" as I do, and I don't mean English! A real advantage of The Master Marketer is its concise explanations of marketing terms, concepts and vocabulary. A copy in the hands of your client can save a lot of lost time and money for both of you.

A Textbook by Pros for Pros

It would be wonderful, too, to see more books such as this one in college and university marketing classrooms. All too often the marketing texts are written by those who "teach" marketing, not those who actually "practise it." This book is written by practising professionals who understand marketing in Europe, in the US and around the globe. It is about the real, not theoretical, world of marketing.

Jo Anne Parke
President
International Marketing Resources, Inc.
December 1993

ACKNOWLEDGEMENTS

Erik Carlgren and Howard Schwartz had a great deal to do with bringing the book alive in a unique way. Erik and Howard developed the wizard theme and the many cartoons. Erik pulled double duty by laying out the book and creating every illustration. I am sure the readers of this book will appreciate Erik's superb handiwork as much as I do.

My appreciation to Susan Belttari for her many editorial suggestions, which are reflected throughout the book. My friends and colleagues Maureen Mudd and Sunny Quay also made important editorial contributions. I am also in the debt of the clients, co-workers and associates who seem to teach me something new every day. Included in this number are Stacy Dean, Susan Fenley, Tom Hight, Dennis Kless, Joel Ratner, Alan Ritchie, Eric Rosenberg, Mick Sutter, Admiral William Thompson, Jennifer Walker, Steve Yinger and my fellow board members of the Direct Marketing Association of Washington.

Thanks to those who inspired me with their wisdom and writings, including Mary Carroll, Bernie Goldberg, Denny Hatch. Norman Hecht, Roland Kuniholm, Donald Libey, Catherine Lincoln, Bruce McBrearty, John McCullough, Richard Miller, Barbara Rains, Anita Shelare, Robert Strock and Julie White. My long-time friend Ginger Miller also provided much needed encouragement and many practical suggestions that helped get the book off to a good start.

A special note of gratitude to Drayton Bird for his excellent chapter on international marketing, and to my publisher, Philip Mudd, who made the entire process pain-free. And I can't forget Jo Anne Parke, who not only wrote an excellent Foreword, but whose wise counsel and friendship have had an important impact on my career. Jo Anne has often proved the old adage: one person can make a big difference.

This book is dedicated with love
to two future Master Marketers,
my sons Michael Harrison Ryan and
Colin Matthew Ryan.

INTRODUCTION

*"The Great Obstacle to Progress is Not
Ignorance but the Illusion of Knowledge"*
Daniel Boorstin

*W*elcome to <u>The Master Marketer</u>. Since you and I will be spending many hours together throughout these pages, I thought you would like to know why I wrote this book and what you can expect to get out of reading <u>The Master Marketer</u>.

Technology, as well as lifestyle and demographic changes, has transformed the face of marketing. We not only have different means for delivering our messages to potential consumers, but those consumers themselves have changed quite a bit. For example, if you market to businesses, you will be more likely to deal with a Ms. Rodriguez, and less likely to deal with a Mr. Smith.

If you market to consumers at home, your audience is matur-

ing rapidly, both in years and in their level of marketing sophisti-
cation. Amazingly, the average first year pupil today is exposed to
more advertising in one year than was Benjamin Franklin over
his entire lifetime. This does not necessarily make the student a
more discerning consumer, but it certainly makes it harder to capture his attention.

I believe it is not just the social change that we find difficult
to cope with, but the very pace of that change. Experts believe that
mankind has gained more knowledge in the past 40 years than in
all recorded history up to that point. Many (including this author)
feel that our understanding of the inner core of human emotions
and intellect has not kept up with our technological evolution.
This is why we are a nation of so many "haves" and "have-nots,"
and why, at the dawn of "genetic engineering" and "virtual reality," as much as one-quarter of the adult population is functionally
illiterate.

How is one to cope with these seismic shifts in audience and
technology? The answer is two-fold. First, you must make a
commitment to learning. The half-life of a technical undergraduate
college education is now less than five years. Understand what
this means; five years after you graduate, 50 percent of what you
learned will be obsolete, or at the least it will be out-of-date.

Despite this fact, fully 60 percent of Americans never read a
complete book after their formal education is complete. Equally
surprising, only four percent of the population own library cards,
even though they are free in most communities. I confess I have a
hard time understanding this, because to me, a library card has
always been like holding the keys to the sweet shop.

When interviewing candidates for positions at my agency, you
would be surprised how many become speechless when I ask,
"What's the name of the last book you've read on advertising or
marketing?" Often, an individual who has been out of school for
ten years or more will give me the name of his college textbook.
This is inexcusable in an era of intense global competition. Or, as

my late grandfather used to put it so eloquently, "Ignorance is not a valid excuse for not being able to feed your family."

Fortunately, the last several paragraphs don't apply to you. You are definitely committed to learning, or you wouldn't be reading these words. So what is the second secret, the one that you can use to stay on top of the marketing game and ahead of your competition?

Secret number two is to become a "Master Marketer." And that is the purpose of this book: to teach you how to be a Master Marketer. But let's get down to brass tacks. How do I define a Master Marketer and how will you know if you feel comfortable claiming that title for yourself? As a Master Marketer:

- You have a thorough grounding in the timeless fundamentals of marketing
- You understand people and what motivates them
- You are open to the newest ideas and techniques
- You have fully developed your creative potential
- You possess the confidence to take risks (educated risks)
- You aren't afraid to make mistakes and treat them as learning opportunities.

I sincerely hope that you will find this book a great help in your quest to become a Master Marketer. It is a collection of ideas, strategies and techniques honed from my years of experience on both the client and agency side. If your organization markets directly to businesses or consumers, you will find a wealth of practical, how-to ideas and techniques.

On the other hand, if like me, you make your living on the agency side of the business, you will learn many new strategies to help you better serve your clients and keep them away from the hungry competition.

While I have been fortunate to have achieved many successes, some of which you will read about, perhaps my most valuable lessons came from mistakes, which I will also share. The pain of these mistakes is a poignant reminder that knowing what NOT to do is often more important than knowing what to do.

The book's 35 chapters are organized into seven sections. The first is Master Marketing Concepts, which includes fundamentals that will lay the groundwork for every marketing project as well as explore some of the harmful myths prevalent in marketing. Section Two, Basic Master Marketing Skills, covers marketing research, positioning, creative strategy, copywriting, and how to find good suppliers.

Section Three, Choosing the Best Marketing Weapons, demonstrates how to select the best media tools from the print, broadcast, television, seminar, trade show, public relations, and other media choices available, and also explains how to get the best results from each. Section Four, Direct Marketing, provides an in-depth look at this powerful marketing medium, including finding the best prospects, direct mail, telemarketing, database marketing, and how to use the computer as a marketing tool.

Section Five, Marketing Strategies for Unique Circumstances, covers strategies to use if you are involved in business-to-business marketing, lead generation, fund-raising, or international marketing. It also includes chapters on how to bring a new product to market and how you can make a large impact when working with a small budget.

Section Six is called Master Marketing Graduate School, and outlines skills that will move you ahead of your competitors, such as: how to be super creative, relationship marketing, how to keep customers for life, self promotional strategies, and how to prepare for the future. Section Seven leaves you with four important resources: a series of worksheets you can use to plan and implement a marketing campaign, a guide to advertising and marketing industry groups, a guide to helpful publications, and a glossary of useful terms.

As for the wizard...you might wonder why he is used as a

symbol throughout the book. The idea was conceived in a strategy meeting with my colleagues Joel Ratner, Howard Schwartz and Pam Whitlinger. We were searching for a graphic symbol that conveyed the message of the book - timeless fundamentals combined with the newest technology.

Voila! the wizard was born. He is modeled after Merlin, from the fable of Camelot. If you recall, according to legend, Merlin was King Arthur's "Master Marketer." He would appear in desperate situations to supply Arthur with suitable advice (timeless fundamentals) and, if necessary, cast an appropriate spell (newest technology).

I hope the wizard helps convince you that marketing can be fun. Finally, I wish you the best of success in all of your Master Marketing endeavors.

SECTION I

MASTER MARKETING CONCEPTS

CORE PRINCIPLE TEN: "DO NO HARM"

CORE MASTER MARKETING PRINCIPLES

*S*uccessful individuals in business, sports and the arts all have one thing in common: they practice the fundamentals. The broadcaster Alistair Cook recalled a story of the famous jazz pianist Earl Hines who spent two to three hours every morning practising just to keep the fingers loose!

While I make no claim to be a marketing equivalent of Earl Hines I would like to share with you 11 basic principles of marketing that can build a solid foundation for all your future marketing efforts. This is a good way for us to start our journey together in this book because, by following these core principles you will always achieve success, regardless of your product, budget, target audience or choice of marketing media.

Core Principle One - Start with a Clear Set of Objectives.
Just as an archer cannot hit a target he doesn't see, so too are we
prevented from achieving marketing objectives we have not
thought through and quantified. Master Marketers can always tell
you their objectives because they know that marketing programmes
without objectives are rarely successful. The method of setting
objectives is covered in detail in the chapters on creating a marketing plan.

**Core Principle Two - Make Identification of Your
Prospects a Top Priority.** It may sound simplistic, but you only
need to ask yourself two questions to start identifying your market.
First, who are the people most likely to do business with me (buy
my product, use my services, join my organization or donate to my
cause)? Second, who are the people who are least likely to do
business with me?

Although these questions seem easy, coming up with the
answers is not. As you will read later, identifying your target
audience can be a tricky proposition. Knowing only the rough
parameters of your market universe is not enough. I don't know
how many times I've asked a new client to define his prospect base
only to be answered, "the Fortune 500." When you hear this often
enough you know you are going to have to dig much deeper to get
a realistic picture of the true market.

**Core Principle Three - Build Your Marketing Programs
Around a BIG IDEA.** We've all heard the Better Mousetrap
Theory - "Build a better mousetrap and the world will beat a path
to your door." Or as Lee Iacocca put it, "When the product is
right, you don't have to be a great marketer." While both state-

4

ments are well intentioned, they are wrong.

The truth is, even a great product has to be marketed properly to succeed. Cream may always rise to the top but products and companies must be pushed to the top. And the best way of pushing a product to the top is through the development of a <u>BIG IDEA</u>. Your BIG IDEA is that competitive point-of-difference. It is the value-added extra that makes what you offer unique and better than your competitors.

As they say in Alaska, unless you're the lead sled dog, the view is always the same. So develop your <u>BIG IDEA</u> and change your view for the better.

Core Principle Four - Be a Target Marketer, Not a Mass Marketer. Marketing used to be a mass-market game. Competition was weaker, advertising costs were lower, and companies could make a lot of money running scores of advertisements or sending out tons of direct mail packages.

Today, costs are higher and prospects are bombarded with more advertising messages than they can absorb. As a result, response rates have dropped — in some industries they are only one-third to one-half of previous levels.

The solution to this problem is called "target marketing." With target marketing, we spend more on each prospect communication, but because we have qualified the audience so precisely, we run fewer ads, and put fewer packages into the mail. The bottom-line benefit is that, even in times of declining response, your marketing efforts can beat the trend and the cost of achieving each new dollar of sales can decrease.

Core Principle Five - All Good Marketing is Based on Relationship Building. Organizations will only be successful in the future to the degree that they are able to build relationships between their firms and their prospects, whether they are customers, donors or members. A later chapter will show you how to use each part of your marketing campaign to build the relationship, including the advertising medium, offer, target audience, message and graphics.

Core Principle Six - Test, Test, Test, if You Want to Sell, Sell, Sell! Testing is the marketing activity that can help improve your results the most. Renowned advertising genius David Ogilvy said, "The most important word in the vocabulary of advertising is TEST."

An ideal test has three requirements. First, it must be measurable. Never test something you can't measure.

Second, the test must be valid. For instance, testing which of two print ads works best is fine, unless you are testing each ad in a different publication. Then the test would be invalid because you are introducing two variables — the ads themselves and the publications.

The third test requirement is significance. Changing one test variable should have the potential to have a big impact on results.

Five components to consider when testing: the offer, the make-up of your audience, the price of your product or service, the copy and the graphics. Develop the habit of testing and you will definitely improve your marketing results over time.

Core Principle Seven - Practice Integrity and Congruence in Your Marketing Communications. The best virtue you can achieve in advertising is congruence. By "congruence," I mean the message communicated should match the reality of what the customer can expect at the point-of-service.

Unfortunately, examples of advertising that lack congruence are all too available. When a bank advertises that "long lines are a thing of the past," and you go to that bank and wait in a long line, that's incongruent. When a company promises a full-satisfaction guarantee, and you practically have to beg to get your money back, that's incongruent. Customers will never forgive you if you betray their faith, so you are far better off leaving inaccurate messages out of your copy.

To be an effective marketer, make sure all your advertising carries a message of integrity and congruence.

Core Principle Eight - If You Can't Measure It — Don't Do It. Early in my career, I worked as a marketing director for a large company. Whenever I would complain about the lack of results achieved on a campaign, our ad agency would give me a song and dance about how we were improving our image in the marketplace and building up goodwill.

I learned quickly that I couldn't feed my family with "image," and my boss wouldn't give me a raise based on all the "goodwill" I was generating. He rightly wanted tangible proof of my efforts, in the form of leads and sales. So, I hired a new agency that focused on results, and I built a tracking system to carefully measure those results.

In the shift from a mass- to a target-marketing environment, a results measurement system will keep you ahead of competitors who view marketing as a game of numbers, and not precision.

Core Principle Nine - Focus on the Right Numbers. Too many marketers have a shortsighted view of their objectives. They may rightly be concerned with a campaign's efficiency in generating leads or sales, and evaluate the results in terms of the total amount of money spent and the short-term gain achieved.

By contrast, the Master Marketer knows that marketing is a long-term process. He knows that the true value of each new sale is not just the immediate profit received; it is in the "lifetime value" of the new customer. He knows it costs only one-tenth as much to sell to an existing customer as it does to acquire a new customer.

After calculating lifetime value, two things should become apparent to you. First, because of the long-term profit potential, most organizations should be willing to raise the price they are willing to pay to acquire a new customer. Second, individual customers are more important (and profitable) than most of us realize, and should be treated accordingly.

Core Principle Ten - Do No Harm. There is a tendency in advertising today to do whatever it takes to get attention, regardless of the long-term effect. This has created a harsh climate, where it is legitimate to offend a small portion of the audience as long as enough people buy. The worst offenders in my opinion are:

- Advertisements that insult any single group of people, such as business people, women, minorities, ethnic groups, or the physically or mentally disabled.
- Ads that use sex to get attention when it has nothing to do with the product.
- Ads that encourage or glorify violence.
- Ads that denigrate any religion or religious practice.

There is no limit to how tasteless one can get. A supplier of portable toilets mailed a brochure with the headline "S__t Happens." The Radio Band of America ran a print ad showing a young woman, sitting in bed, howling with laughter. Facing her, with his back to the camera, is the torso of a naked man. The copy reads, "As her date removed his pants, Sheila suddenly recalled a hilarious radio spot she'd heard that morning. Later, when pressed, she'd admit the timing was unfortunate."

In an interview recently run in Business Marketing, the president of RBA admitted that the ad had provoked vehement response. But because of the number of positive responses, he promised to run it again. While I have no doubt that this "slash and burn" attitude can show results in a short time period, sooner or later you will offend a group or individual that could have been very important to your success.

Entire mediums can be negatively influenced by the actions of the bad actors. Witness what has happened in the telemarketing industry where a very few scam operators have poisoned the atmosphere for many legitimate firms.

So do yourself a favor. Don't resort to the easy, the cheap or the crude. Market in such a way that you help improve the culture, not destroy it.

Core Principle Eleven - When in Doubt, do Something. The following quote appears in The 6 Imperatives of Marketing by Allan J. Magrath.

> *"Every morning in Africa, a gazelle wakes up. It knows it must run faster than the fastest lion or it will be killed. Every morning a lion wakes up. It knows it must outrun the slowest gazelle or it will starve to death. It doesn't matter if you're a lion or a gazelle; when the sun comes up you'd better be running."*
>
> Unknown

This quote holds an important lesson for the Master Marketer. Whether you are the largest organization in your industry or the smallest, inactivity is a sure path to failure. In marketing, there is no such thing as perfect timing. The best time to act is always now. While you cannot expect that everything you do will be successful, you can expect that you will learn from your mistakes and improve, provided that you just do something.

Keep these 11 principles in mind as you read through The Master Marketer. They will serve you well every day in every marketing campaign.

SOME MARKETING MYTHS ARE HARDER
TO EXPOSE THAN OTHERS.

EXPOSING CONVENTIONAL
MARKETING MYTHS

The world of marketing and advertising has changed a great deal over the past decade. What was true as recently as the mid-1980s is patently untrue today, and blindly following yesterday's rules is a sure recipe for failure.

I am not suggesting that all the conventional wisdom is wrong. But you must be able to separate the correct information from the misleading myths. While this is a daunting task, unlearning prevailing misconceptions is an important step in learning new and better information. Or to paraphrase a great adage, it is difficult to pour fresh tea into a full cup.

You might wonder how so much inaccurate information gets to be prevailing wisdom. Here are the primary reasons why you can't always believe what you read or hear:

- What was once true is now old information that refuses to die a well-deserved death. Speakers and authors who never change their themes to reflect changing times do their audiences a major disservice by passing on such worn-out ideas.
- The data may be correct only in a specific context. For example, what is true for a business audience may not apply to the consumer market and vice versa.
- The information may reflect a speaker's/writer's bias toward certain marketing methods or media. Or worse, it may be calculated solely to sell you something.
- Occasionally, the information may have always been incorrect but has been passed down for years as marketing "doctrine." If you have trouble believing this, consider that for decades there was an almost universal belief among doctors that the best cure for most ailments was to bleed the patient. Many advertising agencies still practice the marketing equivalent of "bleeding the patient" by spending large sums on ineffective mass media advertising.

EXPOSING MARKETING MYTHS

To help you empty your "mental cup" of common myths and half-truths, let's explore some examples of inaccurate conventional wisdom about marketing.

Conventional Wisdom: There is a "Right Way" to advertise.
Truth: While there are several wrong ways to advertise, there is no right way. There is only that which works and that which

doesn't work. People who try to do things the "right way" almost never produce outstanding success. Average is not good enough in today's competitive climate.

Conventional Wisdom: Following the rules and statistics of marketing guarantees success.

Truth: The only two things guaranteed in this life aren't worth talking about. Competition and over-stimulation of the consumer work against advertisers. Today, you must be careful to ensure that the rules you follow are not based on yesterday's markets and techniques.

If there is one thing more dangerous than a rule, it's a statistic. Someone with his head in the oven and his feet in a bucket of ice water may have an average temperature in the comfortable range, but don't try to tell him so. Relying solely on rules and statistics is a guarantee to make your advertising boring, and boring doesn't sell. If you want to be a Master Marketer, don't be afraid to break a few rules.

Conventional Wisdom: Creativity is the most important factor in marketing.

Truth: While copy and graphic presentation are important elements in all advertising, they are not the most critical factors. First, you must market to the proper audience; second, you must have a compelling offer; and third, your promotions must appear in the right media. Good creative work won't attract clients if the audience is wrong, if the offer is poorly conceived, or if the choice of media does not match the message.

Conventional Wisdom: The best advertising is the most creative advertising.

Truth: The best advertising is the advertising that produces the best results. Unfortunately, much advertising is created to serve the ad agency's ego and not the client's best interest. Even award-winning ads may be ineffectual at moving products and services. How many times have you noticed an ad but forgot the name of the advertiser (or even worse, believed the ad was run by the advertiser's competitor)?

A good example is the long-running television campaign for Eveready Battery. The ads feature a mechanical rabbit that marches through various improbable scenarios. Creative - yes. Award winning - yes. Effective - no. In surveys conducted by Video Storyboard Tests, Inc., 40 percent of consumers who voted the ad as outstanding attributed it to Eveready's arch competitor, Duracell. Even worse, despite repeated showings of these ads, reports indicate that Eveready's sales are declining while Duracell's are growing.

An advertisement can only be considered effective if it accomplishes one of two things: (1) it causes consumers to purchase a product or service now, or (2) it predisposes consumers to buy that particular product or service the next time they are in the market. Anything else is a waste of time and money.

Conventional Wisdom: Marketing is always expensive.

Truth: Expensive is not always necessary or better. Many marketers over-emphasize the up-front cost of an advertising programme, such as the cost to reach a certain number of people, rather than the more important gauges that tell you if your programme is profitable, such as cost-per-sale or cost-per-dollar-of-revenue. The techniques in this book explain how you can spend less on marketing while producing greater results.

Conventional Wisdom: Consumers are so inundated with promotional messages that response to advertising is decreasing.

Truth: There is some validity to this statement. In general, large-scale, mass-marketing campaigns are producing fewer responses for reasons ranging from declining viewership of network television to increased competition in every industry.

However, Master Marketers are bucking this trend by using target marketing techniques such as those discussed throughout this book.

Conventional Wisdom: Direct marketing doesn't work well for certain industries.

Truth: While it is true that direct marketing can't solve every marketing problem, I have never seen an organization that could not benefit in some way from direct marketing. There are two primary reasons organizations give up on direct marketing:

1. Direct marketing may have been tried once but failed because of poor planning or improper execution of a good plan.

2. Direct marketing may be viewed only as a tool to generate leads or sell products or services. What is missed is the potential of direct marketing to help the organization in other ways, such as image building, new product announcements, attracting attendance at exhibitions and seminars, marketing research, and employee recruitment.

Conventional Wisdom: Consumers are no longer loyal to products or organizations.

Truth: Consumers are not inherently disloyal and they display this trait only to the degree they have been conditioned to be disloyal. Companies who place major emphasis on attracting new customers and minor emphasis on retaining existing customers should not be surprised when the latter leave the fold.

As you will read later in <u>The Master Marketer</u>, relationship marketing techniques can forge strong bonds of loyalty between you and your customers. Relationship building not only transcends the marketing function but is one of the major components of a well-run organization.

Conventional Wisdom: Having the best product will ensure your success.

Truth: Even the best products and services must be promoted aggressively. A recent University of Michigan study determined that more businesses fail due to inadequate marketing than for any other reason. The fact is, most of our products are not as superior to the competition as we would like to believe. As marketers, our task is to make our products stand out from the many choices available to consumers.

SOURCES OF MARKETING INFORMATION

Where can you go for the newest and most relevant marketing information? The following are several sources of information, each with its own benefits and disadvantages:

College Courses - Remember your marketing professor (fondly, I hope)? Was this person a practicing professional who taught as a sideline or a full-time teacher? If the latter was the case, the professor had one luxury that most of us lack; he didn't have to prove anything. And as most of us have discovered, Real World 101 can be quite different from the rarefied atmosphere of the classroom.

Advertising Agencies - Agencies can bring you one major benefit. They can use the experience gained from all of their other clients on your behalf. Of course, this does not mean the experience will always work in your favor. Failures can be repeated as easily as successes.

It is important to ensure that your agency is providing advice for your benefit instead of its own. For instance, many traditional agencies rely far too heavily on broadcast and print media advertisements, and it is no coincidence that media is a primary source of revenue for these agencies. This book will give you many suggestions for evaluating whether or not you are using the right media mix.

Industry Groups - An excellent source of timely marketing information. Such groups not only offer worthwhile information, but are also excellent places to network. But you should keep an eye out for the "old-boy network." Some industry groups are controlled by individuals whose primary purpose is to promote themselves, their friends and business associates. Such a group will be of little use in your professional development.

A list of industry groups is included at the end of this book in the resource section.

Conferences and Seminars - These are great places to learn and network, with certain exceptions. My favorite is the Direct Marketing Association Annual Conference, which includes some of the world's brightest marketing minds on its programme. While once devoted almost exclusively to direct marketing, the DMA has broadened its scope to include integrated marketing campaigns.

Books and Cassette Tapes - Another excellent source of information, provided that the information is timely (look for recent copyright dates) and the authors are practitioners and not just theorists (like full-time professors). Several excellent books and cassettes are listed in the resource section.

Fellow Marketing Practitioners - When I was a marketing manager in the software industry, I belonged to a high-tech marketing group. All of the members performed similar roles on the client side, with no suppliers allowed. Our monthly luncheons were filled with useful information from sources we could trust completely because they were not trying to sell us anything. Perhaps your industry has a similar group.

KEEPING A SCEPTICAL MIND

As I mentioned in the introduction, my career in marketing has spanned both sides of the client/agency relationship. This experience, combined with a solid foundation in the highly measurable discipline of direct marketing, has given me a somewhat cynical view of traditional marketing wisdom. I say the words "show me" so often, I should be made an honorary citizen of Missouri.

My recommendation is that you adopt this same healthy scepticism about marketing. I hope to make my case for the Christopher Ryan view of the marketing world, and I back up my point of view with case histories, proven results, and a lot of practical experience. But I don't have all the answers, and neither does anyone else you will come in contact with.

WRITING A WINNING MARKETING PLAN

*E*very Master Marketer will tell you that planning is a key part of the promotional process. Failure to perform the planning function can lead to disaster. Yet, while most of us know this intuitively, we sometimes fail to devote the necessary time to planning. Let's explore a few reasons why this is so:

- Market planning is hard work with few shortcuts. It is an easy activity to forego when more pleasant and time-sensitive tasks beckon.
- Many marketers lack the knowledge to be effective planners. University courses on the subject offer only confusion, not enlightenment, because they approach

the subject with far more complexity than is needed by the average marketing manager or business owner. Also, many courses approach market planning from a large company, product sales, media-based perspective, which is hard to adapt to situations faced by small to medium-size organizations.

■ Planning puts the marketing manager on the spot. If the plan is loaded with measurable objectives (as it should be), the optimistic manager may find his own figures used against him. As some have painfully discovered, there is a certain degree of comfort in ambiguity. In some organizations, this is known as "aiming high and promising low."

■ Circumstances change so often that marketers become afraid to commit, preferring to operate by the "seat-of-the-pants" method. Although seemingly effective in the short-term, this "reactive" management style rarely leads to success.

Having developed marketing plans for organizations that range from small start-up groups with a small amount of money in seed capital, to a financial institution with millions in assets, I can assure you that the basic market planning steps are the same for all organizations, even though the level of detail required varies.

In simple terms, the marketing plan is similar to a road map. First, you have to decide where it is you want to go, then you must determine the most efficient route to take you there. Until you have this road map, it is wise to refrain from all marketing activities. This is not to say that you will always adhere exactly to your plan. Marketing plans must be constantly monitored and mid-course corrections are a necessity. But until you have a written marketing plan as a guide, it is unwise to think about sharing your promotional message with the marketplace.

BENEFITS OF MARKET PLANNING

Although every organization will receive unique benefits, the following are a few reasons why you should spend the time it takes to design and implement a marketing plan. A well-defined marketing plan:

- Helps you establish priorities in your marketing activities.
- Provides you with a timetable for implementing each marketing activity.
- Gives you specific targets to aim for in the form of marketing objectives.
- Is a barometer for measuring progress or lack of progress in achieving your objectives.
- Helps you discover the most cost-effective marketing activities for your product/service.
- Gives the marketing team an action programme, possibly eliminating the need to clear every decision and expenditure with senior management.

ELEMENTS OF THE MARKETING PLAN

The following outline is one that can be adapted successfully to almost any size company.

SECTION I - Executive Summary or Statement of Purpose

Many textbooks suggest starting your plan with a two- to five-page executive summary which includes a short synopsis of the plan, your conclusions and your recommendations. I believe that an executive summary is necessary only if your plan is over 20 pages. However, many plans will not be this long, and if you can say everything you have to say in 20 pages or less, then it is permissible to skip the executive summary.

As an alternative to the executive summary, you might want to substitute a short statement of purpose which states the basic mission of your organization as well as the scope of the market plan. For example, your plan could cover the entire organization, or it may be limited to a particular division, territory, or product line. The scope of the plan should be clearly explained in the statement of purpose.

SECTION II - Situation Analysis

The situation analysis contains a list of all relevant facts and a brief overview of the progress (or lack of progress) your organization made in the past year. It should cover a number of key areas, such as financial, marketing and product development.

Since every situation is different, there is no fixed way to fill out this section. Be flexible and include any information that you feel will help the reader gain a current and historical perspective of your organization. Some suggestions include:

- Revenue and profit figures broken down by product line, including annual numbers for the past five years and monthly numbers for the past year.
- Market share by product line.
- Position of the company and its products versus its major competitors.
- New products introduced in the past year and those expected to be introduced in the coming year.
- Key market segments served by your products and services.
- Financial performance as measured against last year's objectives.

The situation analysis should also address all significant problems and opportunities anticipated by your firm in the near future.

Problems include things such as shrinking markets, declining profits, major competitive inroads, public relations problems, and personnel shortages. Opportunities include unexplored market niches, changing technologies, windfall profits, pricing advantages, geographic strengths, and favorable press treatment.

Much of the information required for this section, such as product trends, may be contained in the company's business plan and will overlap, so you shouldn't go into great detail. Basically, the situation analysis should provide the reader with whatever background information is needed to evaluate the remainder of the plan.

SECTION III – Previous Year's Programmes and Expenditures

Section III of you plan should describe, in general terms the marketing programmes that you implemented over the past financial year, your expenditures on these programmes, and the results you achieved.

As an example, you may note that £50,000 was spent on direct mail activities spread over 16 different mailings. From this, 1,500 leads were generated, which ultimately resulted in £175,000 in sales revenue. If you have been tracking your marketing activities and expenditures carefully, you should have these details.

Even in those cases where results are more difficult to track precisely (e.g. public relations), you should relate how the expenditures helped contribute to your organization's objectives, such as enhancing the corporate image or causing a better perception of quality control among your customers.

Just as with the situation analysis, a synopsis of last year's programmes and expenditures will create the proper framework on which to build this year's programme and will provide the reader the necessary background information to evaluate the remainder of the current year's plan.

SECTION IV - Marketing Objectives

As I noted in the opening chapter, establishing clear objectives is a core marketing fundamental. For this reason, this section is the heart and soul of a well-designed marketing plan and it demands careful attention. Objectives serve as the justification for every marketing activity and each pound you spend. The objective statement is your marketing destination and it bears repeating: You can't draw a road map until you know where you are going.

Marketing objectives fall into many different categories, including positioning, vertical marketing, lead generation, revenue, and public relations. Let's explore each of these categories.

A. Positioning Objectives

Positioning, while not as measurable as other objectives, is a crucial element of your game plan. In this section, you should state your goals in terms of:

- How you want the market to perceive your company.
- How you wish to shift customers' and prospects' perceptions of your products and services.
- Building customer awareness for a new product.
- Developing major new distribution channels for your products and/or services.
- Your positioning versus chief competitors'.
- Goals for market changes in awareness, technical reputation and customer service perception.

A mechanism should be established to measure your performance in meeting these objectives. One method is periodic surveys of your prospects and/or customer base. These surveys can be in the form of written questionnaires, telephone interviews, or person-to-person contact such as one-on-one interviews or focus-groups.

B. Vertical Market Objectives

A second category of marketing objectives is vertical, or target-marketing objectives. A surprisingly large number of organizations skip this step because they can't tell you the precise makeup, by industry, of their current customer base.

To set vertical market objectives, analyze the composition of your existing customer file, determine if you are satisfied with this distribution, and set specific guidelines for those industries in which you want to increase your penetration.

Vertical market goals can be expressed in percentages: "Increase our share of the market among financial institutions from 12 percent to 14 percent." Or they can be expressed in monetary terms: "Increase annual sales to financial institutions from £220,000 to £310,000."

Deciding which industries to target can be difficult. Some of the factors you will want to consider are:

- Where is the market going? Are certain industries on the decline? Are others on the upswing? What is the best way to take advantage of these market forces?
- Which industries are most profitable for your products or services? Which contribute little to profit?
- Where are your tactical strengths? In what areas are you strongest and the competition weakest? Which profitable niches remain untapped?

C. Revenue Objectives

As a marketing manager, you may not be the individual responsible for setting revenue goals. However, your input will most likely be given great weight in determining these numbers, since you are so close to the marketplace. This is even more likely to be true in organizations where the sales and marketing functions are closely related or part of the same department.

In most cases, your mission will be to develop and implement a programme to assist the sales department achieve its revenue goals. You can probably transfer these numbers directly from your company's business plan. Even if the revenue goals are outlined in some depth in the business plan, it is still useful to list them in your marketing plan. Because there is probably no more important objective to the organization than reaching its sales projections, tying these numbers directly to your marketing programmes is always a good idea.

In addition to presenting the overall revenue numbers, you may want to break them down by product line and/or geographic sales territory.

D. Lead Generation Objectives

If your organization uses a two-step instead of a one-step sales process, you will need to become well-acquainted with the subject of lead generation. In a later chapter I will introduce the subject of conversion ratios. But if you are already doing a good job of tracking leads using conversion ratios you should know how many leads at the front end of the process it will take to achieve a certain amount of sales revenue.

Another way of computing lead requirements is to calculate how many leads each salesperson requires to achieve a given sales quota and to multiply these numbers to establish yearly lead requirements.

After setting total yearly lead objectives, two breakdowns will be helpful. First, allocate your lead-flow requirements into monthly goals. Second, apportion the leads by specific marketing category. To show you what I mean, a marketing plan I developed recently contained the following lead source breakdown:

LEAD SOURCE OBJECTIVES

Marketing Category	Count	% of Total
Direct Mail	1200	35%
Telemarketing (outbound)	400	12%
Print Advertising	600	18%
Exhibitions	450	13%
Seminars	250	08%
Public Relations	300	09%
Referrals & Other	175	05%
TOTAL	3425	100%

As you can see, leads are broken down by the total number and percentage of leads to be generated from each activity.

E. Public Relations Objectives

Public relations is considered such a soft marketing art that many organizations never set specific goals for public relations activities. This is a mistake for two reasons:

1. Mediocre PR people hide behind ambiguity in order to hide poor performance. A specific public relations goal makes the PR practitioner accountable for his effort.
2. Solid public relations can strengthen the total marketing mix at very low cost.

Public relations objectives can include:

- Positive press messages you intend to receive for product and corporate news. Goals for this activity can be broken down by media type.
- Publishing a certain number of articles in leading trade publications under a byline of an official of your organization.

■ Placing your executives as speakers at key industry conferences.

■ Improvements in prospect and customer perceptions of your company, products, and/or services.

F. Other Objectives

List objectives in this category that do not fit comfortably into one of the above categories. Following are examples taken from a marketing plan that I developed for a national software company:

1. Continually upgrade the quality of leads by increasing the conversion percentage of leads to sales from 4.3 percent in the current fiscal year to 5.8 percent in the coming fiscal year.

2. Develop and implement a more efficient lead tracking system to establish tighter control over marketing expenditures. The system chosen must allow for quick lead follow-up and precise tracking of cost-per-lead and cost-per-sale.

3. Support the national account sales programme by helping the sales department achieve its goal of closing 40 percent of targeted accounts.

SECTION V - Creative Strategies

In this section we begin the fun part of the market planning process. We have established our destination from the laborious work we did in defining our objectives. It is now time to construct the road map that will ensure we reach the destination on-schedule and on-budget.

I prefer to begin this section with a discussion of unique selling propositions (USP). Your USP is the factor (or factors) that make your company, products, or services better and more saleable than those of the competition.

Copy themes should be covered next. Copy themes are generally statements which describe the key selling points of your products or services. These will be stressed in your marketing, sales, and public relations activities. While not cast in concrete, these themes can be considered a good foundation for future promotions and advertisements. Copy themes must always reinforce your unique selling propositions.

The following are examples of copy themes for the mythical ABC Company:

1. ABC Company's products are technically superior to any others available.
2. Our products do exactly what we say they do. Our customers can depend on our product integrity.
3. ABC offers its customers excellent technical support.
4. ABC products are extremely cost-effective and contribute to the bottom-line success of our customers.

While these copy themes are expressed in general terms, it is best to be as specific as possible.

The third category of creative strategies is visual themes. As with copy themes, these are general statements of your creative thrust, expressed in visual terms. Here are a few examples:

ABC Company will create audiovisual, exhibition, and print materials with the following characteristics:

1. A high-quality, professional image.
2. Consistency of image across product line and marketing vehicles.
3. Futuristic graphics that reflect high-technology solutions to the problems of today as well as tomorrow.

SECTION VI - Prospect Identification

As I will reiterate throughout this book, the most effective marketers are those who can skillfully identify qualified prospects. Start by listing all known market segments by product, industry, geography, company size, and any other criteria you can use as identifiers.

Next, develop a "customer profile" for each of these market segments. The customer profile goes into great detail about specific purchasers of your products and services, including demographic and psychographic information. The following is a simplified example of a customer profile that I developed for a client in the publishing industry in the USA:

"The primary market for this publication consists of commercial banks in the Northeastern United States, ranging in size from $200 million to $5 billion in assets. Our target audience within these banks consists of senior mortgage loan officers who hold the title of either vice president, executive vice president, or senior vice president.

In smaller institutions, the appropriate title may be president. These well-read and affluent executives are responsible for setting or recommending mortgage policy at their institutions and consider it crucial to stay abreast of trends in mortgage rates, real estate values and lending issues."

After describing your customer profile, the section should end with an outline of the automated or manual system you will use to capture data and a listing of the exact data to be maintained in your system.

For example, our agency maintains the following information on prospects and clients:

- Name
- Title
- Organization name
- Full address information

- Telephone and fax numbers
- Industry type
- Contact type
- Date of entry into system
- Last contact date
- Notes on last contact
- Source code

While this should give you an idea, the information you maintain in your in-house file depends on your specific needs.

SECTION VII - Media Strategies

The media strategy portion of your plan should list the marketing vehicles you will use in your promotional efforts, outline who is responsible for carrying out these activities, and tell how and when these strategies will be implemented.

Media vehicles include:

Direct Marketing

The section on direct marketing should contain an in-depth discussion of the outside mailing lists and/or internal database on which you will find the prospects identified in the previous section. Next, the mailing and telemarketing programs you will use to reach these prospects should be outlined. A knowledge of direct mail and telemarketing response rates is crucial, as is knowing the number of leads or sales you need to achieve your revenue objectives.

It is highly unlikely you will know in more than general terms the content of individual mailing packages or the strategy for each telemarketing programme you will undertake over the next year. However, you will know what your lead generation or sales objectives are, and how many mailing packages you will have to send or telephone calls you will need to make to achieve these objectives.

Print Advertising

Review your goals for print advertising at the beginning of this section. For instance, state whether you will be running lead generation or image-building advertisements. Next, review the major publications to be used in your print media plan, with a brief description on how each publication's readership fits your target prospect profile. Outline a proposed media schedule and include the name of each publication to be used, the number of insertions, and the size of each ad.

Broadcast Advertising

If television or radio is part of your media strategy, list the media outlets to be used with the same type of schedules and profiles as for print advertising.

SECTION VIII - Other Marketing Activities

Marketing Research

Marketing research is an often neglected, but vitally important marketing area. An outline should be completed for all marketing research projects including the completion dates and estimated costs for each project. Because market research is extremely labour-oriented, don't forget to account for the in-house personnel costs involved.

Exhibitions

This section includes a discussion of each show at which you plan to exhibit or visit, a profile of expected attendees, and the objectives to be achieved at each event. Dates for each show should be listed, as well as an approximate budget, including stand space, promotion, travel, and entertainment expenses for all employees.

Sales Seminars

A later chapter explores the enormous potential of sales seminars as a sales and lead generation vehicle. If you plan to use seminars, make sure you list them in your marketing plan. As with the other strategies, discuss why you are using seminars and what you intend to accomplish with your seminar programme. Remember to budget for hotels, travel, exhibition space, marketing promotion, and hand-out materials.

Public Relations

Public relations activities to be listed in your marketing plan include the writing and distribution of newsletters, preparation and mailing of press releases (including mailing costs), customer success stories, speaking trips for company officials, press tours by the public relations manager, and the activities and costs of an outside public relations firm.

Collateral Materials

List your anticipated expenditures for all collateral materials, including brochures, portfolios, audio/visual materials, and user application articles.

Contingency and Miscellaneous Expenses

Contingency expenses cover opportunities that are unforeseen at the time the budget is adopted such as special media buys, trade shows, collateral materials and public relations activities, as well as expenses not fitting neatly into other categories. Most organizations find five to 10 percent of the marketing budget to be a sufficient allocation for contingencies and miscellaneous expenses.

SECTION IX - Marketing Budget Summary

Your marketing budget summary is a listing of all anticipated marketing expenditures by general category, summing up all the programme expenses detailed in the preceding sections.

Outline of a Winning Marketing Plan

Section I - Executive Summary or Statement of Purpose

Section II - Situation Analysis
    A. Current market position
    B. Product background
    C. Competitive environment
    D. Market segments

Section III – Previous Year's Programmes and Expenditures
    A. Programmes
    B. Expenditures
    C. Results

Section IV - Marketing Objectives
    A. Positioning
    B. Vertical Marketing
    C. Revenue
    D. Lead Generation
    E. Public Relations
    F. Other

Section V - Creative Strategies
    A. Unique Selling Propositions
    B. Copy Themes
    C. Visual Themes

Section VI - Prospect Identification
    A. Market Segments
    B. Customer Profile
    C. Database Marketing

Section VII - Media Strategies
        A. Direct Marketing
        B. Print Advertising
        C. Broadcast Advertising
        D. Outdoor Advertising

Section VIII - Other Marketing Activities
        A. Marketing Research
        B. Exhibitions
        C. Sales Seminars
        D. Public Relations
        E. Collateral Materials
        F. Contingencies and Miscellaneous Expenses

Section IX - Marketing Budget Summary

SECTION II

BASIC MASTER MARKETING SKILLS

4

MARKETING RESEARCH BASICS

The subject of marketing research has been known to send shivers down the spine of even experienced marketers. They view marketing research as somewhat mysterious and based on complex scientific principles and costly statistical analysis.

Yet, the fact is, research doesn't have to be expensive. And you don't necessarily have to pay an outside expert to conduct research for you, although it may be a very prudent move. What you must do, regardless of the size or scope of the project, is practice certain time-tested fundamentals. If you fail to do so, the data you generate may be useless, or even worse, counter-productive, because it may be inaccurate.

This chapter will show you the fundamentals, outline the uses for marketing research and give you many good ideas for conducting low-cost research yourself. If you choose to use a research firm, this chapter will also help you to select the best company for your needs and properly evaluate its methods and conclusions.

USES FOR MARKETING RESEARCH

Marketing research can be defined as "any activity that involves gathering and/or evaluating information to be used to assist the business decision-making process." Using this definition, marketing research can be used for a great many purposes, including:

- Identifying new markets for products and services.
- Classifying new business and consumer markets by their demographic, geographic and psychographic characteristics.
- Testing the viability of new products and services. Smart companies want to have an idea of the potential for a new product before spending large sums on development costs. Research often points out modifications that can save a product that would otherwise be a failure.
- Defining narrow market niches. Submarkets or unique uses for products can be found through research.
- Locating decision makers and influencers. Advertising aimed at the wrong prospect is wasted. Locating the right prospect is particularly important in business marketing as there can be many people involved with the decision-making process.
- Defining the sales cycle for products and services. Research can help discover two important questions about the sales cycle. First, how much time does it take from initial contact through the close of business? Second, what is the internal process that prospects go through when evaluating and purchasing products?
- Reducing the risk of product or marketing decisions. In

a fast-changing, technical world, business executives cannot afford to make major mistakes in product development or marketing. Research is a valuable tool when it comes to improving the quality of decisions.

■ Testing advertising copy, graphic, offer and message impact before and/or after the ads are seen by consumers. Pre-testing ads increases the chance for success. Post-testing helps refine future advertising.

■ Evaluating product or service benefits. It is amazing how often a company is wrong about why consumers purchase its products and services. The only way to be truly sure about your advantages is to ask the people who know best - your customers.

■ Determining brand strength and positioning versus the competition. The market is comprised of more than you and your prospects and customers; it also includes competitors. Your position versus the competition is constantly changing, sometimes in subtle ways, and it is imperative for you to understand these changes.

■ Selecting the best media tools. Poor media selection is fatal to marketing programmes. Planners can use research to help develop media schedules that maximize the cost-effectiveness of every dollar spent on print, broadcast, direct mail and other marketing vehicles.

■ Tracking customer satisfaction. Research can be used to get a moving picture of your customers' attitudes about your products, services, pricing, personnel, policies, and so forth. Trends spotted in customer satisfaction can be used to head-off serious problems later.

WHAT RESEARCH CAN'T DO

As we have seen, research can be used to help the marketer make decisions that are more likely to produce the desired outcome. But you must always remember that research is a support tool. It does not, and should not, dictate the decision. A manager's intuition and experience must be factored into the equation. Examples are numerous where the business leader made a decision opposite of that indicated by research and saved the day.

A well-known instance of this is Sony Corporation's decision to produce the Walkman after research suggested the product would fail. Despite the research, Sony's chairman had a feeling that the product would sell and history has proven him right.

THE DANGERS OF POOR MARKETING RESEARCH

Inaccurate marketing research can be deadly to an organization. It can cause resources to be dedicated to a product or marketing effort with a confidence unwarranted by the true facts. Here are some of the causes of substandard marketing research:

- The research methodology was flawed. Proper techniques were not followed, making the information suspect. One example of this would be using too small a sample size.
- The information collected was accurate but analyzed improperly. We have all seen examples where the identical data was used to support two different conclusions. Properly designed surveys help ensure that this does not happen.
- The data collected was incomplete. I recently read an interesting article that demonstrates this point. The story was based on a study of survivors of airline crashes. According to the data, 90 percent of survivors noticed where the exits were when they boarded the aeroplane. The writer drew the conclusion that your chances of surviving an aeroplane accident are greater if you know where the exits are.

As a common sense opinion, this conclusion would seem to be based on a certain amount of logic. However, as an analysis of the available survey data, it was deeply flawed. The fact is, the writer only knew about the survivors. He had no way of knowing what percentage of the people who didn't survive were aware of the location of the exits. Thus, since his information was incomplete, his well-meaning conclusion could not be supported.

■ The research project was biased. For various reasons, individuals can be more interested in promoting a particular viewpoint than in finding the truth. An advertising agency may want to prove that its commercials are increasing its client's brand image. A product manager may want to prove that his "pet" product has huge market potential. A director of customer service may want to prove that his department is doing a superb job and deserves more funding.

Several years ago a client actually said to me, "Chris, I want your firm to conduct a marketing study for me and this is what I want the study to prove." He wasn't joking. Although most people aren't this blatant about it, my client did have a vested interest in the outcome and didn't want to take any chances.

Despite our client's wishes, we undertook the project on the condition that we would follow proper procedure and present an unbiased report. Luckily, the data supported the position held by the client.

Biased research can be hard to detect because the people who review the research reports may have little knowledge of proper research techniques. Often, the person responsible for the project has the most to gain (or lose) from its results. The problem is compounded by the fact that it only takes subtle changes in research methodology to achieve a certain outcome, and these changes can be hard to spot.

The above are reasons why you may wish to use an established marketing research firm that is responsible to one or more people in your organization who want the unblemished truth.

STEPS INVOLVED IN MARKETING RESEARCH

Marketing research is such a specialized subject area that we will not go into the mechanics in great detail here. There are many fine books on the subject. But for most applications, these are the basic steps involved in planning and conducting a research project:

1. Establishing the study objectives. You must be very clear as to the exact nature of the data to be gathered and the specific purposes for which the information will be used. The beginning of the project is also a good time to ask if the benefits of conducting the research are worth the cost involved.

2. Researching secondary sources of data. Sometimes the information you're after has been compiled by an indirect third-party source such as a government agency, industry publication, trade association or re-search firm. Primary research is very expensive and time-consuming. While secondary data may not be quite as relevant or timely as primary information, the cost benefits are obvious.
    Another benefit of secondary research is that it can help you discover new questions to ask or new information to gather through your primary research techniques.

3. Developing the survey methodology. After exhausting

secondary sources, determine how you will go about collecting the additional data needed. Sources of direct data include personal interviews, focus groups, consumer opinion panels, telephone surveys and written questionnaires.

4. Designing a sample. Unless you are working with a small, finite universe of potential subjects, you will probably want to restrict your research to a sample of the audience. The key characteristic of a sample is that it accurately reflects the universe.

For a simplified example, if 40 per cent of the individuals in the entire universe live in Eastern Europe then roughly 40 percent of the sample audience should also live in those countries. A sample drawing only 10 percent of its individuals from Eastern Europe would be heavily biased toward those who live in the West.

Sample bias is a significant problem in survey research. In order to get a true "random sample" of the universe, every person in the universe should have an equal chance of being chosen as a member of the sample. Likewise, all segments of the audience must be included. If any group of individuals is left out of the sample, the results cannot be projected to the entire universe.

Most of the time, it is not the size of the universe that determines the viability of a sample but the size of the sample itself. Often, only a small percentage of the audience has to be queried to draw inferences about the entire audience. For example, during a general election, only a few hundred people are surveyed nationally to determine how each candidate is doing. These 500–600 people can accurately portray how millions of voters feel about the election on any given day.

of millions of Americans feel about the election on any given day.

5. Writing a questionnaire. Regardless of the techniques used to gather your data, some type of questionnaire will be necessary. Hopefully, your project includes time for exploratory interviews or focus groups which will help to bring up valuable (but previously unexplored) issues, and also to refine the questionnaire itself.

6. Collecting data. At the information gathering stage of the project, your task is to conduct personal interviews, make phone calls, mail out questionnaires, or do whatever else is required to collect the needed data.

7. Compiling data. Once the appropriate amount of data has been collected, it must be sorted and organized. For simple projects this can be a manual process, but more often the information is fed into a computer. Electronic methods of compilation allow for sophisticated data manipulation techniques such as regression analysis.

8. Analysis and reporting. After all information is collected and compiled, you must decide which data is important, what it indicates, and how to present the data. When preparing your final reports remember that the individuals reading them may not have enough background in market research to accurately interpret mountains of data, so keep your reports short and simple.

PRIMARY RESEARCH DATA COLLECTION METHODS

Focus Groups

Focus groups are used to explore broad themes and general perceptions of audience members, since their small size limits their ability to be used as precise measurement instruments. Groups usually consist of four to 12 participants who share similar characteristics.

For example, a group of tennis players may be gathered to explore the criteria they use to purchase tennis rackets. Or the same group may be asked to respond to a series of advertising slogans or to react to a group of test television commercials.

Information gained from focus groups is usually not sufficient to serve as a basis for business decisions. Rather, the data is used to help design follow-up survey questionnaires that cover the subject matter in-depth.

It is very important to hold your focus group in a relaxed, comfortable setting. No pressure to buy your product or service should ever be put on group participants because their answers will be very different if they feel the purpose of the meeting is to sell them something. You want to do everything possible to encourage these people to speak candidly and freely.

When conducting a focus group be very careful to ask open-ended questions that give no hint of your anticipated or hoped-for answer. Certain people will try to be helpful by answering in the desired manner, regardless of their true feelings. In fact, it is usually a good idea to keep the name of your product and company unknown to the participants.

Personal Interviews

One-on-one interviews are a very accurate means of collecting data. In the hands of a trained interviewer, individuals will be very forthcoming with their opinions on almost any subject. The interviewer is there to gauge the level of understanding of the subject and can personally choose subjects to match the desired sample. Personal interviews can also be used in the early stages of a project to help develop questionnaires for later use.

However, it must be noted that personal interviews are a very expensive way to collect data. Another problem stems from the reluctance of certain people to answer an interviewer's questions. And the days of door-to-door opinion polling are almost over since people are afraid to open their doors to strangers.

Direct Mail Questionnaires

Direct mail can be used to obtain research data by utilizing written questionnaires. Often, the questionnaire is developed as a result of person-to-person interviews, or through focus groups. Direct mail survey projects are fairly expensive and time consuming so you want to make sure the mailed questionnaire is complete, and not lacking in any substantive way.

Today, written questionnaires serve as the foundation of most research projects. For certain applications, such as when the universe list does not contain telephone numbers, written questionnaires may be the only way to collect the data.

To get the best response rate out of your written survey questionnaire, adhere to the following guidelines:

- Make sure you interview individuals who have a genuine or perceived interest in the survey's subject matter.
- The questionnaire should be easy to read, both from a copy and layout standpoint. To increase legibility, leave plenty of white space on the page.
- Keep the questionnaire as short and uncomplicated as you can. Overly long or complex surveys are quickly consigned to recipients' wastebaskets.
- A questionnaire is supposed to measure how the marketplace feels about a particular subject at a certain point of time. It is a snapshot, not a moving picture.

- Survey questionnaires should always be accompanied by a letter. The letter should be personalized if possible, and convince the respondent that he is important and his answers are valuable.
- Tell the respondent how the findings from the research report will benefit the person in his professional and/or personal life.
- Give your survey an impressive title, such as "Survey of Leading Executives in the Transportation Industry."
- Assure the respondent that his or her participation in the research project will be held in strict confidence. If possible, allow the recipient to answer the questionnaire without revealing his name.
- Offer each respondent a summary report on the survey's conclusions. Assuming your list contains those who have an interest in the subject matter, this alone will induce many to respond.
- Put a stamp on the pre-addressed return envelope. At the least, include a postage-paid business reply envelope. Never ask the recipient to pay the return postage.
- Use a before and/or after response booster. One week before the questionnaire is mailed, send a postcard notifying the subject that an important survey will be arriving shortly. If the response rate on the first mailing is small, mail a copy of the questionnaire to non-respondents, with a note suggesting they may not have received the original and that you are waiting for their reply.
- Consider including a premium with your questionnaire. The right premium can double or even triple response. Successful premiums include vouchers and advertising gifts such as pens and calendars. Be careful not to imply that you are buying the respondent's time with the premium, but rather are including it "as a token of appreciation."

time with the premium, but rather are including it "as a token of appreciation."

Telephone Research

Telephone surveys have a number of advantages over written questionnaires. For starters, the information can be obtained much faster. I have been involved with telephone survey programmes that were developed, tested, conducted, compiled and reported in two weeks.

Telephone surveys also allow for considerable flexibility. For example, perhaps you've conducted fifty phone interviews and an unexpected issue continues to be raised. Simply revise the questionnaire and include the new questions on all subsequent calls. This level of flexibility is not possible with written questionnaires.

Many consumers, though, are extremely wary of telephone surveys because they have been subject to "phony" surveys where the real purpose of the call was to sell a product or service, instead of conducting legitimate research. Because of these abuses and the inherent intrusive nature of the medium, a high percentage of individuals will no longer participate in telephone research.

To increase the likelihood of getting your questions answered, follow these guidelines:

- Keep the questions short and simple. Unless the recipient of the call is deeply involved in the subject matter (or getting paid), it is very difficult to keep someone on the phone more than a few minutes.
- Make sure a cross-section of the universe is represented in your survey. Don't just tear off a section of the mailing list and start calling. You may be limiting the callers to a certain geographic area or other segment.
- Try to complete the calls in a compressed time period and inform the respondent approximately how long the interview will last.

- Although other types of telephone marketing lend themselves to ad-libbing, keep it to a minimum when telephone surveying. Even slight differences in wording can cause statistical variances in the data.

HOW TO FIND OUT WHAT YOUR CUSTOMERS THINK

There are several important reasons to periodically ask your customers and best prospects what they think about your organization:

- To learn their perceptions of your organization, products and/or services.
- To track key indicators of satisfaction.
- To discover new product/service opportunities.
- To build the relationship and prevent competitive inroads. Customers and prospects like to be asked for their opinions.
- To keep your database file clean and up-to-date.

If your database is small and well-defined, you can survey the customer base by telephone. The telephone is a more personal medium than mail and you can pick up nuances in the individual's miss on a written questionnaire. The type of information you will want to request includes:

- Correct name, company and address data.
- Direct-dial telephone numbers.
- Updated titles.
- Areas of functional responsibility.
- Whether the individual is a decision maker, influencer or recommender.
- Satisfaction levels with service from current suppliers.
- Buying cycle for products/services.

■ Size of company/agency and/or size of department.

Whether you are conducting the survey by phone or mail, it is important to keep the questions very brief and simple. The written questionnaire should take no more than 10 minutes (preferably less) to fill out and the phone interview should last no more than five minutes. An incentive can be used to increase response, either in the form of a small gift or discount coupon. At the least, you should make the case that the person will benefit from better service by answering your questions.

A CASE STUDY

Several years ago, we created a customer satisfaction survey for Chase Manhattan Bank's credit card division. Chase felt it was important to know how well the bank was meeting the needs of its six million credit card holders. Since the bank receives tens of thousands of calls monthly at its customer service centre, we decided to query those who called or wrote the centre during a particular time period.

A written questionnaire was developed which asked 12 questions about the individual's recent experience with Chase and his/her overall level of satisfaction with the bank and its credit card programme. We mailed the questionnaire to 5,000 card holders and received over 2,000 responses. We then set-up a programme to survey several thousand card holders every three months. By using the responses to the initial survey as a benchmark, Chase was able to precisely track the performance of its customer service department, make necessary changes, and improve customer satisfaction.

CUSTOMER SERVICE SURVEY
for Preferred Chase Accountholders

1. Was your recent inquiry to our customer service department:
1 ☐ By mail
2 ☐ By telephone

2. If your inquiry was by telephone:

	Yes	No
Were you put on hold more than once?	3 ☐	4 ☐
Were you re-directed to more than one person?	5 ☐	6 ☐
Were you asked to call back?	7 ☐	8 ☐
Did you have to repeat your question or problem more than once?	9 ☐	10 ☐

3. If your inquiry was by mail:

	Yes	No
Was the response from Chase clear and complete?	11 ☐	12 ☐
Was the response from Chase understandable and written in a polite and friendly manner?	13 ☐	14 ☐

4. Certain inquiries require additional research. What do you consider a reasonable time-frame for such an inquiry to be resolved:
15 ☐ within one week   16 ☐ 1-2 weeks
17 ☐ 2-3 weeks   18 ☐ more than 3 weeks

5. Was your inquiry resolved in a satisfactory time?

Yes	No
19 ☐	20 ☐

6. How satisfied were you with the quality of service you received from Chase on your inquiry:
21 ☐ Very Satisfied   22 ☐ Somewhat Satisfied
23 ☐ Not Satisfied

7. How many times did you contact Chase before your inquiry was resolved:
24 ☐ One time   25 ☐ Two times
26 ☐ Three or more times   27 ☐ I'm still waiting

8. Please rate your satisfaction with the Chase representative who handled your inquiry in the following areas:

	Very Satisfied	Somewhat Satisfied	Not Satisfied
Courtesy	28 ☐	29 ☐	30 ☐
Understanding your inquiry	31 ☐	32 ☐	33 ☐
Having authority to make decisions	34 ☐	35 ☐	36 ☐
Showing concern about your problem	37 ☐	38 ☐	39 ☐
Follow through on your inquiry	40 ☐	41 ☐	42 ☐

9. What is the most convenient day or days for you to contact our customer service department: (please check all answers that apply)
43 ☐ Sunday   44 ☐ Monday   45 ☐ Tuesday
46 ☐ Wednesday   47 ☐ Thursday
48 ☐ Friday   49 ☐ Saturday

10. What times are most convenient for you to contact Chase: (Eastern time)
50 ☐ 8-12 noon   51 ☐ noon-4 p.m.
52 ☐ 4-8 p.m.   53 ☐ 8 p.m.-midnight
54 ☐ midnight-4 a.m.   55 ☐ 4-8 a.m.

11. How likely are you to renew your account(s) when it (they) come(s) up for renewal:
56 ☐ Very likely   57 ☐ Somewhat likely
58 ☐ Not likely

12. Do you have any comments or suggestions on how we can improve our service to you? _____
_____
_____
_____
(please use the back if you need more space)

PLEASE FOLD COMPLETED QUESTIONNAIRE AND MAIL IN ENCLOSED POSTAGE-PAID ENVELOPE
Or send to Chase Manhattan Bank (USA), N.A., P.O. Box 15008, Wilmington, DE 19885-9800

Sample Customer Survey

HOW TO SELECT A MARKET RESEARCH COMPANY

Research is a complicated subject and although I've given you basic information here, when the research is complex or of critical importance to your organization, it may be in your best interest to hire an outside research company. If the need arises, keep these pointers in mind.

First, ask for an initial discussion. Most credible research firms will be happy to meet with you and provide a proposal before any fees are incurred.

Second, evaluate companies that specialize in your industry. At the very least, don't choose a firm that has the greatest expertise in consumer research if you are a business-to-business marketer, and vice versa.

Third, ask for several references from organizations whose needs are similar to your own. Call these references.

Fourth, meet with the people who would actually be working on your account. Are you being serviced by an experienced senior manager or a recent graduate? Is the chemistry right between you and these people? Will they work hard on your behalf?

Fifth, are their services reasonably priced? Not necessarily cheap, but reasonable. Also, are they looking out for ways to conduct your research in a proper manner within your budget?

Sixth, will they let you be a full-partner in the research process? They may know research but they can never hope to understand your company, products and customers the way you do. It is the combination of your knowledge with their research expertise that will produce the greatest results.

Should you use your ad agency to do research? The answer to this question is that it depends on their level of experience. Most small- to medium-size agencies are not marketing research experts, so do you really want to educate them at your expense? However, if the agency has expertise in this area, and provided they have no great stake in the outcome, then by all means entertain a proposal from your agency for research work. There's a good chance that if they don't have the expertise in-house, they will sub-contract a research firm and pass on the costs to you...with a healthy mark-up of course.

The best combination is to have the outside research company, your agency, and your own staff involved in the project. Although this option can prove very expensive, you will benefit from each party's unique perspective.

5

DEVELOPING A WINNING POSITIONING AND CREATIVE STRATEGY

"The Meek Shall Inherit the Earth,
But They'll Never Increase Market Share"
-William G. McGowan

*P*ositioning is the most misunderstood, unappreciated and neglected part of the marketing process. David Ogilvy, founder of Ogilvy & Mather, stated that positioning is the most important decision made in advertising a product or service. He also correctly noted that successful positioning had far more to do with the results of a promotion than how an advertisement was designed and written.

In marketing, the word "position" can be defined as "that place an organization and its products or services occupies in the minds of its prospects and customers." Every organization, as well as each product or service offered by an organization, has its own unique "position," or more accurately, its own "series of positions." A company can occupy different positions among various audience segments. Or, despite attempts to promote consistency through all product lines, individual products can occupy different positions.

Although positioning can consist of dozens of subtle factors, the three primary elements that define an organization's position are price, quality (performance) and service. An organization can be known for its low prices or high prices, for its high-performance products or low-performance products, and for superior service or inferior service.

Of course, most organizations are positioned somewhere between these extremes. For instance, you can become known as a moderate-priced supplier of medium quality goods. It must also be noted that these terms are highly subjective.

The three positioning elements of price, service and quality can be shown on a "Triangle of Excellence."

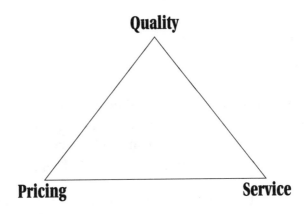

The "Triangle of Excellence"

While it would be highly favorable to be viewed by the market-place as being superior in price, service and quality, it is extremely difficult to achieve excellence in all three areas. It is however, very possible for a company to occupy two of the three points of the triangle. For instance, a company that has a reputation as a low cost supplier with excellent service would not be expected to have the highest quality products.

Likewise, given competitive economic realities, a company known for its first-class products and services will usually be unable to sell its products at the lowest cost. Consumers are sophisticated enough to understand that there is a strong correlation between pricing and quality.

The point to remember is that each element of the positioning triangle is evaluated in relation to the other two elements. For instance, price will always be evaluated on the basis of how costly the product or service is, given the performance of that product related to similar products and also on the anticipated level of service expected after the sale. Thus, a high-priced product can only support its price so long as the customer perceives good value in the performance and service criteria.

As you can see, positioning is highly fluid. Not only is it subject to the changing whims of the prospect's perceptions of your own company and product strengths and weaknesses, it is also dependent on the perceived strengths and weaknesses of all known competitors.

A good example of how the positioning triangle works can be found in the motor industry, where European manufacturers are faced with a double burden. First, a dealer must convince the consumer that the asking price for a European car is worth it, given the perceptions of quality and service. Then, the dealer must overcome the general perception that Japanese cars are superior in quality to their European counterparts and in many cases offer the consumer greater value for money.

Note my use of the word "perception" in the preceding paragraphs. Even though European automobiles are statistically close to the Japanese in quality, the perception is otherwise. And unfortunately, the marketplace often operates on perception, not facts. Always remember this important point: In marketing, perception is reality. This can be a blessing or a curse, depending on how adept you and your competitors are at manipulating consumer perceptions.

Of course, the most effective positioning does not rely on manipulation but takes full advantage of your true strengths and the weaknesses of your competitors. This is why it is always a good idea to start developing your positioning strategy by asking three questions:

1. What is our organization good at?
2. What can we do better than anyone else?
3. How can we translate our existing strengths into a unique selling proposition?

POSITIONING BY COST OR DIFFERENTIATION

Michael Porter, professor of the Harvard University School of Business Administration, shows organizations how to position themselves by creating a competitive positioning strategy. Porter says that organizations have two major ways to distinguish themselves within an industry: either through low cost or differentiation.

According to Porter, to be successful with a "cost leadership" strategy, you must:

- Deliver a GOOD product or service at the lowest possible cost, or
- Open a significant and sustainable cost gap over all other competitors, or
- Create an advantage through superior management of key cost drivers.

Keep two points in mind when considering a cost strategy. One, even with a low-cost strategy, you must maintain parity with competitors in satisfying buyer needs. Two, accept the fact that cost leadership will often require tradeoffs with differentiation.

To be successful with a differentiation strategy, you must:

- Select one or more needs VALUED by the consumer.
- Selectively add costs in these areas if necessary.
- Achieve and sustain superior performance by serving these buyer needs immediately.

Just as with the cost-based strategy, a differentiation strategy has two requirements. One, you must maintain cost parity with competitors to achieve above-average profitability. Two, you must be careful to pick cost-effective forms of differentiation.

To explain this principle in simple terms: when you spend £1.00 to add extra performance or quality to a product, you must make sure that the consumer places a value of more than £1.00 on the improvements and is willing to pay more than £1.00 extra for the product than he would otherwise have paid. If the improvements fail this test, they are not cost-effective.

HOW TO DEVELOP A SUCCESSFUL POSITIONING STRATEGY

The first step in developing a positioning strategy is to determine your starting point through a series of questions:

1. What is the scope of your positioning problem - to position an entire organization or simply to position a product or series of products?
2. In an ideal world, what is the position you would like to hold in the marketplace?

3. What is the position that you currently hold? You must be brutally honest with the answer to this question. If you do not know the answer, conduct research to find out.
4. What is the position of each of your competitors?
5. Is the positioning statement for the current product or service compatible with your organization's overall position?
6. Does your positioning strategy violate the true nature of the organization?
7. Where is the product on the life cycle? Is it a new, pioneering product where the consumer asks, "What is this product?" Or, are you in a mature market where the consumer asks, "Why should I buy this model?"
8. Do you have the resources to offer a comparable product to the consumer at a lower cost?
9. Given the competition, do you have the necessary resources to reach and maintain the desired position in the marketplace?

Answer all marketing positioning questions in the context of overall corporate objectives, such as profit, return on investment (ROI), levels of financial risk desired, new technologies and so forth.

The questions are fairly general in nature and are intended to provide the framework in which you can develop the best possible creative strategy. The output of this process is a position statement, which can be as short as one sentence or as long as a paragraph. Do not attempt to develop the creative strategy until you have complete agreement on the position statement from all concerned individuals (marketing, sales, research, customer service, finance, administration, etc.).

NINE POSITIONING MODELS

Here are nine examples of the many ways that your organization can be positioned:

1. The "Hot Company." To be a "hot company," you must be associated with an important and current issue.
2. The "Technology Leader." This works if you can reach and maintain a position of technology leadership (this is becoming increasingly harder to do).
3. The "Warm and Fuzzy Company." A "warm and fuzzy" company builds a great deal of trust with the public and can therefore command premium prices.
4. The "All-Knowing Company." This type of organization and its employees are known as the industry experts.
5. The "First Company." The first company to market a certain type of product can have a significant advantage.
6. The "Largest Organization." The biggest company may not be the best, but it is often perceived as such.
7. The "One and Only Organization." If you can convince the marketplace that you are the one and only company that does something or produces something of value, your success is assured.
8. The "Fastest Company." Even if you're not the best, you can appeal to those who need immediate service.
9. The "Cheapest Company." This is the cost leadership strategy. Companies that practice it successfully will always have a good share of the market, especially if they can combine low price with quality service.

One last thought about positioning. Whatever strategy you choose, it must be very simple to present to the consumer and it must be very consistent. Always express your positioning as clearly and as focused as possible.

ON TO THE CREATIVE STRATEGY

Development of the creative strategy moves the process from the general to the specific. And although it has much in common with the positioning statement, the output of a creative strategy will go directly into your advertisements and marketing materials.

A winning creative strategy should always be based on a unique selling proposition (USP). Your USP is that competitive point-of-difference that makes your product better than any other on the market. If you are not sure you have a unique and saleable difference, ask the real experts, your customers.

Products and services with well-defined USPs can be termed "value-added" products and services. The easiest way to determine if you have a value-added product or service is to ask if you have a differentiation that consumers are willing to pay extra for. If not, you probably have a "commodity" product. Commodity products are those which are so similar in nature that they must be sold on the basis of something not intrinsic to the product, such as price, terms, service or speed of delivery.

A unique selling proposition is often based on a strategic advantage that you have over the competition. Strategic advantages can include:

- Superior technology, particularly if protected by a patent.
- Distribution advantages, such as those gained from an existing system.
- Marketing superiority.
- Location. Being at the right place can mean everything.
- Personnel. Your team can be a significant edge.

■ Vertical or horizontal control. Ready access to "house" customers and/or abundant sources of supply can be advantageous.

HOW TO ADD VALUE TO PRODUCTS AND SERVICES

Although many marketers refuse to believe this, widespread access to technical advancements in most industries has led to the "death of the product solution." And since so many products are similar in quality and functionality, the secret is not to differentiate what your product is but rather to differentiate what it can do for the prospect. This is, after all, the only thing that really concerns the buyer.

In this world of commodity products, you must find a way to set yourself apart. And it is not only substance that will set you apart, it is also style.

One of the best examples of this is the clothing industry. Do you ever wonder why one pair of jeans sells for two to three times the price of another, or why a pair of "Air Jordan" tennis shoes sells for four times the price of the run-of-the-mill brand. I challenge the average consumer to tell me what makes the expensive shoe so valuable.

For another example, how about the lowly potato? Take a potato, slice it, boil it in oil, and sell it at the local fastfood restaurant. Or take the same potato, present it with garnish on fine china, and sell it for 12 times the price at an elegant French restaurant. Obviously, the second potato is not worth 12 times as much. The added value is the atmosphere in which it is served and in the presentation.

These examples prove that commodity products can be differentiated. Here are some additional value-added ideas:

■ Enhance the product or service with technical improvements. As noted above, this strategy has limitations because competitors will counter with their own improvements.

- Offer add-on services with your products. For instance, a car dealer can offer lifetime oil changes with the purchase of a new car or a software supplier can offer a 24-hour assistance hotline.
- Provide your customers with up-to-date information about their industries or job functions. Everyone can use information on how to do his or her job better.
- Offer expanded satisfaction guarantees and extended warranties. In fact, do anything you can to reduce the anxiety and fear the prospect has of making a bad decision.
- Offer new delivery methods and/or shorten delivery times for your products.
- Change the packaging or appearance of your product. The food industry has done this successfully in two very different ways. First by packaging prepared entrees and vegetables in single-serving containers. And at the opposite end of the spectrum, by offering commodity foods in bulk quantities.
- Find new uses for your product or service. Probably the most famous example of this is Arm & Hammer, which re-positioned its faltering baking soda product very successfully as a refrigerator deodorizer.

Be very careful about selecting your unique selling proposition. It can be an expensive, or even fatal mistake, to focus on a USP that is of little interest to the consumer. Once you have advertised your USP, it is very difficult to change your marketplace image. Test USPs prior to making large investments in media.

SEVEN ELEMENTS OF A CREATIVE STRATEGY

The following elements should be considered when developing a creative strategy:

1. A thorough understanding of the objectives. What do you want the advertising to accomplish? How is the advertising intended to support the organization's position statement?
2. Who is our primary target audience? What are their needs and interests?
3. What is the most important benefit of our product or service?
4. How can we prove our product claims? This information will be necessary for the copy that supports the headline statements.
5. What is our offer? What exactly are we going to give the prospect for his money? The offer is second in importance only to the choice of the audience.
6. Who is our competition? What is their marketing strategy and where are they running their advertisements?
7. What is the marketing budget? Do we have the necessary resources to overcome the competition and achieve our objectives?

Never forget to give each of these elements thorough consideration when developing your creative strategy.

HOW TO WRITE COPY
THAT GETS RESULTS

*E*ven Master Marketers find the subject of writing copy confusing and sometimes intimidating. There are hundreds of books and thousands of articles on the art of writing copy, each with its own unique viewpoint. Certain authors would have you believe that writing copy is like painting by numbers: "Just follow ten easy steps and wait for the orders to come pouring in." If life could only be that easy!

Writing winning promotional copy is getting tougher for several reasons. Competition is fierce, since more marketers are forced to compete for a slow-growing number of prospects. Consumers are better educated, more sophisticated, more aware of promotional strategies, and less likely to fall for hype or gross exaggeration. And advertising clutter is everywhere since prospects are exposed to hundreds of advertising claims daily, very few of which are actually targeted to their individual needs and desires.

The good news is that each of these problems leads to its own opportunity. Good copy can definitely make your organization compete successfully for your prospect's attention and dollars. But whether you write your own copy or use an outside resource, you need to be able to judge its effectiveness. I believe that good copy should always meet these five criteria:

1. It works. The copy achieves its stated objective, whether that objective is to sell products, generate leads, acquire new members or improve your organization's image. The good copywriter always keeps his "eyes on the prize."

2. It is targeted at the correct audience. You absolutely must understand your audience thoroughly to write good copy. Amateurs write copy first and then ask if it fits the audience. A true professional asks many questions about the audience before developing creative themes.

3. The copy advances your cause. The advertisement should make friends for your organization, not lose them. This means that you should not follow a short-term strategy of hyperbole and exaggerations, or deliberately mislead your audience. Nor should you write "shock value" copy. Yes, it does bring you attention. But rarely does it pay off in the long-term.

   But rarely does it pay off in the long-term.

4. It is memorable. No copywriter can attain immortality, but the closest one can come to it is to create advertisements that so capture the imagination of the audience that the ads are remembered long after they stopped running.

5. It is unique. In a world full of "me-too" advertising, fresh, vibrant copy will always stand out. Response rates for almost all industries have dropped to the point where the safe approach is no longer guaranteed to produce adequate

results. Being different does have its risks, but also offers the greatest rewards.

BEFORE SITTING AT THE TYPEWRITER

As a great admirer of Wolfgang Amadeus Mozart, I have always been intrigued by how he created such beautiful music. Mozart credited much of his success to his in-depth musical training as a youngster. In fact, Mozart never stopped studying music until his untimely death at the age of 35.

Yet, what is truly fascinating about Mozart is that he first composed his works "in his mind," then simply recorded the notes on paper. He never had to change a manuscript once it was written. It was always perfect THE FIRST TIME. Mozart kept no copies of the original score because he could always reconstruct the manuscript from memory. This is one reason why many people believe his music was divinely inspired.

I have often pondered (often over the sixth draft of something) how wonderful it must be to have such a talent. Unfortunately, the fact is that genius and divine inspiration are in very short supply (although our creative director, Howard Schwartz, once claimed that God speaks to him through a chihuahua named Pepe.) Most of us find writing to be a difficult and tedious process. The problem is not that we suffer from a lack of divine inspiration, but rather, from a failure to properly prepare for the writing assignment.

If you can afford to hire an advertising agency or freelance writer, I highly recommend that you do so. However, if your budget doesn't allow for this, you must prepare yourself for the task.

The best preparation for writing is in-depth knowledge of your product or service, backed up by a well-conceived offer. I suggest you spend a greater percentage of your time in the preliminary disciplines of research and offer development. While these are not the glamorous parts of the writing process, the extra preparation will make your copy more effective and much easier to write.

After conducting research and developing the offer, you should list every benefit you can think of for your product or service. Then rank these benefits in the order that you perceive them to be important to your prospects. Your goal is to find the single most important benefit, plus two or three secondary benefits to emphasize throughout the copy.

Remember that when you are developing the offer, ranking benefits or writing copy, you should always be thinking of one individual, not a group of nameless, faceless prospects. If you cringe at the thought that your writing will be read by thousands of individuals, then you will definitely benefit from this technique.

This method of focusing on one individual is often taught in public speaking classes as a cure for nervousness. It is easily transferrable to copywriting by visualizing one prospect and writing copy for only that specific individual. In fact, it helps if you speak to someone who fits the profile of the target audience about your product or service. Then, write something that you believe would capture attention and persuade that particular individual to accept your offer.

MOTIVATORS THAT WORK

Humans can be motivated in a surprising variety of ways. Using the correct incentive for a specific audience is a hallmark of good copywriting. Following are examples of appeals that have proven successful for many different types of offers:

Greed – Everyone is susceptible to greed to some degree. While greed is usually thought of as a negative emotion, it is really just the desire to get a better deal than our neighbour, or to enhance our position at a low cost. Copywriters that effectively push the greed button sell a lot of products.

Fear, Uncertainty and Doubt (FUD) - FUD is selling from

the negative perspective. Instead of saying "If you buy our product, these good things will happen to you," FUD copy implies "If you don't buy our product, these bad things will happen to you." Fear has been used in financial marketing to persuade prospects that their current investments are suspect, and in the computer industry to convince prospects that their current technology has shortcomings that leave them in a weak competitive posture.

Guilt – Although it must be used carefully, implied guilt can be a powerful motivator. A good example of this type of appeal is the telephone companies' "get in touch with someone" campaigns designed to make you feel guilty for not calling your mother.

Curiosity - This appeal is most effective with so-called "early adapters" of products. Some people have a strong need to own, or at least know about, the newest products and services. If you have the task of generating leads for a new product or service, create the curiosity in your advertising by withholding a little information. A satisfied curiosity-seeker does not respond to advertising.

Status or Exclusivity - People who have children know this as the reverse psychology approach. As soon as you tell your child he can't have something, his interest in the forbidden object increases dramatically. Likewise, for many individuals, the desirability of a product rises in direct proportion to its difficulty of attainment. The type of people who respond to this type of "snob appeal" can be found on lists of exclusive department stores such as Harrods.

Time Pressure - This appeal works better in a supporting role. Time pressure creates a sense of urgency by saying "buy me today because it will cost you more tomorrow" or "only the first 200 respondents can take advantage of this offer."

Convenience – Most people feel a great deal of time pressure in their lives. Advertisers that show people how their products and services will save them time and/or make their lives easier have a significant selling benefit.

Financial - The financial hot buttons of your prospects can be pushed two ways. First, by demonstrating how your product or service will save money and second, by demonstrating how your product or service will help generate more income.

THE AIDA FORMULA

One of the better known and time-tested copywriting formulas is "AIDA." I first read about this technique 15 years ago and have used it for hundreds of applications since. AIDA is simple to remember and, most important, it works.

The first "A" in AIDA stands for **"Attention."** You must always capture your prospect's attention as a first step to convincing him to respond affirmatively to your offer. Without gaining his attention, there is no sale. Depending on the media used, attention-getting devices can include bold benefit statements, curiosity-provoking questions, strong graphic images, give-away offers, official looking formats, and many others.

The "I" in AIDA stands for **"Interest."** Once you have captured a prospect's attention you must then arouse his interest in hearing more about your product or service. Many sales are lost at the border between attention and interest. For instance, it would be relatively easy to capture attention simply by printing the word **"FREE"** in large bold letters on the face of your advertisement. Most people will stop to find out what is being given away. But unless your message quickly builds on the attention getting message, the ad will fail.

One technique for building interest is to open your copy with strong benefit statements. Sales trainers teach the concept of "selling benefits, not features." This concept is equally valid in advertising. Your audience doesn't give a hoot what the product does (at least not at this stage). They want to know whether it will make them happier, wealthier, wiser, or make their job easier.

The following two headlines illustrate this point.

"Brand X has the most technologically advanced components."

"Brand X will save you one hour a day in processing time."

Headline number one is <u>us</u> oriented. It says "Look how good we are." Headline number two is <u>you</u> oriented. It says "Look what Brand X can do for you."

For an easy way to remember this principle, imagine that every one of your prospects keeps his radio tuned to the same station, and its call letters are WIIFM. WIIFM stands for "What's In It For Me." Copy that is not written to answer the prospect's question, "What's in it for me?," is ineffective copy.

The "D" in AIDA stands for "**Desire**." Even after you have captured the prospect's attention and built interest in your product or service, you must convince the prospect that what you are offering is worth more than what he will have to give you to receive it. This is known as "proving the value equation."

Remember that you must prove the value equation by building a strong case for the value of your product or service as it relates to a specific prospect. Different people have different value systems, so don't make the mistake of confusing what is important to you with what is important to the prospect. This is another good reason to gain a thorough understanding of your audience before you start to write copy.

The final "A" in AIDA stands for **"Action."** This is where you give your prospect sufficient motivation to send in the order card, or pick up the phone and call, or go to the nearest retail outlet to buy your product. Since you have been building the motivation to respond from the beginning of the advertisement, the favourable action of the prospect should be the logical conclusion to the process.

Just as it is important to lead the prospect to say YES, you must never give him a reason to say NO. Terms should be crystal clear and, in a direct mail package or coupon, the order coupon should be easy to read and fill out. It is also advisable to restate the major benefit, and security-blanket reinforcers such as money-back guarantees should be included as well.

THE PAPA FORMULA

PAPA is another easy-to-remember formula for writing copy in various media. Its letters stand for PROMISE, AMPLIFY, PROOF and ACTION.

Promise - Use the headline to promise the reader or listener a significant benefit that your product or service provides.

Amplify - After the promise is made, it should be covered in as much detail as possible. Amplification can include secondary benefits, product features and product specifications.

Proof - Even after the promise has been made and amplified, you must convince a sceptical prospect that your organization is legitimate, that your product will do exactly what you claim it will do, or that your service will be performed to the customer's specifications.

There are three basic methods of establishing this proof: product usage demonstrations, testimonials and satisfaction guarantees.

Action - As with the AIDA formula, everything you do or say must lead the reader or listener to take action. You must tell the prospect, in specific and understandable terms, how and where to take advantage of your offer.

THE PERSONAL SELLING FORMULA

Marketing and personal selling have a great deal in common. Good salespeople follow a series of steps that are designed to conclude in a purchase decision. They learn that each step is critical and must be followed in sequence to achieve the desired outcome. Likewise, each of these selling steps has its equivalent procedure in advertising copy.

Step One - Create an atmosphere of credibility. Credibility can be achieved with image advertising, public relations and mass-marketing techniques. The object is to predispose the prospect to accept your offer, whether it is the next time he sees your product on the supermarket shelf or the next time he receives a direct mail offer from you at home.

Step Two - Establish rapport. People prefer to buy from someone they like. This is why a salesperson will try to quickly find common ground with a prospect, such as shared hobbies or mutual friends. Advertisers build rapport with warm and inviting graphics and copy, while direct marketers build rapport with personalization and database marketing techniques.

Step Three - Grab attention. The number one tool salespeople use to grab attention is the strong benefit statement: "Mr. Prospect, my product will give you 50 percent greater output at the same cost." Likewise, marketers lead with a strong, opening primary benefit or a curiosity provoking headline.

Step Four - Support the benefit statement. This is the "prove it" stage. Salespeople "prove it" with product demonstrations and lists of product features. Marketers "prove it" with demonstrations, user testimonials and satisfaction guarantees.

Step Five - Overcome objections. Sales trainers teach their pupils a series of answers to common prospect objections. Since the advertiser may not have the ability to personally respond to a spoken objection, he must learn to anticipate potential objections and answer them within the advertisement or direct mail package.

Step Six - Close the sale. Whether face-to-face, as in personal selling, or through an advertising medium, it all comes down to closing the sale. A good salesperson asks for the order again and again. Marketers should be equally bold in asking for the order telling prospects exactly what you want them to do.

IMPORTANCE OF THE EMOTIONAL APPEAL

Whether you use the AIDA Formula, PAPA Formula, Personal Selling Formula, or any other process for writing copy, you must keep one important point in mind:

LOGIC FOLLOWS EMOTION

Writers who approach the copy process by attempting to logically prove the merits of their product or service are making a big mistake. The fact is, most individuals first make the buying decision for emotional reasons and then look for logical arguments to justify the decision they have already made.

Herman Holtz, in his excellent book, Persuasive Writing, makes this point well by offering three basic principles of persuasion:

1. A basic emotional appeal to cause the subject to want to be persuaded.
2. The need to be offered plausible rationalizations.
3. The reassurance that being persuaded is a wise decision.

Note that Holtz suggests first appealing to the emotions and then offering rationalizations. His formula would not work if it were reversed. Follow the Master Marketer method of writing copy, "Lead with the heart, and follow with the brain."

For copywriters, the weapon of choice is "words." Words can either evoke images that generate desire and spur people to action, or they can lie flat and wasted. Consider how words are used in the following examples:

"We have nothing to give but blood, sweat, toil and tears."

or

"We are going to fight very hard."

"Ask not what your country can do for you, but ask what you can do for your country."

or

"It is important to be civic-minded."

"Friends, Romans and Countrymen. I have not come to praise Caesar, but to bury him."

or

"Let me tell you what I think about Julius Caesar."

"The fresh, delicate pastries are mouth-watering."

or

"The pastries are good this morning."

In each of our examples, the images evoked by the first statement are much more powerful than the second. Whether you are writing to stir a country to action or to sell a household product, the words you choose can make an enormous difference.

26 Advertising Words that Sell

The following 26 words are known to evoke positive emotions. Begin incorporating them in your advertising and promotional materials and watch your results soar:

- Announcing
- Astonishing
- Exciting
- Exclusive
- Fantastic
- Fascinating
- First
- Free
- Guaranteed
- Incredible
- Initial
- Improved
- Limited offer

- Love
- Phenomenal
- Powerful
- Revealing
- Revolutionary
- Special
- Successful
- Super
- Time-sensitive
- Unique
- Urgent
- Wonderful
- You

The most important word in this list is YOU. The word "you" should be used often and the word "I" sparingly. In a letter that I received at my office recently I counted the word "I" 17 times and the word "you" only twice. It would have been a great letter had the I/you counts been reversed.

SPECIAL RULES FOR WRITING DIRECT MAIL COPY

In direct mail, copy is king, and always will be. Direct mail is simply not a graphic medium, as compared to television or magazines. The only thing more important than what you say in direct mail is saying it to the right people. Here are four major differences between writing for direct mail and other media:

1. The length of direct mail copy is elastic. While the volume of copy of a broadcast commercial is limited by the length of the radio or television spot, and print by the physical size of the ad, direct mail copy has no such restrictions. It is possible to use either a one page letter or ten page letter to accomplish the same purpose. Of course, one will out-perform the other and the trick is to know just how much copy is enough.

2. Direct mail is a conversational medium. I urge direct mail copywriters to think verbally, then transfer their thoughts to paper. While it is true this requires an occasional violation of the King's Rules of English, such transgressions can produce superior results. You don't have to be an English graduate to write good direct mail copy, and it may even hurt more than help.

3. Direct mail is truly a one-on-one marketing vehicle. Recognize this fact and write your copy accordingly.

4. By definition, direct mail, as part of the direct response family, usually requires a call-to-action. Your copy must produce results and those results should be measurable.

TIPS FOR WRITING DIRECT MAIL

- Always include a P.S. in your letter. People tend to read the P.S. before the body copy of a letter because they first look to see who signed the letter. Two ways to use the P.S. are to restate your most important benefit or to repeat your call-to-action.
- Keep your words, sentences and paragraphs short.
- Repeat your major benefits at the beginning and end of the letter. Also consider repeating them in the P.S., lift-

note and response device.
- Use statistics to support your claims. And remember the old expression, "If the statistics don't prove your viewpoint, you need more statistics."
- Test different copy approaches and offers. I have seen even a minor copy change in the P.S. lead to a significant increase in response.
- Remember always that your job is to sell. Copy that sells is good. Copy that doesn't sell is useless.

THE IMPORTANCE OF BEING A GOOD COMMUNICATOR

I once expressed my concern to a freelance copywriter that a particular print advertisement seemed a little too sophisticated and trendy for the audience. His creative ego defense shot up immediately as he informed me that "If the people reading the ad were too stupid to understand it, that was their problem." He went on to tell me that he wasn't about to change his style to suit a bunch of illiterate prospects. Of course, we found a new writer for the project.

What this person failed to understand is that it is irrelevant whether or not the audience was "illiterate" according to his lofty standards. The audience was what it was. These were the people who were either going to buy our client's products or not buy them. As such, during the time we spent working on that account, they were the most important people in our lives.

As the person charged with writing the words that convey the message, you must accept 100 percent responsibility for the quality of that communication. It is your burden to ensure that your message is not only heard, but that it is understood, in exactly the way that you intended. And you must do this on your prospect's terms, not your terms.

Always keep in mind that the prospect owes you nothing. He or she has no obligation to listen to you or even acknowledge your existence. Your challenge is to convince these preoccupied individuals, one at a time, to temporarily make your organization and its product or service the most important thing in their lives. This is a humbling and important task.

7

HOW TO FIND THE BEST SUPPLIER
AND AGENCY PARTNERS

*E*ven Master Marketers can't do it alone. We all need business associates to help us achieve our objectives. That is the purpose of this chapter; to demonstrate the best way to locate and get the most from your suppliers.

Before founding the agency which was to later become Ryan King Renninger, I worked for a decade on the client side, which gave me a great deal of experience working with advertising agencies and other service firms. In fact, one of the reasons I changed to the agency side of the business was the continual frustration with the poor level of service I received from suppliers and advertising agencies.

Specifically, I found the following to be negative characteristics of service providers:

Lack of expertise – In ten minutes with a new agency or supplier, it is obvious to me whether or not the account executive knows anything about marketing. Too often, I find myself dealing with an individual who tries to overcome his lack of expertise with a contrived sales pitch. When such a person is giving me a canned presentation, he is often genuinely surprised when I don't parrot back the expected response.

The worst offenders in the "lack of expertise club" are general purpose advertising agencies that lack basic marketing expertise. Often, they know just enough to be dangerous, but not enough to guarantee their clients good results.

Failure to stay within the budget – Estimating complex marketing projects is not for the inexperienced. One inaccuracy on a specification sheet can mean a large difference in price. If you are dealing with a supplier not experienced in estimating, you can almost count on cost overruns.

Failure to meet scheduled project completion dates – Sometimes this problem is caused by a supplier's lack of experience. But it can also be caused by inattention to details, or simply a poor attitude when it comes to meeting clients' deadlines. Of course, knowing the reason why your agency misses your completion date is no consolation when your time-sensitive offer reaches the prospects two days after the end of the sale, or your annual report is not printed in time for the board of directors meeting.

Inflexibility – Most agencies, including our own, work on hundreds of unique projects every year. Of these, perhaps 40 percent go exactly as planned. With the remainder, the changes can range from the minor to a complete overhaul of the project. We accept this fact, and build extra days into the schedule for anticipated changes. And, regardless of whether these changes were caused by the client, it is the agency's job to make the project come out all right in the end.

Unfortunately, many suppliers fail the flexibility test. A data processing shop may react negatively because the mailing file layout is different than expected. Printers push you back in the schedule because two extra half-tones are included with the artwork. Mailing houses are offended because you decide to change from franking the outside carrier to stamping.

Sometimes suppliers have legitimate complaints about clients. But more often than not, problems are exacerbated by the supplier's unwillingness to be flexible. Instead of fighting clients, these suppliers should learn to accept the world of marketing as it actually is, not the way they wish it to be.

Non-accessibility – This type of firm can be recognized by its habits. When a big job is coming up, the supplier will be practically camped at your doorstep. When the job is small, your account executive will be nowhere to be found. And when your job goes awry it's guaranteed that the person you need to solve the problem will be "in a meeting" or "out on appointments."

POSITIVE SUPPLIER QUALITIES

Let's consider the other side of the coin and discuss what types of traits you should look for when hiring a new advertising agency, direct marketing firm or production supplier.

Results-Orientation – Perhaps the most important quality, in my opinion, is a focus on results. By this, I mean that the agency is committed to achieving some specific outcome as a result of its efforts. Ask the supplier what results his latest programmes have produced for similar clients. Better yet, ask those clients yourself.

Experience – You will also want to find out about your prospective supplier's general experience in marketing and also how

89

much experience he has in your specific industry. While it is true that most marketing skills are transferable, it is also true that experience in a specific industry will give one supplier a significant edge over those without such experience.

Pricing – Another are you should assess is pricing, estimating and billing. When the supplier gives you an estimate, does he honour that estimate even when his costs are higher than anticipated? Does he produce his own work or use subcontractors for parts of the job? Remember, for every subcontractor used, there is an additional markup to pay. Try to use an agency that will give you a price for the entire project and honour that price unless you change the specifications of that project.

Attention to Detail – Try to discover how detail-oriented a particular supplier is. This is a critical factor, especially when implementing multi-media campaigns. A recent study showed that there are over 150 separate decisions to make on the average multi-media marketing project. To make each of these decisions and complete the project on time, it is important that a supplier has personnel who are good at managing details.

Responsiveness – You may want to call a random sample of a supplier's current clients to gauge how responsive and accessible the supplier will be. Many companies are great at selling new business but not so great at servicing the clients they already have.

GETTING THE MOST OUT OF YOUR VENDORS

Once you have found capable marketing firms to work with, there are certain things you can do to ensure their best effort on your behalf:

1. Meet the people who will be responsible for your

account. Often, the smiling account executive/sales representative who sold you on the merits of using his agency, actually has little to do with the day-to-day management of your account.

For production issues you may be dealing with people who have titles such as production manager, production coordinator, traffic manager or customer service representative. On the creative side, these people may be creative directors, art directors, copywriters and graphic artists.

Whatever the titles, you will want to meet all major participants on your account face-to-face. You not only get a better feeling for their specific strengths and weaknesses, but most people work harder for those customers with whom they have had personal contact.

2. Insist that the company's top personnel participate in the management of your account. The bigger the agency you are working with, the more likely you are to be delegated to personnel with less experience and authority. As one of my clients put it when describing his experience with another agency, "They sent in the A team to sell us and left the C team to service us." This is more likely to happen if your account is so small that it represents only a small fraction of the agency's business. It is only human nature to give more time and attention to top accounts. The message is: give your business to a supplier who will consider your organization an important account and accord you the type of treatment an important account deserves.

3. Try the supplier on small jobs first. Many managers have been burned by trusting a major project to a first-time supplier. No matter how impressive the supplier's

portfolio, or how glowing its references, you can only accurately judge the competence of a supplier after he has worked on a few projects for your organization. At our agency, we never mind beginning a relationship with a new client by working on small projects. It gives my staff and the client's staff a chance to get to know each other's habits and to develop a productive working relationship. Equally important, the client appreciates our willingness to put out full effort, even on small projects. And, assuming everything goes smoothly, they often reward us with larger jobs or the entire account.

4. Ask the vendor to put it in writing. In all marketing disciplines, there are so many details involved that it is easy to produce misunderstandings. Two common problems in communications are pricing and scheduling. There is nothing quite so frustrating as receiving an invoice for considerably more than you expected, or finding that your direct mail packages were dropped at the post office two weeks later than you were told, or that your print ad ran in the wrong issue.

To prevent the pricing problem, make sure you get a written estimate before the project starts. Hopefully, you can receive a firm quotation but, if not, at least insist that the estimate be honoured within an established range, such as plus-or-minus 10 percent. Also, be careful that all possible additional costs are spelled out before the additional work is performed.

To handle the scheduling problem, a written time-table should be provided by the supplier, outlining the project start and completion dates and major benchmark dates in between. Suppliers should welcome this request, because the schedule lists not only the responsibilities of the supplier but the client's as well. With a schedule, delays can be pinpointed and corrected.

5. Be loyal to your suppliers. This is not only important from an ethical point of view, but it also serves a practical purpose. Certain companies are known to have the loyalty of Benedict Arnold toward their suppliers. No matter how well you execute their projects, another supplier can come in and take the business away by providing a slightly better price on the next job. Naturally, the supplier who buys the business with price, knowing full well that it got the business solely on price, has no great incentive to provide outstanding service. There are degrees of loyalty between clients and suppliers, and I urge you to adopt a high degree. The best relationship between a client and supplier is similar to that of a partnership, where it is in each party's interest to keep the relationship alive and well.

6. Encourage an open relationship with your suppliers. Many times I've heard an agency employee say something similar to the following about his client: "I know that what my client is doing is wrong, but he doesn't want my advice on how to make it right." If your agency is afraid to share its frank and honest opinion about anything related to your account, you are missing a golden opportunity. Presumably the supplier is an expert in their area of specialty, or you shouldn't be working with them in the first place. Why not take full advantage of this expertise?

REASONS TO HIRE A FULL-SERVICE AGENCY

Should you use an outside advertising agency? Consider these benefits before deciding:

- An agency will offer a fresh, unique perspective on marketing issues (at least, they should).
- As an outsider, the agency will presumably be less affected by the internal politics of your organization.
- The agency will almost certainly have more specialized knowledge in certain areas than your staff.
- An agency will free your staff for other valuable tasks. You may be able to operate with a smaller payroll by using an agency judiciously.
- A good agency will gain an in-depth knowledge of your products and markets. The longer the agency works with you, the more valuable this accumulated knowledge becomes.
- If your agency is well-versed in cost-effective, target marketing strategies, it will save you, not cost you money, over time.

REASONS NOT TO HIRE A FULL-SERVICE AGENCY

If the following applies to you, then you should consider using in-house or freelance resources instead of an advertising agency:

- You cannot find an agency which understands your products and marketplace.
- You can't afford the monthly agency retainer.
- You have little or no media to place.
- You require little or no market research.
- You have an experienced in-house staff.

■ You would rather have a number of differing viewpoints based on limited knowledge, than one outside perspective based on in-depth knowledge.

ASKING THE RIGHT QUESTIONS

One secret to success in finding new suppliers is to ask the right questions. The checklists on the following pages can be used to help you choose a new advertising agency, direct response firm, list broker, printer, data processing firm and mailing house. The questions can be adapted for other vendors as well.

CHECKLIST FOR CHOOSING AN ADVERTISING AGENCY

1. How long have you been in business?
2. What are your yearly billings?
3. What did the agency principals and senior managers do prior to starting the agency?
4. What is your largest account? What is your smallest account?
5. Which of your other accounts are in my industry?
6. What is your area of greatest strength?
7. What is your area of greatest weakness?
8. Which parts of my projects would you handle inside and which will you subcontract?
9. Are you results-oriented? What are some of the specific results achieved by your clients?
10. Have you had projects that were failures or didn't go as well as expected? (If the agency answers no to this question it is either lying or brand-new in business)
11. Who will work on my account? What are their backgrounds?
12. Will I have access to <u>all</u> senior management of the agency?

13. How flexible are you about billing? Do you work on a retainer, project, or hourly fee basis?
14. Do you have a minimum project charge?
15. Do you charge for project incidentals such as faxes, mileage and long-distance phone calls?
16. Do you honour your project estimates? What is the plus or minus range on your estimates?

CHECKLIST FOR CHOOSING A DIRECT RESPONSE AGENCY

1. How long have you been in business?
2. What are your yearly billings?
3. What did the agency principals and senior managers do prior to starting the agency? Specifically, what was their prior involvement in direct marketing?
4. What is your largest account? What is your smallest account?
5. Which of your other accounts are in my industry?
6. What do you consider your area of greatest strength?
7. What is your area of greatest weakness?
8. Which parts of my projects would you handle inside and which will you subcontract? Do you have staff copywriters and artists? Do you own or control any of the production process?
9. What are some of the specific results achieved by your clients? (Do not hire an agency that can't answer this)
10. Have you had projects that were failures or didn't go as well as expected? (If the agency answers no to this question it is either lying or brand-new in business)
11. Who will work on my account? What are their backgrounds?
12. Will I have access to all senior management of the agency?

13. Do you have a minimum project charge or mailing size?
14. Do you bill by project or by package?
15. Do you honour your project estimates? What is the plus or minus range on your estimates?

CHECKLIST FOR CHOOSING A MAILING LIST BROKER

1. How long have you been in business?
2. What are your yearly billings?
3. What did the agency principals and senior managers do prior to starting the list brokerage?
4. What is your largest account? What is your smallest account?
5. Which of your other accounts are in my industry?
6. Are you better at business lists or consumer lists?
7. Do you own or manage any of your own lists?
8. If you are a list owner/manager, what pressure do you place on clients to use your lists?
9. Do you conduct back-end analysis for your clients?
10. Do you create list-performance analysis systems for your clients? Can I see samples?
11. What are some of the specific results achieved by your clients on lists you've recommended?
12. Have you recommended lists that were failures or didn't work as well as expected? (If the broker answers no to this question he is either lying or brand-new in business)
13. Who will work on my account? What are their backgrounds?
14. How flexible are you about billing? Will I have to prepay for any of my lists?
15. How much up-front research will you do for me before an order is placed?

CHECKLIST FOR CHOOSING A PRINTER

1. Who are your other customers?
2. What types and sizes of presses are in the shop? Are there Web or sheet-fed presses?
3. What are the smallest and largest jobs handled and the approximate turnaround times?
4. Is there an extra charge for rush jobs? How many shifts are normally working?
5. How many colours can be printed in one pass?
6. Are written estimates furnished for each job?
7. What type, weight and colour paper is kept in stock?
8. Can over-printing be done on a previously printed job?
9. Is die-cutting and perforating equipment available?
10. Is there a bindery on the premises?
11. Can printed materials be folded on the press?
12. How are printed materials shipped? (shrink-wrapped, pallets, or cartons)
13. How are charges for "overs" determined?
14. Can the printer create mechanical artwork?
15. Can material be stored and for how long? What is the fee for this service?
16. Are the materials on the premises insured?

CHECKLIST FOR CHOOSING A MAILING HOUSE

1. Who are your other customers?
2. What are the smallest and largest volumes handled? What is the turnaround time?
3. Is there an equipment list available?
4. Is there an inside person to coordinate and expedite projects?
5. What types of labels can be affixed?
6. What are the capabilities of the inserting machines?

7. How are the receipt of materials, drop dates and inventory reported?
8. Can you meter postage on-line?
9. Can you handle folding, coding, bursting and trimming?
10. Are stamps affixed by hand or machine?
11. How is payment of postage handled – directly to the post office or through the mailing house?
12. Can you fulfill premium offers?
13. Are standard prices given for services or is each job quoted?
14. What postage permits are applicable and who arranged for the permit?
15. Are postal receipts sent directly to the customer?
16. Are samples available showing acceptable folds, sizes and envelopes?

CHECKLIST FOR CHOOSING A
COMPUTER SERVICE BUREAU

1. Who are your other customers?
2. Is input acceptable on tape, floppy disk, or both? Can you convert from one format to another?
3. Is title and address expanding and abbreviating available?
4. Is upper/lower case converting and gender coding available?
5. Can you clean Postal Code and street address information?
6. Can the file be appended with Postal Codes?
7. Is postal presorting available for first-class and second-class?
8. Does the merge/purge system use a match code or evaluate field-by-field? (preferred for business-to-business)

9. Can software be customized to meet special needs? What is the hourly programming cost? Is there a minimum or maximum charge?
10. What standard reports are available?
11. Can the service bureau do data entry?
12. What types of barcoding services are available?
13. What types of personalized printing (laser, impact) are available?
14. Can you laser print sheet-fed and continuous forms?
15. Can signatures and logos be digitized?
16. What is the minimum job charge?
17. What quantity discounts are available?

SECTION III

CHOOSING THE BEST MARKETING WEAPONS

THE STRATEGIC WEB METHOD
OF SELECTING MEDIA

For several years, "multi-media advertising" and "integrated marketing" have been discussed at great length in advertising agency, client and academic circles. Both of these terms simply mean ensuring that all advertisements, promotions and marketing efforts present a consistent image for a company and its products or services.

Yet, despite all the talk, and the vast potential of integrated media, few advertisers are practicing it effectively. We will explore why this is so in a moment. For now, consider the fact that over $130 billion was spent in the US on various forms of advertising in 1991, of which a large portion was totally wasted, or at best, only partially effective. Even those who do make an attempt at integrating their media sometimes fail to realize the subtle influences various media have on each other.

Instead of viewing media as layers of independent promotional vehicles, each of which generates an incremental increase in overall results, the Master Marketer views media as a web of interconnecting and synergistic marketing tools. This "web effect" is why we refer to the art of selecting and planning media as the "Strategic Web" method.

Traditional marketing methods treat each media as separate unrelated entities.

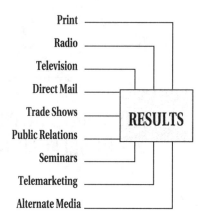

The Strategic Web uses each marketing tool to create a synergy and yield greater results.

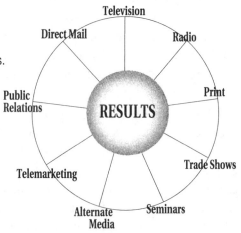

The primary cause of uncoordinated media is that schedules and strategies for each media vehicle (broadcast, print, direct response, etc.) are set independently of one another. In large companies, these separate media are even handled by different departments, each with its own agenda, budget and territory to protect. Sometimes these departments even work with different outside agencies. The company may have one agency handling mass-media advertising (print and broadcast), another handling direct mail, and still a third handling sales promotion.

Because it runs promotions in several types of media, this type of organization often claims that it is practicing multi-media marketing. While this is technically true, the conflicting schedules of the various media almost always prevent a successful program.

Image-splintering is an equally serious problem. Image-splintering occurs when an organization has unique creative thrusts for promotions run in each different media type. At best, these diverse messages have no effect on the audience and certainly do not support each other. At worst, they conflict with one other and confuse the audience.

Image-splintering can occur despite the best intentions. Marketers may purposely tailor their creative to take advantage of the nuances of a particular media, such as the demonstration ability of television or the ability to personalize direct mail copy. More about this shortly.

RULES FOR STRATEGIC WEB CAMPAIGNS

The Strategic Web method is based on the proven fact that each marketing vehicle can positively influence the results achieved by all other vehicles, provided that you follow three very important rules:

1. Each media must contain a similar message. Please note that I said a "similar" message, not "identical." By

this I mean that you should definitely use a familiar creative theme, graphic look and copy thrust. But I also recommend that you take the differences of various media into account and fine-tune the promotions accordingly.

2. The choice of media must be carefully coordinated. There are no magic formulas to do this because the media-mix varies from campaign to campaign. And while the choice of media in a Strategic Web pro-
    gramme may look very similar to the media used in a traditional programme it is the *way* they are used that truly separates the two approaches.

3. All media used are scheduled with much greater precision and are executed in very close time proximity to one another. For this reason, much greater levels of memorability and impact are achieved. As an added bonus, results will be seen much faster than with traditional programmes.

BENEFITS OF THE STRATEGIC WEB METHOD

Practitioners of the Strategic Web method of integrated marketing realize the following advantages over traditional methods:

■ Much greater results than from traditional programmes. This is true regardless of the programme's objectives (sales, leads, members, image, etc.).

■ Lower cost-per-sale or cost-per-lead. Leads and sales generated by the Strategic Web method often cost only one-half to two-thirds of those generated with traditional methods.

- Improved quality of response in terms of size of order, lifetime value of customer, etc.
- Longer recall of promotional messages by the audience.
- Overall savings in creative and media costs.

A COMPARISON OF TRADITIONAL VS. STRATEGIC WEB RESULTS

The following simplified data from actual campaigns will give you an example of how effective coordinated media can be. The purpose of both of these campaigns was to generate leads to be followed up by the company's sales force. Both campaigns utilized print advertising, direct mail and telemarketing.

CAMPAIGN ONE

January - March	Print campaign runs
March 10	Direct mail to 10,000 prospects (outside mailing lists)
April 5-25	Telemarketing to 5,000 prospects (internal list)

CAMPAIGN TWO

September-October	Print campaign runs
October 5	Direct mail to 10,000 prospects (outside mailing lists)
October 13-26	Telemarketing to 10,000 prospects (outside mailing lists)

Note the three major differences between these two campaigns.

- The total length of campaign two was eight weeks, versus 16 weeks for campaign one.
- Telemarketing began eight days after the mail drop in campaign two, versus 25 days for campaign one.

■ The same list was used for mail and telemarketing in campaign two. Two different lists were used in the first campaign.

How did these differences affect response rates?

CAMPAIGN ONE

	Budget		Audience
Print Advertising	£12,000		75,000
Direct Mail	£6,000		10,000
Telemarketing	£8,000		5,000
TOTAL	£26,000		90,000

	Response %	No. of Leads	Cost per Lead
Print Advertising	.001	75	£160
Direct Mail	.008	80	£75
Telemarketing	.014	70	£115
TOTAL PROGRAMME	.023	225	£115

CAMPAIGN TWO

	Budget		Audience
Print Advertising	£8,000		50,000
Direct Mail	£6,000		10,000
Telemarketing	£16,000		10,000
TOTAL	£30,000		70,000

	Response %	No. of Leads	Cost per Lead
Print Advertising	.0014	70	£115
Direct Mail	.012	120	£50
Telemarketing	.023	230	£70
TOTAL PROGRAMME	.036	420	£72

In this example, while it did cost £4,000 more, the coordinated campaign produced 195 more leads, with a 56% higher response rate and a cost-per-lead only 62% of the traditional media method. These response figures are not at all unusual. We have been involved with campaigns where applying the Strategic Web method has led to a 200 to 300 percent increase in the effectiveness of the programme.

BASIC STEPS IN INTEGRATED MEDIA PLANNING

Successful media planning is always based on a thorough understanding of the audience, organization, products and/or services being promoted. Without this solid foundation of knowledge, the media plan will almost certainly be ineffective.

Master Marketers do not follow the traditional model of media planning whereby media selection is made after the creative strategy is developed. They realize that the choice of the audience can be the most important decision made in a campaign. Choosing the audience to fit an existing creative theme is definitely an example of putting the cart before the horse.

The exception to this rule occurs when you have a creative strategy that is already working very well. In this case, you might want to tailor the choice of media to those which are compatible with the successful creative theme.

The following steps will help you create a media plan that supports the entire marketing process:

Step 1 - Reach firm agreement on the objectives of the marketing program. These objectives should be quantified where possible and expressed in terms of dollars or units of sale, numbers of leads, share of market, etc. All client and agency personnel involved must sign off on these objectives.

Step 2 – Make sure you fully understand the desired positioning of the organization and the product or service being promoted. For example, if your organization is known for quality and integrity, you will not want your commercials screened during controversial programmes.

While the overall organizational position should remain constant, there are times when a product can be positioned two different ways for two different audiences. For example, a media schedule may call for a product to be promoted in technical publications with one set of ads (appealing to the technical audience), and in general business or financial publications with a different set of ads (appealing to the financial audience). This is fine, as long as the creative themes of these ads complement, and don't conflict with each other.

Step 3 - Describe, in the greatest detail possible, the characteristics of your target audience. First, define the audience in demographic terms, such as: gender, age, income, marital status, family size, education, and ethnic background for consumer groups; and occupation, industry, location, company size, and purchasing authority, for business groups. Next, analyze the audience in psychographic terms such as interests, attitudes and lifestyles. Psychographics can be even more important than demographics in predicting future buying behavior. Defining the target audience can be best accomplished by first profiling your current customer base, because the people most likely to purchase from you in the future may be very similar to those who have purchased from you in the past. However, don't limit yourself to the study of past customers. Go outside the circle to find new potential audiences. This is where the art meets the science of media planning. If you are working with an outside agency, make sure the media director helps by suggesting new audience segments.

Step 4 - Define the geographic boundaries of the campaign. Determine the effective distribution area for your product or service. Will you need a national, regional or local plan? Consider the value of testing the programme in small selective areas at low cost before spending lots of money for a national campaign. There are many ways to localize a campaign. You can run ads in regional issues of national publications or buy inexpensive spot local or cable TV instead of network television.

Step 5 - Determine the budget limitations for the campaign. Optimally, the media plan should not be based on a pre-defined budget, but rather on the combination of media which will achieve the desired objectives at the lowest dollar cost. However, on those occasions where you have a preset budget amount to work with, it is much better to know this up front.

Step 6 - Establish the optimal levels of "reach", "frequency" and "continuity." These terms are defined later in this chapter. Each media programme will contain its own level of reach, frequency and continuity based on the unique characteristics of the product, audience and campaign objectives.

Step 7 - Choose the correct media-mix. The media-mix refers to the media categories you will use to best reach the target audience. Knowing how and when to use each advertising medium is a hallmark of a Master Marketer.

Traditional approaches to media planning often concentrate most of the advertising budget on one category, while the Strategic Web method requires multiple media channels. In fact, the same advertising budget spread over multiple media can be more effective than if used in a single medium, for these reasons:

■ People tend to ignore the same commercial run over and over on the same advertising medium, particularly if they feel you are contributing to annoying "advertising clutter." With a single channel plan, you may have a high absolute exposure level but a low effective exposure level.

■ With multiple media, you can reach the same people in different environments. Everyone has varying degrees of receptivity to messages depending on where and when they are exposed to the advertising. For instance, many people use radio as background accompaniment when driving or carrying out other activities. Therefore, it is not a strong direct response tool, although it can be very effective when used in conjunction with mail, telemarking or direct response print advertising.

■ Your message will remain interesting for a longer peiod of time if seen in multiple media especially if it is tailored for the unique characteristics of each medium.

Step 8 - Write the media plan. The media plan is the document the media planner prepares that provides all important information about the media aspects of the campaign. At a minimum, the media plan should include:
- Background on the advertiser and the product or service being promoted
- Objectives of the advertising campaign
- Length of time the campaign is to run

- Geographic boundaries of the campaign
- Budget for the media portion of the campaign
- Profiles of the target audience by unique segment
- Rationale for the recommended levels of reach, frequency and continuity
- Media mix strategy
- Media schedule, detailing the exact media to be used, timetables and costs

REACH, FREQUENCY AND CONTINUITY

It is necessary to understand the principles of reach, frequency and continuity to be an effective media planner.

"Reach" refers to the total number of households or businesses that are exposed to a message in a specific advertising vehicle at least once over a given period of time. Reach can be expressed as a cumulative number of households exposed, or as a percentage of the total universe exposed. Thus, if 30% of the prospects in your market have been exposed to your message, you have achieved a reach of 30.

"Frequency" refers to the average number of times each household is exposed to a message. With mass media it is very difficult to control exactly how many times each individual prospect sees your message. For instance, if your media plan calls for an average frequency of five, certain prospects may see the message 12 times or more, while others may never be exposed. This is one of the reasons target marketing is so effective; it gives you much greater control over the level of market penetration.

"Continuity" refers to the length of time an advertising program is run. In an ideal world, you would simply run your campaign perpetually at high levels, and eventually reach every prospect. But since budget limitations prevent all but the largest advertisers from achieving this level of continuity, consider the techniques of "flighting" and "pulsing."

With flighting, you concentrate your advertising during certain periods of time (flights), with scheduled breaks where you run little or no advertising. For example, if you are running ads in monthly trade publications, you might schedule them four months on and two months off. In a one year period, your ad would run eight times. This type of flight, properly conducted, can generate 80 to 90 percent of the results of a full-time schedule, at only 65 to 70 percent of the cost.

Pulsing schedules employ lower levels of steady advertising, mixed in with occasional bursts of heavy advertising. Pulsing works especially well with special promotions and seasonal products and services. In such cases, you keep "top of mind" awareness with your steady advertising and concentrate larger volumes of ads during those periods the prospect is most likely to need your product or service.

The precise blend of reach, frequency and continuity is the most difficult decision to be made by media planners. Except in rare circumstances, trade-offs will be necessary. For instance, it is possible to achieve high levels of reach but this may leave you with few resources for frequency. And it is the combination of frequency and reach that makes for a successful campaign.

WHEN TO GO WITH A HIGH REACH PLAN

Build greater levels of reach into your media plan if these circumstances apply to you:

- When you have a broad market
- When your company or product line is unknown
- When your product is unique or revolutionary
- When the commercial or advertising venue is very dramatic

WHEN TO GO WITH A HIGH FREQUENCY PLAN

Build greater levels of frequency into your media plan if these circumstances apply to you:

- When you have a small market.
- When you have a well-defined target audience.
- When you face a large, entrenched competitor.
- When your products are not easily distinguishable from the competition.
- When you are selling a high-ticket product.
- When your target audience consists of affluent individuals or senior executives.
- When your offer is time sensitive (tied to breaking news or a special promotion).

Advertisers more often err on the side of too much reach at the expense of frequency. Sometimes, organizations choose media plans that promise to reach a large number of people at a very low cost-per-thousand (CPM). But when the composition of the audience is analyzed, it is apparent that only a fraction of the total number are viable prospects.

This is why cost-per-thousand can be a very unreliable measurement of a program's chance for success. If you choose to evaluate media on a CPM basis, make sure you compute the number based on qualified prospects only, not the total circulation or universe reached.

For a simple example, if a magazine ad costs £10,000, and the magazine's circulation is 100,000, CPM would normally be calculated as £100 (£10,000 divided by 100). However, if only 10,000 of the circulation were viable prospects, we would compute the effective CPM as £1,000 (£10,000 divided by 10). As you can see, this makes a tremendous difference and is a far more productive way to compare media alternatives.

115

IDEAL EXPOSURE LEVELS

Unless you have a very broad market, it is almost always preferable to find media that contain a smaller number of qualified prospects and to advertise with higher frequency.

The ideal number of times a prospect should be exposed to your message will vary by product, medium and the competition. Generally, I recommend three to four "effective exposures." An effective exposure occurs when the prospect actually notices your commercial or reads your direct mail letter or print ad. If the prospect mutes the television or goes to the kitchen when your commercial airs, this is not an effective exposure. If she leafs past the page in a magazine that contains your ad, it is likewise not an effective exposure.

In traditional media programmes, to achieve three or more effective exposures, you would usually have to place your advertisement where it could potentially be seen by the average prospect eight to 12 times. The good news is that this number of required contacts can be much lower when you practice the Strategic Web method of integrated marketing. This is true because of the intense time compression in which the various media are run and the unified creative theme of all media.

COMPARISONS OF ADVERTISING MEDIA

The following are some of the pros and cons of the major media:

TELEVISION   <u>Strengths</u>
Extremely large reach
Best visual medium
Good for demonstrating products
Reaches a younger audience
Works well with emotional appeals

Entertainment possibilities
High frequency medium

Weaknesses
Network television is very expensive
Poor for targeted audience segments
Not good for selling complex products
Over-saturated
Mute buttons

RADIO   Strengths
Very flexible
Wide variety of formats/stations
Relatively inexpensive
Short production time
High frequency medium
Low production costs

Weaknesses
High cost for broad coverage
Extreme commercial clutter
Less attentive audience
Poor response vehicle

MAGAZINE   Strengths
Specific audience targeting
Demographic & geographic selectivity
Creates high recall
Long message life
Good visual medium
Reaches affluent audience

Weaknesses
Very low frequency

Limited demonstration capabilities
Long production times

NEWSPAPERS

Strengths
Pinpoint geographic selection
Good for immediacy and news value
Large reach within a defined area
Short production times

Weaknesses
Expensive for national advertisers
Little or no demographic selectivity
Short shelf life
Poor color reproduction
Ad clutter

DIRECT MAIL

Strengths
Personal communication tool
Very targetable
Large variety of formats
Strong response
Good response measurements

Weaknesses
High cost per contact
Mailbox clutter
Poor public perception
Environmental & privacy issues
Poor list quality

TELEMARKETING Strengths
Cost-effective
Very measurable
Highly targetable

Fast start-up time
Very flexible
Great partner with other mediums

Weaknesses
Not good for complex offers
Intrusive and annoying to certain prospects
Good lists may not be available
Poor public perception
Personnel training/retention problems

OBSTACLES TO IMPLEMENTING INTEGRATED MARKETING

There is no doubt that the advantages of integrated marketing are numerous and well worth the effort. So why haven't more organizations and ad agencies coordinated their creative and media plans? Here are the major obstacles that must be overcome:

■ Advertising agencies rely too heavily on mass media. Even though the percentage of audience captured by the TV networks has declined in the past ten years, television ad revenues still accounted for the highest percentage of revenue at the largest ad agencies. Agencies push mass media on their clients because it is very lucrative for them to do so.

■ Lack of expertise on certain media. Many agencies know little about target marketing methods such as direct mail and telemarketing. Rather than viewing these tools as full-partners, they are often shunted off to separate divisions. The target marketing people then become the enemy, trying to take money from the "important" mass media profit center.

■ Clients sometimes mistrust agencies and have a great

reluctance to put all their marketing eggs in one basket. Thus, they give mass media to one agency, direct response to another, and occasionally, sales promotion to a third. As I can assure you from experience, getting two or more agencies to cooperate on a campaign is about as hard as teaching a fish to walk on dry land.

■ Clients are misled into believing that awards equal success. Mass media agencies evaluate themselves and each other by the number of awards they receive.

The problem with overemphasizing awards is that they are usually won on the basis of creativity and memorability of the commercial; not on the basis of results achieved. We have, for example, a well-known Japanese auto manufacturer that featured a caricature of a "lying" car salesman in its US ads. The ads won many awards but the car company saw sales diminish during and after the period the campaign ran.

If you are working with an agency that prides itself on the number of awards it has won, instead of the number of success stories it has achieved for its clients, do yourself a favor. Find yourself a results-motivated agency that practices the Strategic Web method of integrated media.

ONE OF THE DANGERS OF PASS-ALONG READERSHIP.

9

BASICS OF MAGAZINE ADVERTISING

here are thousands of magazines that accept paid advertising, ranging from general audience publications such as Reader's Digest and Time, to very select, special interest publications with circulations in the low thousands (or even hundreds). Magazines offer a number of significant benefits to the advertiser, including:

■ Audience targeting - Advertisers can buy space in consumer magazines that appeal to specific types of readers, such as sports enthusiasts, financial investors, working women, men, hobbyists, etc. Business publications are even more narrowly focused, with most industries being represented by one or more trade publications. For instance, the marketing industry has <u>Marketing</u>, <u>Marketing Week Campaign</u>, <u>Creative Today</u> and <u>Direct Marketing International</u>.

■ Geographic selectivity – Every major city and region has at least one local interest magazine. Many national publications also offer regional editions which give the advertiser the impact of appearing in a national publication, at a much lower rate.

■ Demographic selectivity – As with regional editions, many consumer publications provide space in editions going only to subscribers that match certain demographic criteria (e.g. college students, the wealthy, or families with small children). Likewise, business publications offer the ability to target readers by job function and/or spending authority.

Detailed information on European consumer and business magazines is now available in the UK through British Rate and Data's subscription service so that you can plan pan-European advertising campaigns.

■ Long lives – While most broadcast, direct mail and newspaper promotions are quickly forgotten, magazine advertisements can continue to produce for months, or even years. Magazine ads for my first book, The Direct Marketing Challenge, still produce an occasional response three years after the ads stopped appearing.

■ Pass-along readership – Magazines often are seen by far more people than their circulation figures indicate. They are given to friends (and co-workers), left on buses, trains and airplanes, and sit in waiting rooms for months.

■ Magazine ads generate higher recall than other media. Readers of magazines tend to peruse ads at greater length and remember more of what they read.

■ Use of colour – Some of the most beautiful and effective full-colour advertising is run in magazines, which makes it a strong image medium; particularly for products and services which lend themselves to colour presentation such as food, cars and travel.

MAGAZINE DISADVANTAGES

Advertisers should also consider the following negative characteristics of magazines when deciding whether to use this medium:

- **Low frequency** - Since most magazines are published monthly or weekly, advertisers are limited in their ability to place their messages in front of the same individuals with any reasonable frequency. This contrasts with high frequency media such as television, radio and newspapers, where the ad can be repeated hourly or daily.

- **Long closing dates** - Many monthly magazines require the advertiser to reserve space five to six weeks before the issue's publication date, and to submit camera ready materials three to five weeks in advance. This allows limited flexibility in designing ads to take advantage of fast-breaking news or hot consumer issues.

  For example, when running ads for an investment fund, I found that in times of rising interest rates our most effective technique was to print the current interest rate or yield of a particular fund in large, bold letters. This worked well for newspaper ads because the closing date was one or two days prior to the publication date. In contrast, because of the long lead times required, the information in our ads would be out-of-date by the time they appeared, so we were forced to use ads that were not rate specific.

■ Slow response - Related to the problem of long closing dates is the slowness at which response is received. This makes a magazine a poor vehicle when immediate feedback or sales are needed.

■ Advertising clutter - As with every other advertising medium, magazines are overflowing with promotional messages. If you are a small-space or infrequent advertiser you may find your ad buried among a sea of giants.

CHOOSING THE BEST MAGAZINES

Selecting the best publications for your advertising budget starts with gathering information. A directory such as British Rate and Data (BRAD) covers over 4500 business publications and 2000 consumer magazines. Information listed in BRAD includes an editorial profile, rates and discount policies, production requirements, closing dates, circulation figures, and much more.

Refer to these directories to get the names of publications in your area of interest, then contact the specific magazines and ask for a "media pack." A media pack should include a sample issue of the publication, plus its rates, circulation and production requirements. Audience composition data and an audit statement from a reputable organization should also be included.

Business publications can be divided into two broad categories; "horizontal" and "vertical" magazines. Horizontal magazines serve people who have the same type of job function, regardless of industry. For example, Personal Computer World appeals to executives involved in strategic data processing issues, and Management Today serves senior managers. Both publications are read by individuals in dozens of different industries.

Vertical publications primarily service those people within a specific industry and are read by individuals with many different job classifications. Almost every industry group, from accounting to veterinary medicine, has its own "must read" publication(s).

Business publications are distributed in two distinct ways, "paid circulation" and "controlled circulation." Paid circulation, as the name implies, means that the subscribers pay a subscription fee for the magazine. Controlled circulation means that the magazine is distributed free to individuals who match certain qualification criteria. Many publications have both paid and controlled subscribers on their distribution lists.

Paid circulation publications derive their income from a mix of subscription fees and advertising fees while controlled circulation magazines must derive their income solely from advertisers. And while the debate rages between proponents of paid and controlled circulation magazines, I have found that the most important factors are the composition of the reader audience and the cost of reaching that audience, not whether the readers have paid for the magazine.

Consumer publications can be categorized in two general ways. First, by method of distribution, which refers to whether the magazine is sold by subscription or at the newsstand (retail). Second, by the type of publication, such as general interest, sports, youth, women's, hobbyist, etc.

In the UK magazine circulation figures are audited by the Audit Bureau of Circulations (ABC). ABC verify both the publications' circulation claims and the quality of the methodology the magazine uses to calculate its circulation figures.

To qualify for ABC certification, each magazine must submit its circulation figures annually in the form of a "Publisher's Statement." Annual in-depth audits either confirm these statements or correct them.

The following information is available from publishers:

- The industries and individuals reading the magazine.
- The names of the associations and their members who receive copies.
- The types of people who have received copies addressed to them individually or by job title.
- Breakdown of paid and unpaid (controlled) circulation.
- Number of copies sold through the news trade.
- Methods of distribution and geographical breakdown.
- Full price, discounted price and cost of subscription.

PROTOTYPE

CLASS, INDUSTRY OR FIELD SERVED: Travel, customs of people, products and related human interest, subject to geographical and sociological nature.

1. AVERAGE PAID CIRCULATION FOR 6 MONTHS ENDED DECEMBER 31, (YEAR)

Subscriptions:	295,069
Single Copy Sales:	109,721
AVERAGE TOTAL PAID CIRCULATION	404,790
Advertising Rate Base	400,000
Average Total Non-Paid Distribution 12,050	

1a. AVERAGE PAID CIRCULATION of Regional, Metro and Demographic Editions

Edition & number of issues

Eastern (6)	149,772
Central (6)	161,916
Western (6)	93,102

2. PAID CIRCULATION by Issues

Issue	Subscriptions	Single Copy Sales	Total Paid	Issue	Subscriptions	Single Copy Sales	Total Paid
July	285,960	116,637	402,597	Oct.	301,738	105,764	407,502
Aug.	297,181	107,749	404,930	Nov.	290,590	109,495	400,085
Sept.	300,315	102,700	403,015	Dec.	294,630	115,979	410,609

ANALYSIS OF TOTAL NEW AND RENEWAL SUBSCRIPTIONS

Sold during 6 Month Period Ended December 31, (Year)

3. AUTHORIZED PRICES

(a) Basic Prices: Single Copy: $1.50.	
Subscriptions: 1 yr. $12.00; 2 yrs. $22.00; 3 yrs. $30.00	19,431
(b) Higher than basic prices:	None
(c) Lower than basic prices: 1 yr. $7.00; $8.00, $8.99; 2 yrs. $13.99	78,924
(d) Association subscription prices	None
Total Subscriptions Sold in Period	98,355

4. DURATION OF SUBSCRIPTIONS SOLD:

(a) One to six months (1 to 6 issues)	660
(b) Seven to twelve months (7 to 12 issues)	85,669
(c) Thirteen to twenty-four months	1,021
(d) Twenty-five to thirty-six months	143
(e) Thirty-seven to forty-eight months	9,100
(f) Forty-nine months and more	1,822
Total Subscriptions Sold in Period	98,355

5. CHANNELS OF SUBSCRIPTION SALES:

(a) Ordered by mail and/or direct request	68,501
(b) Ordered through salespeople:	
1. Catalog agencies and individual agents	8,644
2. Publisher's own and other publisher's salespeople	590
3. Independent agencies' salespeople	14,100
4. Newspaper agencies	None
5. Members of schools, churches, fraternal and similar organizations	6,317
(c) Association memberships	None
(d) All other channels, See Par. 11(a)	203
Total Subscriptions Sold in Period	98,355

Sample page from ABC Audit Statement

Reliable data is crucial in constructing an effective media plan. When you consider a publication, make sure that it is an audited publication and insist on seeing its most recent audit statements. Most reputable magazines routinely provide audit statements with their media packs. As an advertiser, you can rely on audited statements to be fairly accurate, so don't accept a publication's own, unaudited circulation figures. While they may be correct, they may also be the result of someone's fertile imagination.

EIGHT IMPORTANT MEDIA PLANNING QUESTIONS

Ask these eight questions to determine if a particular magazine is the right place to promote your product or service:

1. Are the readers of this publication similar to the people who currently use my product or service or are they similar to those whom I believe will be good prospects?

2. What is the overall cost per thousand (CPM) to reach the publication's readership? What is the effective CPM to reach the portion of the audience that are qualified prospects?

3. What is the CPM and effective CPM when pass-along readership is factored?

4. Is the magazine one which will enhance the credibility of my organization or will it be decreased? Will my ad be in good company?

5. Is advertising in this publication consistent with all other promotions I am undertaking and the image I am creating for my company and its products?

6. Does the publication contain a high percentage of repeat advertisers? This is a good sign since repeat advertisers usually indicate long-term effectiveness.

7. Is the publication flexible on positioning and production issues?

8. Can I receive a special rate to try the magazine (such as a six or 12 time rate for one or two insertions)? Is there a discount for local advertisers or mail-order suppliers?

TEN QUESTIONS TO ASK ABOUT DIRECT RESPONSE ADS

Barbara Rains, associate publisher of North American Publishing Company (Philadelphia, PA), advises her direct response clients to ask these 11 questions of publications in which they are considering running direct response ads:

1. What other direct response advertisers are in your magazine?

2. What statistics do you have on their response?

3. What kind of advertising schedule do they carry in your magazine?

4. What discounts do you offer to direct response advertisers?

5. What kind of frequency discounts are available for multiple insertions?

6. Can I take the 15% agency discount if I place the ad

through my "in-house" agency?

7. What special editorial sections cover my product or speak to my portion of the audience?

8. Can you guarantee positioning within these editorial sections?

9. Do you offer any merchandising programs?

10. Can I gain access to your subscriber list for direct mail follow-up?

AD SIZES AND POSITIONING

There is always lively debate within the advertising community on ad size and positioning issues. Confusion often reigns because of conflicting studies showing the value and relative effectiveness of various sizes and positions. Here are my thoughts on the matter:

■ Advertising positioning in order of priority:
  1. Back cover
  2. First right hand page
  3. Second right hand page
  4. Inside front cover (2nd cover)
  5. Inside back cover (3rd cover)
  6. Page facing 3rd cover
  7. Center spread
  8. Front of publication positions
  9. Back of publication positions

■ Advertising facing or alongside editorial matter is more effective but only if the ad message is related to the editorial story-line.

■ Right hand position is a little more effective than left hand position but not worth paying extra for.

■ When running a response ad with coupon, the coupon must run along an outer edge, preferably on the right-hand side.

■ If the magazine has a mail-order section, direct response ads placed there will usually pull better than in editorial sections (many publications also offer discounts of as much as 20% to direct response marketers).

■ Certain non-standard size ads can give an advertisement large impact. For example:
  - Small ads placed in identical locations on sequential odd or even pages
  - Checkerboards - Supporting ads placed diagonally on the page or across pages
  - Half- or third-page ads running vertically or horizontally across the page
  - Gatefold or centerfold ads
  - Island ads surrounded by editorial matter

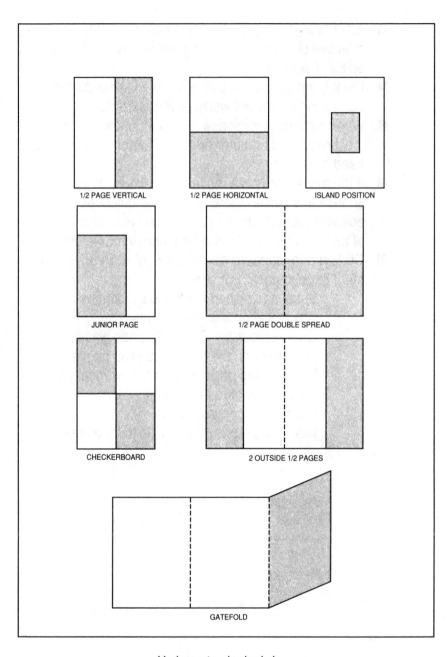

Various standard ad sizes

Two alternatives to traditional space ads that reach the same audience are response cards and card decks. Response cards can be bound into the publication to be torn-off by the reader or they can be freestanding inserts. Card decks are packages of postcard size advertisements that usually contain selling copy on one side and the advertiser's mailing address and postage-paid information on the other side. These decks are mailed from one to 12 times per year to the magazine's subscribers.

Card decks and insert cards will usually generate more leads than the space ad itself but the leads are often of inferior quality.

PURCHASING MAGAZINE SPACE

All of the information you need to purchase advertising space in a particular publication can be found in BRAD and the magazine's media pack. The media pack will contain a rate card which lists all the ad sizes available and the rate for each size. Consider the rate card prices to be negotiable because publications are often willing to work out special arrangements, especially if you have the potential of becoming a frequent advertiser.

Almost all publications discount rates to advertisers who agree to run ads more than once. For example, a management magazine's rate card notes that the publication charges about £8,500 for a full-page, four-colour ad. Advertisers who run the same size ad six times pay 10 percent less and those that agree to run 12 times get a 20 percent discount.

As soon as the decision to reserve space in a publication is made, you or the advertising agency should fill out, fax or mail an "insertion order" to hold the space. An insertion order should contain the following information:

- Name and address of publication.
- Name and address of advertiser and agency.
- Billing instructions (bill advertiser or agency).
- Publication issue date.

■ Description of ad (it is a good idea to include the ad's headline and key number).

■ Size and number of colours of the ad.

■ Position instructions such as Run of Publication (ROP) or special placement.

■ Rate, whether published rate or negotiated rate. Also include any extra production costs.

■ Special instructions, if applicable.

1 Advertising Rates (black and white)

Size	1X	6X	13X*
2-Page Spread	$16,625	$16,060	$14,255
1 Page	8,315	8,200	7,425
⅔ Page	6,700	6,555	6,085
½ Page Island	5,700	5,580	5,180
½ Page	5,025	4,920	4,565
⅓ Page	3,355	3,280	3,045

Size	24X	48X	60X
2-Page Spread	$13,670	$13,500	$13,280
1 Page	7,225	6,890	6,785
⅔ Page	5,815	5,680	5,410
½ Page Island	4,945	4,830	4,600
½ Page	4,365	4,260	4,055
⅓ Page	2,910	2,845	2,710

* This special 13X rate is for advertisers who run in every issue in 1992—the 12 regular monthly issues plus the June Special Issue.

Color Rates

Color	Page	Spread
Standard AAAA (red, yellow, blue or green)	$745	$1,225
Matched	925	1,535
4-color Process	1,550	2,095
Metallic Sheen	1,505	2,045

Cover Rates

	6X	12X
Cover 2	$10,695	$9,735
Cover 3	9,500	8,675
Cover 4	11,355	10,695

Software Magazine rate card.

Insertion Order No. _____

Date _____

Client _____

_____

RYAN KING RENNINGER

rkr

MARKETING ADVERTISING

Media Issue _____

Date of Issue _____

_____

_____

Media
Insertion
Order

Size _____ Color(s) _____

Position _____

Headline _____

Product(s) _____

Costs

_____	Space Cost: _____
_____	Color: _____
_____	Other: _____
_____	%Commission: _____
_____	Net to us: _____

Payment

☐ Bill Agency
☐ No Charge
☐ Trade
☐ Bill Client
☐ See Special Instructions

Invoicing

Your invoice must show RKR Insertion No._____and must have tear sheets attached. Invoices will not be considered for payment until printed material has been received and reviewed with client.

Special Instructions: _____

_____

_____

_____

_____

Insertion for (Client): _____

Media Director: _____

Inserted by Ryan King Renninger

Ryan King Renninger acts only as an agent for the above named client and as such is entitled to any and all standard agency discounts and commissions from the magazine of insertion.

1901 Research Blvd ▪ Suite 310 ▪ Rockville MD ▪ Phone: 301-251-4708 ▪ FAX: 301-762-2049

Ryan King Renninger's insertion order.

137

HOW TO CREATE A WINNING PRINT AD

Before developing a concept for the ad, and certainly before writing a word of copy, make sure you have a well-defined creative strategy. Your creative strategy will depend on the answers to the following questions:

1. What is the unique selling proposition of my product or service? What makes it better or unique?

2. What exactly do I want the ad to accomplish?

3. What are the characteristics of the publication? What is the editorial environment in which the ad will run?

4. What is the competitive situation? Who else is advertising in this magazine?

5. How will I achieve consistency with all my other marketing and advertising?

The actual creation of a print ad begins with a concept. I like to think of the concept as the "BIG IDEA," or the major theme of the ad. A good concept is a blend of a hard-hitting headline and a compelling visual. No matter how strong the headline and graphic are individually, they must work together well to create a powerful concept.

By far the most important part of the copy is the headline. In fact, you would be serving yourself well to spend as much time working on the headline as on all the rest of the copy. Studies have shown that over 75% of magazine readers never get past the average ad's headline. This means that three out of four times, the headline was not strong enough to draw the reader into the body copy.

What makes a great headline? First, the headline should contain the main message of your ad. Second, it should offer a benefit. Third, the benefit must be readily apparent and not require any interpretation on the part of the prospect. Fourth, it must work in perfect harmony with the ad's visual.

Two headline approaches are the "news bulletin" and the "curiosity provoker." The news bulletin headline can highlight a new product or service or improvements to an existing product or service. The curiosity provoking headline asks a direct question or creates a puzzle for the reader to solve.

How long should your headline be? The answer: as long as is required to accomplish the objective. Research has shown that long headlines usually outsell short headlines, so when in doubt, go with the longer headline version.

Likewise, the length of body copy depends on the purpose of the ad. Image ads require less copy than direct response ads. Direct response ads must contain all the copy necessary for the prospect to take the action requested. Yet, I see this rule violated often with very long image ads and very short direct response ads.

The main purpose of body copy is always to reinforce and support the headline, not to open up new areas. Ads are best written in conversational language. Unless your audience is highly technical, keep the industry jargon to a minimum.

If you have a choice between photographs and illustrations use photographs. Studies show that ads with photos gain 30 percent higher readership than ads with illustrations. Of course, photos are usually more expensive than illustrations, so you must factor the extra cost in the equation. One effective use of photographs is to show a before and after scene.

Other ideas to get the most out of your print ads:

- Use captions under your photographs. Captions are read as much or more than headlines.
- Avoid cluttered layouts. Make the ad easy to read.

- Use testimonials. They add credibility.
- Four-colour ads gain 40% more readers than two-colour ads but usually cost a great deal more.
- Use subheads and keep your paragraphs short.
- If you are using a premium in your ad, sell the premium, not the product.
- Keep reverse type to a minimum. It may look nice but it reduces readability.
- Develop one layout format and stick with it. You should have such consistency that readers know that the ad is yours even before seeing your name.
- Strive to create ads that are unique. Be an advertising leader, not a follower.

10

BASICS OF NEWSPAPER ADVERTISING

*T*here are three basic varieties of newspaper publications to advertise in: national publications such as <u>The Times,</u> <u>Financial Times</u> and the <u>Sun;</u> regional and local publications which cover a limited geographic area. Together, all forms of newspaper advertising account for approximately 30 percent of total advertising expenditures.

Newspapers can also be classified by frequency of publication. The greatest number are dailies and weeklies but there are also papers published only on Sundays, as well as monthlies and bi-weeklies. Newspapers, like magazines, can also have either "paid" or "controlled" circulation. Paid circulation means that the recipient pays to receive the paper. Controlled circulation refers to those papers that are distributed free, such as community and "shopper" newspapers that contain many advertisements and little or no editorial material.

ADVANTAGES OF NEWSPAPER ADVERTISING

Advantages of newspaper advertising include:

- Large reach. The vast majority of households subscribe to one or more local newspapers. In some communities, it is possible to reach over 90 percent of households with a single newspaper.
- High frequency (dailies). You have the ability to expose your prospects to your message day after day.
- Good geographic selectivity. Newspapers allow you to reach just the communities you want. Even large, national papers such as The Daily Mirror now offer regional editions to break down their subscriber areas.
- Qualified audience. Newspaper readership rises with income and education level.
- Low cost per thousand (CPM). Newspapers offer a cost-effective way to reach large numbers of people.
- Low production costs. Newspaper ads are inexpensive to create and reproduce.
- Quick turnaround time. Unlike magazines, newspapers can accept your ads on very short notice, which makes it a good medium for timely promotions.

DISADVANTAGES OF NEWSPAPER ADVERTISING

- In general, newspapers offer poor demographic selectivity, since all categories of individuals read the same papers. This is not as true however, for specialized publications such as <u>The Financial Times</u>.

- Short message life. The newspaper which is read each morning is discarded the same evening, along with your advertisement.

- Poor production quality. Although many papers, are using colour, the majority are still printed black only, on low-quality newsprint stock. This does not lend itself to high quality visual images.

- Very expensive for national advertisers. Most papers give a better rate to local advertisers. The greater expense and difficulty of coordinating media buys make newspapers a poor choice for many national advertisers.

HOW TO BUY NEWSPAPER SPACE

Newspaper space can be purchased as either display advertising or classified advertising. Display advertising is placed throughout the paper, mixed in among editorial matter, while classified advertising is most often run in special sections and grouped according to the type of products or services being sold.

Newspapers sell space by the line or column centimetre.

You can purchase newspaper space as either R.O.P. (Run of Paper), or in premium positions. R.O.P. means that your ad can appear anywhere in the paper, and your ad is placed at the publisher's discretion. This is the most economical way to buy space, but not always the most effective. You can also purchase premium positions to place your ad in a particular section, such as the sports pages, next to editorial matter, or at a specific place on the page. Premium positions are especially important for coupon advertisements.

Most newspapers offer series discounts of 10–20% to volume advertisers. It is a good idea to accept the lower rate if there is any possibility you will reach the larger number of lines. For example, if you contracted for 20,000 lines, but only ran 10,000 lines, the paper will simply charge you a "short rate," which is the difference between the 20,000 line rate and the 10,000 line rate. So, when in doubt, sign up for the lowest rate.

Many newspapers also offer lower rates to local retailers, charitable organizations and direct response advertisers. They are also open to special arrangements for new advertisers, since they hope you will become a steady customer.

Because newspapers have different circulations and different rates, you should use the "milline rate" for accurate cost comparison. The milline rate is the cost per line to reach each million of circulation. To calculate the milline rate, multiply the applicable line rate by 1,000,000 and then divide by the circulation. Here are two examples:

NEWSPAPER A: $$\frac{£8.50 \text{ (line rate)} \times 1,000,000}{350,000 \text{ (circulation)}} = £24.29$$

NEWSPAPER B: $$\frac{£6.25 \text{ (line rate)} \times 1,000,000}{280,000 \text{ (circulation)}} = £22.32$$

As you can see, according to this calculation Paper "B" has a milline rate of £22.32, which is lower than that of Paper "A" (£24.29). However, this does not necessarily mean that B is a better media choice. To determine the true efficiency of each publication, it is necessary to calculate the "effective milline rate."

The first step is to determine the percentage of the total circulation of each publication that are qualified prospects for your offer. Then re-calculate the milline rate using the formula above. For our purposes, we will assume that 60 percent of Paper A and 45 percent of Paper B are qualified prospects.

NEWSPAPER A:
$$\frac{£8.50 \text{ (line rate)} \times 1,000,000}{210,000 \text{ (60\% of 350,000)}} = £40.48$$

NEWSPAPER B:
$$\frac{£6.25 \text{ (line rate)} \times 1,000,000}{126,000 \text{ (45\% of 280,000)}} = £49.60$$

As you can see, by using the effective milline rate as our guide, Paper A would be a better use of your advertising dollar, with an effective milline rate of £40.48, versus Paper B, with an effective milline rate of £49.60.

SOURCES OF INFORMATION ON NEWSPAPERS

There are two sources of in-depth information on newspapers. First, you can contact the display advertising department of the appropriate newspapers and ask for their latest rate cards. Rate cards contain all or some of the following data: general and discount advertising rates; commission policies (some papers do not offer commissions to local advertisers); color availability; split run rates; mechanical requirements; classified rates; special position availability and rates; and circulation figures. While collecting rate cards from a few newspapers is fine for a local advertiser, those who market in a wider geographic area should subscribe to British Rate and Data (BRAD). BRAD summarizes the data from the individual rate cards in one comprehensive volume. BRAD subscriptions are fairly expensive, so if you are working with a limited budget you might check to see if BRAD is available at your local library.

Since newspapers base their rates primarily on circulation, it is important that advertisers be able to rely on the accuracy of the numbers supplied by the paper. For this reason, you should verify that the newspapers you advertise in are audited by the Audit Bureau of Circulations (ABC). ABC circulation statements contain useful information, such as: total circulation; circulation by locality; numbers of subscribers brought in with discounts, contests and premiums; and number of papers sold at newsstands, mailed, and delivered to the home.

NEWSPAPER INSERTS AND SUPPLEMENTS

The "insert" is a free-standing piece of advertising literature. Inserts run the gamut from postcards to full-color catalogs with dozens of pages. Usually, the advertiser has the insert printed and delivered to the paper, although many publications are willing to assist the advertiser with production. The advantage of a free-standing insert is that the production quality can be much better than the rest of the paper. Also, there is no editorial matter within the insert to compete for the reader's attention.

A "supplement" is a part of the paper containing general or specialist editorial matter. Examples include "The Magazine" (Sunday Times), The Guardian Media and You Magazine (Mail on Sunday). Many regional editions exist as well. Advertisers like supplements because they usually offer better reproduction quality than newspapers and because rates can be very favourable for regional editions of national supplements.

HOW TO CREATE AN EFFECTIVE NEWSPAPER AD

Follow these tips to produce an effective newspaper advertisement:

- Put major effort into the headline. Just as with magazine advertising, the headline is far and away the most important part of the newspaper ad's structure.
- Use the headline to grab the reader's attention. State a major benefit, provoke curiosity, announce important news, prompt action, or make a genuine promise to the consumer.
- Don't be afraid to lose readers with your headline. Forget the people who aren't legitimate prospects and write your headline to get all genuine prospects to read the ad and take action on your offer.
- Remember to keep it simple. Stick to one main theme, one benefit and one big idea.
- Don't overstate your case. Exaggerations and hyperbole turn people off.
- Keep the layout simple. Newspapers are not good visual mediums, so don't try to do too much with graphics.
- Use a photograph. Photos pull in more readers than illustrations.
- Put a caption under every photograph and illustration. Captions increase readership.
- Go easy on the reverse type. Although designers love reverse type, it has a tendency to wash out in newspapers.
- Create a consistent look for all your newspaper advertising and stick with it. Never give up on a successful ad too early.

11

BASICS OF TELEVISION ADVERTISING

*T*elevision is an extraordinarily powerful medium, with the potential to make or break markets, companies and products. National advertisers such as Procter & Gamble, The Sun and Ford could not have achieved the market share they hold today without television.

Although TV is now being used by almost every type of advertiser, it works particularly well for the following offers:

- National consumer products.
- Products with broad audience profiles (e.g. toothpaste).
- Advertisers with large market shares to protect.
- Advertisers with a hot new product.
- National product and service companies with dispersed retail outlets.

- Products that lend themselves well to a visual presentation (e.g. food and cars).
- Non-complex products.
- Certain direct response offers.

Each of the regional stations provide their own news and local interest programmes; in some cases they supply programmes to the network or buy in programmes produced by other regions. Advertisers can buy spots on the complete network or from local regions. In theory, the ITV regions each have independent sales organizations, but the current round of takeover moves may change the picture considerably. Channel Four is broadcast throughout the country and has its own sales organization.

Satellite and cable television is in relative infancy although recent reports suggest satellite is increasing its share of audience up to around 30 percent. Satellite subscribers' choice currently includes:

- Sky Movies
- The Movie Channel
- Sky Movies Gold
- Sky One
- The Family Channel
- Music Television
- Sky Sports
- Eurosport
- Family Channel
- Children's Channel
- Sky News
- CNN

This proliferation of media gives viewers a much wider choice but makes it equally difficult to select the right channel to reach both consumer and business target audiences.

In the UK, television output is dominated by the BBC which

has two channels, Independent Television (ITV) and Channel Four. The two BBC channels do not accept advertising although there are ongoing debates about replacing the present licence fee system with advertising revenue. Cable and satellite channels are available in the UK and in Europe although they are less developed than the United States.

As well as accepting product and service advertising, the commercial channels also sell sponsorship for complete programmes such as films, popular entertainment series and the weather.

The ITV network, which had advertising revenue of around £1.4 billion in 1992, is structured by regions, although at the time of writing ownership was changing rapidly as the government relaxed the rules on takeovers. The prepublication structure included:

- Carlton
- Central
- Meridian
- Yorkshire/Tyne-Tees
- Granada
- Anglia
- London Weekend Television
- HTV
- Westcountry
- Channel
- Grampian
- Ulster

ADVANTAGES OF TELEVISION ADVERTISING

Consider these benefits when deciding whether to include television in your marketing plans:

- Television offers the largest possible reach. Virtually all European homes contain one or more television sets, and TV viewing occupies around 30 percent of average European leisure time. Whether you are attempting to reach the greatest number of the total population or the greatest number of people in a particular city or region, TV can provide blanket coverage of a market.

■ Television is a high frequency medium. If you can afford the time, TV allows you to drum your message into the minds of your prospects through constant repetition.

■ Television offers powerful demonstration capability. From a sporty car hugging a mountain road, to the famous "Ginsu Knife" slicing through tomatoes, TV has the ability to bring products to life. Television combines pictures, graphics, movement, music and dialogue. The skillful blend of these elements creates an unforgettable and successful advertisement.

■ Television can be inexpensive. While the overall cost of television makes it the most expensive promotional medium, careful media buying can give you a lower cost-per-thousand (CPM) than other marketing vehicles.

■ Television supports other marketing efforts. The selective use of TV to create awareness can dramatically increase response to follow-up marketing tools. This is why the tabloid newspapers are on your TV screen urging you to rush out to buy their paper so that you can have your chance to win millions.

■ Television is a creative medium. The excitement and drama of creating and executing a TV commercial is unmatched in the advertising world. It offers client and agency alike the chance to make a large impact.

DISADVANTAGES OF TELEVISION

There are some drawbacks for you to consider before including television in your media-mix:

- ■ Television time is expensive. Although I made the point that television can be inexpensive when measured in terms of cost-per-thousand, it still requires large amounts of money to achieve the reach and frequency necessary to penetrate a market; especially a market dominated by large competitors.
- ■ Commercial production is expensive. Despite low-cost techniques available, high-quality TV commercials can cost tens of thousands to produce.
- ■ Television has a broad viewership. Although cable and community TV have made this marketing vehicle available to many smaller organizations, many of those with narrow audience niches will not find television to be a good targeting tool.
- ■ Television is not generally good for presenting complex products and services.
- ■ Television suffers from over-saturation. The TV advertiser's worst nightmare is the remote control mute button, which is being used by more and more people who are tired of TV airtime clutter. Subscriber Channels like Sky are also draining the audience base away from network advertisers.

SCHEDULING TELEVISION TIME

Television schedule planners must be concerned with both the reach and frequency of the message. "Reach" refers to the total number of households exposed to the message. In broadcast, reach is measured in "rating points." Each rating point indicates the percentage of the total number of households that own televisions that watched a particular program. "Frequency" refers to the number of times each household is exposed to your message.

Advertisers strive to achieve a certain amount of gross rating points. Gross rating points (GRP) are calculated by multiplying the rating points on each show in which a commercial has been run, by the number of commercials run. Media buyers also rate media in terms of the cumulative number of households which have seen a commercial. The audience number will almost always be lower than the total of gross rating points because of the people who have seen a commercial more than once.

If you have a unique, high-impact product, reach can be more important than frequency because those who are exposed to the commercial only once or twice may very well remember it and take action. Most often though, large reach should not be achieved at the expense of frequency. Due to the problem of over-saturation mentioned above, commercials must usually be seen several times to penetrate the prospect's awareness, let alone cause him to buy the product.

The television day is divided into time sectors, such as breakfast, daytime, prime time and late night. Media planners should take careful note of the sector in which a commercial is to be run. Both the price of television time and the demographics of viewership vary widely throughout the broadcast day.

Programme content is another key factor because there is an inverse relationship between a person's commitment to a particular programme and his willingness to pay attention to a commercial message. This is why so many direct response ads run in non-prime time periods. Late night viewers are less committed to television programmes than prime time viewers, and therefore are more likely to respond to late night direct response ads. The same ads run in prime time spots achieve much lower response rates.

The Broadcaster's Audience Research Board (BARB) as well as individual stations, provide vast amounts of research data on the precise composition of the audience for each programme in the schedule. Viewership figures for specific programmes are measured three ways: 1. Households which keep diaries on their viewing habits, 2. Electronic monitoring devices, and, 3. Telephone or personal interviews.

The Target Group Index surveys the viewing and buying habits of a defined sample of the population, recording their characteristics, media exposure and buying habits in relation to 400 types of product. Media buyers use such data to ensure sufficient overall commercial coverage and to match their products or services to the buying trends in specific market areas.

Television time is highly negotiable and, as noted earlier, can be relatively inexpensive. We have purchased time for local advertisers for as little as £50 per spot on cable or community television. At the other end of the spectrum is national network space, which can cost from a few thousand to over £100,000 per minute.

A reduced rate is available for those willing to place their commercials Run of Station (ROS), which allows the station to run the commercial at any open spot during the broadcast day. As an alternative, you can schedule the commercial to run at any time during a particular daypart.

When developing your TV schedule, keep in mind that quality is usually more important than quantity in media selection. I once violated this rule by making a large buy on a national sports programming network to advertise a money market mutual fund. I was persuaded to try the sports programming by the large amount of gross rating points that could be purchased at a very small price.

The commercials featured a free phone number and we scheduled operators to come in on the weekends to take the expected flood of calls. Unfortunately, the flood turned out to be a trickle. We had an unhappy advertiser but learned an important lesson: Don't be persuaded by large numbers. When in doubt, always choose quality over quantity.

One way to make sure you are reaching people who are likely purchasers of your products or services is to profile existing customers to find out which television programmes they watch on a regular basis. Since like-minded people tend to watch similar programmes, you will be communicating with individuals that match your target audience profile.

TYPES OF COMMERCIAL FORMATS

While by no means a conclusive list, the following are some of the more frequent commercial formats:

Slice of Life - Also referred to as problem/solution. This format shows a typical consumer or business user engaged in some everyday activity. Usually, the commercial starts out with the individual faced with a seemingly unsolvable problem (such as a headache that won't go away). Then, a kindly family member, neighbour or friend, introduces the person to a remedy that has worked for them (such as a certain brand of aspirin). The commercial ends with a smiling user praising the product that has solved his or her problem.

Presentation - One or more individuals appear in front of a camera and talk about the product or service. This format can work equally well in an inexpensive studio setting or out on location. It is most important to have a persuasive presenter who appears to be someone who would actually use the product or service being advertised.

Demonstration - The product is shown in actual use (e.g. a floor cleaner wiping up tough dirt). Consider using this format when you can show a definite competitive advantage, but make sure that the advantage is one that means something to the consumer.

Testimonial - One or more individuals tell the story of how the product or service benefitted them. Testimonials are best used when you need to provide back-up support for a strong product claim. Perhaps the most famous example is Victor Kiam who was "so impressed by the Remington shaver, he bought the company."

Dramatization - In this format, the product is shown being used in a highly exaggerated manner. A well-known example is the Tidy Bowl commercial which showed men rowing a tiny boat inside a toilet bowl filled with water colored blue from the product. Dramatizations can be highly effective in gaining attention for a commercial but you must be very careful that the drama supports, rather than overshadows, the product.

Animation - Animation uses cartoon-like techniques to high-light product features or portray the product in use. Sometimes, well known cartoon figures are utilized.

Documentary - A documentary commercial shows the product in a unique or interesting application. Documentaries often blend aspects of the testimonial and the slice-of-life. One example of this format is the series of spots featuring a young couple who drove their Nissan four-wheel drive vehicle across deserts and through teeming jungles, encountering various adventures along the way. The commercials not only show the strength and durability of the vehicle, but also imply that it is an integral part of the adventurous lifestyle.

Life Style - An effective format when there are only minor differences in product features or quality. Prime users of this type of commercial are beer and wine suppliers. Rather than focus on specific product virtues, which are nebulous and hard to quantify, these commercials show the consumers of the product in happy, exciting situations. The subliminal message: "Drink our product and be part of the in-crowd."

Product versus Product - This format pits your product one-on-one against the competitor's product. This strategy works well when you're not the largest company in the market. If you are number one, direct comparisons only help your competition, since it puts the competitor in the same league as you and increases the enemy's name recognition at your expense.

Probably the most famous examples of the product versus product format are the AVIS "we try harder" commercials, which ran when AVIS was number two in the market.

HOW TO CREATE A WINNING
TELEVISION COMMERCIAL

The most important thing to remember about television is that it is a visual medium. Audio is used to support the visual, not the other way around. Advertisers who do not make extensive use of graphics and movement are failing to take advantage of TV's unique attributes.

As with all advertising vehicles, you must grab the viewer's attention in the first few seconds of the commercial. This is particularly important in television because studies show that attention is highest early in the commercial and tends to drop throughout its length.

If you attempt to create a commercial that starts slowly and builds intensity, you only ensure that you will increase the number of people who hit the mute button. In fact, it is a good idea to visualize the viewer watching your commercial with his finger resting on the mute button. Your objective is to make sure he does not press that button. This can be a terrifying thought, but it will help you create better commercials.

Here are some additional ideas on how you can make better television commercials:

■ Keep the focus on one major concept. Don't spread your limited time too thin by attempting too much. If your product has ten significant benefits, highlight one, but never more than three. Rather than bringing in new product merits, repeat your main message again and again.

■ Always remember that the product is the focal point, not the commercial itself. Your purpose will not be served if you achieve a high degree of recall of the commercial but very little recall of the product.

- Be very careful about using humour. Humour often diverts attention away from the product and tends to wear out its welcome unless replenished.

- When you write your commercial, never forget that the purpose of the commercial is to sell, not to entertain. Save the entertaining for the TV programmes.

- Don't load your commercial with too much copy. Long copy confuses the viewer and distracts from the visuals and sound. Every word must be weighed carefully for its contribution to selling the product or service. In general, a 30 second commercial should contain no more than 65 words, and a 60 second commercial should contain no more than 130 words.

- If you are running a direct response commercial, make sure you ask for the order. Tell the viewer what you want him to do: "Pick up the phone and call now" or "Go to your nearest dealer and ask for product X."

- Always practice honesty and congruence in your television advertising. The commercials must represent the "true" personality of your company and its products and services. Similarly, they must be consistent with all your other marketing and advertising.

- Avoid the urge to use your chairman or managing director as the spokesman. In certain rare instances it is advisable to use your top executive, but make very sure you are not doing this to stroke someone's ego. Amateur spokesmen are hard to coach on camera and often end up wasting valuable and expensive filming and editing time.

- If possible, use live people in your advertising and don't be afraid of creating emotional appeals. Witness the Food and drink campaigns that adds a strong human quality to the commercials.

STEPS IN PRODUCING THE
TELEVISION COMMERCIAL

Production of a television commercial is much more complex than a radio commercial because you are dealing with a visual as well as an audio component. Following are the steps to take in order to bring a TV commercial from concept to air:

Step One: Creative Strategy. The creative strategy takes into account the attributes of the product or service being promoted, the specific target audience, the competitive environment, the choice of media outlets, and the programming around which the commercials will be run.

Step Two: Writing the Script. After the basic creative strategy has been determined, the copywriter first writes an outline, then a detailed script of the commercial. A TV script shows the video portion on the left hand side of the page and the audio portion on the right hand side of the page.

Step Three: Preparing the Storyboard. Storyboards are inexpensive pictorial representations of the entire commercial. A frame is prepared for each scene, usually with a thumbnail sketch of the scene on top, and the corresponding copy under that frame.

TV commercial storyboard.

Step Four: Estimating Production Costs. The storyboard is then sent to one or more production companies or studios in order to get estimates. Costs incurred in producing commercials include:

- Personnel used in the commercial, referred to in the industry as "talent". If you hire professional actors, you will have to pay them standard (Equity) rates for appearing in the commercial as well as repeat fees every time the spot runs.
- Production costs, including the film costs, props, directors, lighting personnel, camera personnel, electricians and so forth.
- Graphics and/or studio animation.
- Original or studio music.
- Travel and location expenses.

Production of television commercials can range in cost from a few hundred pounds to several hundred thousand pounds.

Step Five: Pre-production Planning Meeting. Everyone involved in the production, including the client, agency, production house and talent, should assemble a week or so before the shooting date to go over all details of the commercial. If the shooting is to take place in an unusual location, it is a good idea to have everyone meet at the location to discuss issues such as lighting, camera angles and so forth. Each person should also indicate his complete understanding of every detail concerning the script.

Step Six: Filming the Commercial. Certain commercials can be shot entirely within the studio while others require a great deal of location work. Things will go much smoother if you are working with a quality production house and if you work out most of the details at the pre-production stage.

Step Seven: Editing and Post Filming. Much of the hard and tedious work of the production process takes place at the production house after the shooting. Dozens of takes and hours of film must be reduced to a 30 or 60 second commercial. Post production also includes cleaning up blemishes and overlaying musical and graphic tracks.

DEVELOPMENTS IN TELEVISION

Although satellite channels such as Eurosport and MTV are attempting to introduce an international element into the UK television, the advent of "European" television is a long-way off. The one annual euro event is the Eurovision Song Contest which has survived longer than "Jeux Sans Frontier" an international "sporting" challenge between European towns.

A number of European series are being broadcast on BBC 2 or Channel 4, but the most visible attempts at a euro-series, BBC's Spanish soap opera "Eldorado" foundered in its early stages. Channel 4, partly in response to the reduction in live football to network viewers, now broadcasts regularly on the Italian football scene with a weekly live match.

Breakfast and daytime television seem to be strong growth sectors as programme providers introduce more magazine-type programmes into a sector that was previously dominated by movie repeats. Channel 4's "Big Breakfast" programme has been an outstanding success in 1993 and has demonstrated that not all breakfast programmes need to follow a set pattern. The programme has also taken the breakfast slot to a younger audience and offered advertisers greater opportunities.

Satellite and cable television offers the greatest opportunities for niche marketing on television with strong growth in specialist channels. These include:

- Children – with offerings from Children's Channel, Nickelodeon and Cartoon Network.

- The family sector – with channels such as Family Channel.
- Music, with MTV and CMT which offers country music videos.
- TV Asia.
- QVC, a home shopping channel.
- A woman's channel to be launched shortly.

These will provide advertisers with the opportunity to practise target marketing, but much depends on the ability of the channels to deliver audiences in suitable numbers.

ONE REASON TO TARGET CAREFULLY.

12

BASICS OF RADIO ADVERTISING

Radio advertising has many of the advantages of television at far lower cost. To begin with, radio has tremendous reach, even though its popularity has declined relative to television. Radios can be found in homes, cars, boats, offices, and anywhere else you find human beings. For certain advertisers, radio can be extremely effective. Those who routinely use radio include:

- Local and regional advertisers
- Small businesses
- Retail establishments
- car dealers
- Office product and service suppliers

- Packaged good manufacturers
- The leisure industry

Radio commercials are able to fulfill the major functions of advertising: informing, reinforcing, persuading, and adding value. Other advantages of the radio medium include:

- Radio is a flexible marketing tool. You have an almost unlimited range of options to achieve the right blend of reach and frequency.
- Radio allows you to take advantage of rapidly changing circumstances. It is possible to hear your ads on the air within a day or two after you decide to advertise.
- Radio is an excellent target-marketing medium. With a wide variety of format and audience choices, you can reach just the type of people who are your best prospects. Audience segments run the gamut from affluent classical music enthusiasts, to talk-show listeners to sports fanatics.
- Radio time is relatively inexpensive, with spots in certain daytime sectors available for under £10. This makes radio an excellent tool for low-budget advertisers and those who are testing the viability of a new product or service before committing to an expensive television campaign.
- Radio is the only way to reach certain demographic groups cost-effectively. For instance, radio reaches many teenagers, a segment notoriously difficult to reach with other media.
- Production of radio commercials is easy and inexpensive. If you have few requirements for outside talent, a quality radio commercial can be produced for a few hundred pounds.

DISADVANTAGES OF RADIO

While the disadvantages of radio are few, they make this medium a poor choice for certain advertisers.

First, radio suffers from extreme commercial clutter. Your ad, no matter how clever, will be surrounded by a sea of other commercials crying out for attention. If you doubt this, listen to your radio during end of the year car sales. Somewhere on the dial, 24 hours a day, you will be able to find a car dealer begging you to buy last year's model, at "giveaway" prices.

A second drawback to radio is that it is not a good tool for direct response marketing. This is because radio is a passive activity (most of the time). We are far from the early days of "wireless" broadcasting where entire families would gather around the radio and hang on every word.

Thirdly, radio offers no visual stimulus, like television and print advertising. You must be able to paint a picture of your product in the minds of the listener. Radio directly engages only one of the five senses: hearing, which is often distracted by other activities. This does not make it an ideal medium for complex or high-involvement products or offers.

Today, most of us do our listening while engaged in other activities. Certain of these activities, such as driving and working, command the majority of our concentration. The listener may have little opportunity to heed the advertiser's call-to-action, even if he wanted to. Behind the wheel of an automobile, there is no order form to fill out, no coupon to clip, and phoning may be impossible.

Research suggests that people who listen in their cars tend to be more attentive than home listeners. But while radio sales people will tell you of the vast driving audience with car phones ready and willing to call in, from my experience, this is not the case.

I am not trying to discourage the use of radio for direct response, only alerting you to the facts. If you must use radio for direct response, combine it with other media, particularly television and direct mail. You may also have to advertise with greater frequency to catch enough of your audience at a time when they are willing and able to call. It also helps to have a highly memorable telephone number for those who can't write it down now but wish to call later.

SCHEDULING RADIO TIME

In the UK, there are four main groups of radio stations – national networks such as Radio 1, 2, 3, 4, 5 run by the BBC, independent national networks such as Classic FM and Virgin 1215, local BBC stations and local independent stations. Only the independent stations accept advertising.

When developing a media schedule it is important to match the profile of your target audience with programming formats and audience profiles of each of the stations you are considering. Information on station programming, audience characteristics, rates and policies is published by British Rates and Data (BRAD). BRAD sells its guidebooks by subscription (see Resource Guide) and your local library may also have a copy. Information can also be obtained (more than you ever dreamed of) from the individual station or radio network.

As with all advertising mediums, you should strive to achieve the optimum blend of reach and frequency. "Reach" refers to the number of people reached by a commercial. "Frequency" refers to the number of times each person hears the commercial. Unless you have a very large budget and can achieve both, you will have to decide whether to adopt a campaign with high reach, high frequency, or something in between.

Generally, I recommend programmes with higher frequency. If you have targeted your audience correctly, you should have a large number of potential buyers, but you must usually put your message in front of them several times before they take action. The exception to the "frequency first" plan is when you have a highly distinctive product. In this case, frequency can be sacrificed to achieve greater reach.

Another important concept to understand is the rating point. "Rating points" are defined in radio the same way as in television. Each rating point is equal to one percent of the total potential audience for a program. For instance, if there are 100,000 potential listeners in a market area, and 2,000 of these people are tuned to a particular station during a certain time period, that station has two ratings points.

Many advertisers base their media purchases on achieving a certain Gross Rating Point (GRP). GRP refers to the rating of each programme on which a commercial is run, multiplied by the number of commercials run. For example, three commercials run on successive nights on a programme with two and one-half rating points would equal seven and one-half gross rating points.

$$
\begin{array}{rl}
\text{Rating} & 2.5 \\
\underline{\text{x Frequency}} & \underline{3.0} \\
\text{= GRP} & 7.5
\end{array}
$$

Each radio broadcast day is broken down by time periods which define the type of audience that is likely to be listening to a show's format. Although each station can set its own schedule, typical sectors include:

6 a.m. - 10 a.m. ...Morning drive time
10 a.m. - 3 p.m. ....Daytime
3 p.m. - 7 p.m. .....Evening drive time
7 p.m. - midnight ....Nighttime

Drive time is the most desirable since it usually has the highest ratings. It is also the most expensive. The least expensive radio time is Run of Station (ROS) where the station has the ability to run your commercial at any time of the day or night.

Much radio spot time is sold in packages, which rotate an advertiser's commercial spots equally over the four major sectors. For example, a spot could be run twice each in morning drive, daytime, evening drive and nighttime.

Follow these tips to get the most from your radio schedule:

- Be extremely wary of information provided by radio station sales reps. While most are honest and reliable, they only make money if you buy time on their station. Consult with an independent expert such as an advertising agency or media buying service.
- Don't hesitate to negotiate radio rates. Frequent advertisers and new advertisers have a great deal of leverage with radio stations.
- Choose your stations carefully. If you have a commercial that you believe will work well on any station format, it's probably a weak commercial.
- Remember that target marketing principles are just as important when selecting the media schedule as they are in creating the commercial.
- If in doubt, do what the big advertisers do. Your largest competitors may have spent a great deal of money testing various schedules. Take advantage of their research by testing the same dayparts.

PRODUCING THE RADIO COMMERCIAL

As noted earlier, radio commercial production can be easy and inexpensive. If you use an advertising agency to create your commercials, the agency will most likely arrange for all production details. Even so, it doesn't hurt to know something about the process.

The quickest and least expensive production method is to prepare a script which the radio announcer reads live. You can also record the commercials for repeated playback. Live commercials can give you a high degree of credibility since a loyal radio audience usually likes and respects the announcer.

Be very careful to time the commercial for the unique speaking style of the announcer. On average, a 60-second commercial will contain 140-160 words, a 30-second commercial 70-80 words, and a 10-second commercial 25-30 words. This does not include time for music, special effects or changes in talent (as you would have with a two-way dialogue).

If your advertising is designated for one station, that station will often record your customized commercial in-house. Otherwise, find a good quality recording studio to produce the commercial and reproduce as many copies as needed to send to all the stations on which you intend to advertise (these duplicate copies are known as "dubs"). A good way to find a quality recording studio is to call advertisers who run commercials you admire and ask where their commercial was produced.

Anyone who has a speaking part on a radio commercial is referred to as "talent." There is a wide range of talent available for almost any type of radio spot. Almost all radio talent will have "demo tapes" that demonstrate the variety and range of commercials with which they have been involved. Both radio stations and advertising agencies carry a large number of demo tapes.

When looking for talent for your commercial, request the type of voice you are interested in, such as "middle-age conservative businessman" or "young, urban, professional woman." Another way to find good talent is by listening to other commercials. Simply call the company which advertised (or their advertising agency) and ask for the name and phone number of the talent they used.

Music is very important in radio commercials. The agency and/or studio you are working with will suggest the type of music to use in a particular commercial. Original music is always a good touch. It is not as expensive to create original music as you may think, since it is mixed electronically from a bank of thousands of sounds and dozens of instruments. But you might find a very nice and inexpensive piece of quality music in the studio's archives which fits the bill perfectly. If you still can't find what you're looking for, contact one or more "music houses." Music houses carry thousands of tunes in their libraries and will be glad to send you a demo tape of possibilities.

Sound effects are as important to radio commercials as color and photography are to magazine advertising. Since radio is an auditory medium, it relies on stimulating the imagination of the listener. At one time, sound effects were created live during the taping of the commercial. For instance, if you wanted the sound of rustling leaves in your commercial, someone would actually rustle leaves at the appropriate time during the taping. Today, sound effects are inserted directly into the commercial by the recording studio. As with music, there are thousands of choices available. To indicate placement of sound effects, simply note the sound you are looking for at the appropriate place on the commercial's script.

Be an educated consumer when it comes to production expenses. Make sure you are supplied with a written estimate upfront, which outlines all of the studio and outside charges. Always ask how any change in the production process (such as new or additional talent or music), will affect the estimated price.

HOW TO WRITE A WINNING RADIO COMMERCIAL

The ability to write effective radio commercials is unique and special. Someone who is successful at writing print advertising or direct mail copy may falter when faced with writing a script for a radio commercial. The primary difference is that there is no graphic design to support the radio commercial.

This is not to say that there is no visual element in radio. Quite the contrary. But the visual image must be manufactured by the copywriter. He must stimulate the imagination of the listener with voices, music and special effects, and mentally transport that person to a different time and place. He must break through the clutter of competing sounds and images and cause the listener to stop and listen. Only then does he have the chance to persuade the listener to take action.

Always remember that radio is a _personal_ medium. The listener must feel that the announcer or radio talent is speaking to him directly. Thus, you should write the commercial as if it were to be heard by only one person - and you must get that one person's attention and a positive response.

Follow these additional tips to write a winning radio commercial:

- Create a distinctive mood with music, sound effects or a unique voice. Help the listener disengage himself from his current activity.
- Be consistent with all other marketing vehicles. For instance, if you are running television ads, consider using the same soundtrack and talent as you do in the TV commercial. This consistency will help you achieve boosts in response across all marketing vehicles.
- Don't be clever just to get attention. Always keep your eye firmly fixed on the objective. If someone remembers your ad but can't remember the name of your company, you have failed.
- Target your commercials. Since production costs in radio are relatively low, consider creating different versions for unique audience formats.
- Get to the point quickly. If you are addressing a special audience segment, state this immediately. For ex-

ample, "If you're considering a homeowner loan, come to National Bank, where you receive the lowest rates on home equity loans in five years."

■ Repeat your company and product name. I recommend that you use your company name at least three times in a 60-second commercial and two times in a 30-second spot. This principle also holds true for phone numbers.

■ Stick to your BIG IDEA. Don't try to accomplish too much in one commercial. Instead of confusing the listener with multiple offers, concentrate all your efforts on achieving one objective.

■ Always include a call-to-action in your commercial. Presumably, you are on the air to generate specific action on the part of your audience. Make this very clear to the listeners by telling them exactly what you want them to do.

■ Avoid words that are hard to pronounce. Be especially careful about anything over three syllables. Let the talent read the script before the commercial is taped and change any words he or she has problems with.

HOW TO PREPARE THE RADIO SCRIPT

Script formats vary widely, but all must clearly and precisely convey the words, music and sound effects used in the commercial. There must be complete agreement between advertiser, agency, talent and recording studio. Whatever script format you use, keep these points in mind:

■ Double space the copy for better readability.
■ Do not abbreviate anything.
■ Clearly indicate the exact time sequence and instructions for music and special effects.
■ Indicate where you want pauses by using commas and

dashes. Underline and use exclamation points where you want special emphasis.

■ Don't always follow the rules of written grammar. Remember that you are writing for the ear, not the eye. The commercial has to sound good, not look good.

Sinai Hospital
30-second radio ad
"Natalie's Dad"

SFX:	Baby crying, then pacified.
DOCTOR:	It's okay sweetie ... Daddy's here.
VO:	Being Natalie's father is an important part of Robert Adler's life.
SFX:	Hospital noises
OS:	Hospital PA System: Doctor Adler to delivery.
SFX:	Newborn crying.
VO:	Here at Sinai Hospital, there's another job that he performs with the same dedication. In fact, the qualities that make him so important to Natalie, help him provide the special care his patients deserve.
SFX:	Baby cooing.
VO:	You see, Robert Adler is a very important part of another family ... the family of caring physicians who have made Sinai Hospital their choice.
VO:	Sinai Hospital. The physicians choice.

Radio script

179

180

13

USING SALES SEMINARS TO SELL

*S*eminars are an effective and cost-efficient method of generating leads and selling products and services in consumer and business-to-business applications. The financial and computer software industries have been using sales seminars successfully for years, and other industries are beginning to capitalize on their innovations.

Seminars fall into two general categories: those that support the sale of goods and services and those that run as a separate profit centre. For our purposes we will focus on the former, although I realize that for-profit seminars are a large and growing industry.

BENEFITS OF SALES SEMINARS

Before exploring the mechanics of designing and implementing sales seminars, let's consider some of the reasons why you might want to make seminars an integral part of your marketing programme:

1. Seminars work. They put you directly in front of your prospects. And with a well-planned promotional programme, you can be reasonably certain of attracting a sizeable audience to your seminars.

2. Seminar attendees tend to be well-qualified prospects. Very few people will sit through a two- to four-hour presentation unless they are interested in the subject matter.

3. For complex products, or those with long sales cycles, seminars can move attendees up the selling continuum. Suspects become prospects, prospects become hot prospects, and hot prospects become buyers. Sales can be closed in a much shorter time by adding seminars to the marketing mix.

4. Professionally conducted seminars increase your organization's credibility in the marketplace.

5. If you run your business over the phone or by mail, seminars may be the only opportunity you have to meet your prospects and customers.

6. Seminars give you an excellent opportunity to conduct primary marketing research since they provide a captive audience of qualified prospects.

7. Seminars can change the dynamics of the seller/buyer relationship. If you have provided prospects with valuable information, hosted them in comfort for several hours, and made the experience a pleasant one, there is a certain bond forged that transcends typical buyer/seller relationships and will work to your benefit.

PROBLEMS WITH SALES SEMINARS

While the above list of benefits sounds tempting, conducting seminars poses several possible problems:

1. Seminar programmes can be expensive. While there are low-cost ways of marketing and conducting seminars (which I will present later), these programmes can be expensive compared to other marketing methods.
2. Seminars take valuable staff time. The time you and your staff spend marketing, preparing, and running your seminars is almost always greater than originally anticipated.
3. Murphy's Law applies to seminars time after time. There are usually so many details, and so many people involved in a seminar programme, that mishaps are bound to occur.
4. A bad seminar is worse than no seminar at all. Sales seminars generate high visibility which can work in your favor. However, if the information content of your seminar is mediocre, the visibility you gain will be exactly the type you don't want.

SHOULD YOU TRY SALES SEMINARS?

Given the list of benefits and obstacles, if you feel you have a product or service that lends itself well to this method of promotion, I would definitely urge you to try sales seminars as a marketing tool. The following questions should help you determine whether sales seminars are for you:

- Is your product or service suitable for a seminar? Simple, well-known products do not lend themselves to seminars. You must either offer new information, or provide a new twist to existing information. The following industries are naturals for sales seminars:

- Accounting
- Banking
- Business Management
- Computer Software
- Employment
- Insurance
- Investments
- Legal Services
- Medical and Legal Office Management
- Telecommunications

■ Do you have enough to say about your product(s) or service(s) to make it a worthwhile use of your time and your prospects' time?

■ Do you have a seminar leader? Locating someone in your organization who can speak well in public is probably no problem. Locating someone with extensive knowledge is probably no problem. But finding both traits in the same individual can be a big problem. An alternative is to hire an outside speaker, but this solution carries its own set of problems.

■ Is there a strong likelihood that the prospects who attend your seminar will become customers? Remember, your number one goal is to sell goods and services, not to educate the public.

■ Do the economics justify the investment? Figure out how many attendees you will need to achieve the sales figures necessary to break even on seminars. Be conservative in the numbers you use. To be on the safe side, figure on a lower number of attendees and greater than anticipated costs. If your projections don't look viable, forget the seminar programme.

To give you an example of how the numbers work, following

are the projections we used for a client who used seminars to generate leads for its sales force:

<u>Projected Revenue</u> (five seminars)

Number of attendees	225
Prospects (40% of attendees)	90
Sales (@ 30% closing percentage)	27
Average revenue per sale	X£5,000
TOTAL REVENUE	£135,000

<u>Projected Costs</u> (five seminars)

Marketing/promotion	£80,000
Travel (hotel, airfare, etc.)	£11,000
Facilities (rental, equip., food)	£12,000
Material and handouts	£6,000
Miscellaneous/contingency	£3,000
TOTAL COSTS	£112,000

According to our projections, we expected to net approximately £23,000 after all costs. And this considered only short-term sales. If you take into account the lifetime value of the 27 new customers (£675,000), the seminars were definitely worthwhile

■ Are there other benefits to be gained in addition to direct sales of your products and services? Are there ways to leverage the seminar programme to achieve other objectives, such as national press exposure or introduction to important industry contacts?

HOW TO SET UP A SEMINAR PROGRAM

Once you make the decision to start a seminar programme, there are two vital requirements: you must have a programme agenda and you must know where to find potential attendees.

The first step is to create a general outline of the programme. In a one-half day format there will be approximately two and one-half to three hours of presentation time to fill, not including coffee breaks. If you don't have enough material to cover such a large block of presentation time, consider adding workshops, question and answer sessions, and audio/visuals as filler material.

Once you have a preliminary seminar outline, you should turn your attention to finding the best target audience. A good place to begin is with a list of all known prospects for your product or service. Hopefully, you have this information on an in-house database. If not, it can be compiled by hand. All sales reps should be asked for a list of every prospect they have worked with in the past year.

Customers should also be invited to your program, for three important reasons. First, the seminar will help you further the relationship. Second, you can cross-sell customers new products and services. Third, customers will help you sell business to other attendees since they serve as excellent references. If you are afraid to invite your customers, then you have the type of problem that seminars can't solve and I suggest that you carefully read the chapter on "Keeping Your Customers for Life with Relationship Building."

After you have a general outline and target audience profile, you should develop the in-depth programme. Leave nothing to chance. Don't rely on your product manager or number one sales-person to prepare a presentation. More than once, I've seen a programme turn sour because a technical person got too involved with bits and bytes, or a sales rep gave too strong of a sales pitch from the podium. As the marketing professional, it is your job to know exactly what everyone on the programme is going to say.

GENERATING ATTENDEES FROM OUTSIDE MAILING LISTS

Because it is difficult to fill a seminar with known prospects and customers you will probably have to go elsewhere to find potential seminar attendees. There should be many outside mailing lists of suitable prospects. But choosing the right list(s) from the many possibilities is not easy. My best advice is to consult a mailing list broker that has experience in your industry and in promoting seminars. The subject of choosing a list broker and mailing list research is covered in detail in a later chapter.

Seminar promotion mailings generally pull better than lead-generation mailings. For instance, at two companies where I was involved in nationwide seminar programmes, our seminar mailings generated response rates of three to six percent. Recent mailings for both clients and our own seminar promotions have confirmed that these numbers are not unusual.

To fill a medium-size hotel seminar room, you will need 40 to 60 attendees. However, because 20 to 50 percent of the people who register for a free sales seminar cancel or fail to show up, your goal should be to register one and one-half times as many people as you need in the room. The following simple example will show you how the math works:

Number of seminar cities	10
Target audience for each seminar	x 50
Total attendees needed	500
	x 1.5
Registrants needed	750

Assuming a conservative response rate of three percent, this means you should mail to at least 25,000 prospects (an average of 2,500 per city) to generate 750 registrants (25,000 x .03 = 750). Unless your programme is two days or longer, you will usually need to find your target audience within 100 miles of the seminar location. To continue with the above example, these ten seminars should only be scheduled in cities where there are at least 2,500 prospects within a 100 mile radius.

STEPS TO PROMOTE YOUR SEMINAR PROGRAMME

After you have handled the first two elements necessary for a successful seminar (a programme in outline form and a thorough understanding of your target audience) you can proceed with these proven steps for filling your seminars:

Step One: Schedule your seminars in well-known locations such as hotels. If your seminar is to be held first thing in the morning, be certain traffic problems in the hotel area will not keep your registrants away or cause a large number to be late.

Step Two: Send your first direct mail promotion at least six to eight weeks before the seminar. One format that works well is the personalized letter in a window envelope, including an enclosed business reply card. Many other formats are available and are covered in the chapter on direct mail.

If your programme is intended for a general audience, is free or moderately priced, and there are few mailing lists available, then you should consider running print ads instead of, or in addition to, direct mail.

Step Three: If response to your first mailing is low, send a follow-up mailer. This can be something as simple and inexpensive as a double-postcard, where side one of the card is filled with copy promoting the seminar and side two contains the response card with postage-paid business reply information.

Step Four: Prepare your handout materials for the programme. These can include seminar outlines, schedules, reference materials, sales brochures, case histories, and so forth. However, don't go overboard with materials. Most people will spend little time scrutinizing these materials once the seminar is over. Your sales team can always accommodate those who need additional information about your products or services.

Step Five: Verify all registrants by telephone 48 to 72 hours before the event. Remember, if your seminar is free, you can expect a significant no-show rate. Without telephone verification, sometimes as few as 40 percent of those who registered will show up. Also, if you have a low attendee count, you can use this conversation as an opportunity to ask your registrants to invite co-workers and friends to the seminar.

TIPS ON CONDUCTING A WINNING SEMINAR

Follow these rules to help make your seminar program a success:

- Make sure your programme is informational, not sales-oriented. You will earn more brownie points (and sales) from your audience if you approach the seminar as a chance to share expertise and help your attendees. There are exceptions to this rule, such as when your products are unique and interesting enough to serve as the basis for the presentation. And it goes without saying that in a free seminar, a small amount of self-promotion is tolerated. But outside these constraints, don't insult your audience by turning it into a sales pitch.
- The programme should be interesting and informative. Whatever you can do to add entertainment value will be appreciated by the audience, particularly if the programme content is dry or highly technical.
- Consider asking one of your best customers to appear on the programme and explain how your product or service has been helpful to them. As the saying goes, "It ain't bragging if someone else says it about you." But make sure you have a good idea what the customer will say.

You don't want any surprises here, such as the customer mentioning that he is just as happy using your competitor's product.

■ Use audio/visuals to highlight important points. Most people don't want to sit through a half-day or full-day lecture. Although slides work best, if you are operating on a small budget, overhead transparencies are certainly acceptable.

■ Don't forget to rehearse. If you have more than one person on the programme ask all speakers to rehearse individually. Also have at least one full run-through several days before the seminar to see how well the total program works. I once made the mistake of ignoring my own advice on this point. We were doing a seminar in Boston and the territory sales rep was to meet us the night before the programme to do a quick runthrough. I had sent this person slides and an outline of his part of the presentation and asked him to prepare ahead of time. The rep showed up the night before the programme without his slides and asked, "What do you want me to talk about tomorrow?" Needless to say, his part of the programme was a disaster. Lesson learned.

BE PREPARED FOR THE WORST

Anyone who has conducted seminar programs will tell you there is no shortage of disasters and pitfalls. While by no means complete or conclusive, here are five of the more common problems that give seminar managers ulcers.

Problem One: Missing or malfunctioning audiovisual equipment. This happens so often it almost becomes routine. The solution is to arrive early, thoroughly check out the equipment, and have a back-up available. On a related note, it is important to bring a spare copy of your slides or transparencies, especially if you shipped the original materials separately.

Problem Two: Poor lighting in the seminar room. Quite often, lights either won't dim, meaning your slides or overheads won't be readable, or they won't brighten, leaving you standing in the dark with an audience prone to falling asleep. To prevent this, check out the lighting system before the programme and know where the hotel personnel are in case of problems during the seminar.

Problem Three: Uncomfortable temperatures in the seminar room. Again, forewarned is forearmed. If you show up 10 minutes before the start time there is little that can be done, but given enough time, you can bring the temperature to a comfortable level. My preference is to have the room a little cooler than normal as this promotes sharp thinking.

Problem Four: Weather or traffic that prevents attendees from showing up or seriously delays their arrival. Preventive medicine for this problem is to check out the traffic patterns before scheduling the seminar. But even in severe weather situations when you have many absences, remember that out of respect for those who do arrive, the show must go on.

Problem Five: A scheduled speaker doesn't arrive. This is a serious problem, particularly if you've built the programme around the reputation of the speaker. The only solution is to be prepared with something to say. Always try to get a copy of each of your speakers' outlines and audiovisuals well before the pro-gramme. If necessary, step in yourself to cover the material.

POST-SEMINAR FOLLOW-UP

The post seminar follow-up can be just as important to your

success as the programme itself. And the follow-up begins immediately after the formal session ends. You should have personnel on hand to answer questions and thank people for coming. If you are offering your attendees lunch following a morning seminar, arrange for your employees to be spread throughout the dining area to talk to the prospects.

Within two days after the seminar, send all attendees a thank-you note, along with additional information related to the seminar topic. People who registered and did not attend should be called and/or mailed information as well. All qualified prospects should be turned over to sales representatives for follow up and should be added to your in-house marketing database.

TO CHARGE OR NOT TO CHARGE

Two schools of thought exist about whether to charge people to attend sales seminars. The first says that because you are providing valuable information you should be compensated for the value of that information. Charging an admission fee also discourages the unqualified freeloaders who show up at seminars just to get a free meal and competitors who show up to make contact with your prospects and customers.

Proponents of free seminars counter with three good reasons not to charge a fee:

1. Most people will not sit through an hours-long programme just to get a free meal. They will have at least moderate interest in the subject matter. As for competitors, simply do not allow them to attend. It's your party and you can invite or refuse anyone you want.

2. Many qualified prospects who would otherwise attend, will not do so if they are charged a fee. This is particularly true of low- to mid-level personnel. Although they

are often decision influencers and recommenders, they must get approval from their superiors to attend a fee-based seminar.

3. Most people attend sales seminars because they believe they will learn something of value to help them in their personal or professional lives. Yet, if the seminar is free, they expect a certain amount of sales information about the sponsoring company and its products or services which they would not tolerate if they were forced to pay a fee.

Given the above arguments, I believe that the decision should be one of economics. If the potential for generating significant revenue in your primary business exists from the prospects who attend, then you should consider a free seminar. However, if you can't pay for the seminar programme from product and service sales, then you should charge a fee, or find other ways to promote your organization.

WHEN YOU EXHIBIT AT A TRADE SHOW...

...LOCATION IS EVERYTHING

14

EXHIBITION MARKETING

*T*rade shows and exhibitions rank as one of the most expensive and sometimes frustrating promotional vehicles. Yet, for many organizations, trade shows are considered an essential part of the marketing mix. If your industry has a well-developed network, your company's absence at the big annual conference could be noted as a sign of its impending demise. In such an industry, even if you feel the event is not the best use of your company's marketing budget, you reluctantly go back, year after year.

Here are some of the best reasons to consider adding trade shows to your marketing arsenal:

1. Companies usually send their decision-makers to trade shows, particularly in tough economic times. As long as

you choose the right places to exhibit, the leads you generate should be of excellent quality.

2. If you conduct most of your business by telephone or mail, or have a widely dispersed customer base, trade shows may be the only opportunity you have to meet and greet your customers and prospects.

3. If your competition exhibits at a particular trade show, you may wish to do so as a defensive measure. You don't want your customers and prospects exposed to their products without having the benefit of your presence.

4. Trade shows are excellent forums to present new product ideas, and provide you the opportunity to field test products and services before committing large sums to marketing programmes.

5. Trade shows are great opportunities to make important contacts with industry colleagues, suppliers and association leaders.

6. Industry and financial press routinely attend large conferences and trade shows. These events can be your best opportunity to catch so many editors and reporters at one time and place.

7. Your competitors probably use trade shows to introduce new products and services. For this reason, such events provide an outstanding opportunity to conduct competitive market research. You can learn a lot just by walking around and asking questions.

8. Although it is usually not a primary purpose of trade shows, new business can be conducted at these events. I have participated at several trade shows where a deal made at the show has more than paid the entire cost of exhibiting.

THE CHANGING EXHIBITION DELEGATE

As anyone who regularly exhibits at trade shows will tell you, attendance at most has been declining, a victim of slashed budgets and the move toward direct response marketing methods. Companies can no longer afford to send a dozen people to "make a good showing" or to reward employees for a good year. But even though fewer are attending, the costs of exhibiting remain high. According to Exhibit Surveys, Inc., the cost of reaching each trade show visitor in the US is now over $150 (versus $107 in 1985).

While this may appear to be bad news, the dark cloud does have a silver lining. While fewer in number, attendees are better educated, come from higher levels in their organizations, and are much more serious about the business purpose of the event. There are fewer "leaflet collectors" and more "buyers". Attendees are there to learn more about their industries and to evaluate new products and services.

These changes are definitely good news for the exhibitor, but you must respond to them by changing your perceptions and methods. Treat each person who visits your stand with greater respect reflecting his or her increased value. Be willing to spend the extra time and energy required to convince a more skeptical and serious prospect.

SETTING TRADE SHOW OBJECTIVES

Many organizations have poor experiences with trade shows because they lack a planned, professional approach to preparing for the events. The fact is, it is the work you do before the show that will help determine your success. As a results-driven Master Marketer, you will want to start by establishing specific objectives for each trade show. And by setting objectives, I don't mean "getting a bunch of leads" or "meeting new prospects." You must be very specific. Set precise objectives in each of these areas that apply:

- Volume of sales. As I noted above, even shows focused on generating loads can sometimes produce significant sales revenues. If this is your intention, by all means quantify the amounts.

- Generating a specific number of leads. You should also break these numbers down to account for the quality of the leads you generate. For instance, it is easy to come up with a gimmick that will get a large number of people to drop their business cards into your "fishbowl." Just give away a £50 note once an hour. But could you consider all or a large part of these to be qualified leads? Not likely. Chances are you will find cards ranging from the highly-qualified prospects to your competitors who are themselves exhibitors.

It is also important to establish exactly how much you are willing to spend for each qualified lead. To compute this figure, total all costs associated with the show and divide by the number of leads you intend to generate. For example, the following costs are taken from a client's trade show budget:

Exhibit modifications (new artwork)	£700
Exhibit space (10 x 20 booth)	£4,800
Shipping exhibit and materials	£850
Materials design and printing	£2,200
Pre-conference mailing (2900 postcards)	£1,250
Post-conference mailing (fulfillment)	£400
Lodging, travel and entertainment	£2,700
TOTAL BUDGET	£12,900

This company's objective was to generate 200 qualified leads from the trade show, giving it a cost per lead of approximately £65 (£12,900 divided by 200). Since £65 is considered a reasonable price to pay for a qualified lead, this figure was used as the cost-per-lead (CPL) target.

- Meetings with selected prospects. Because you are likely to have one or more senior managers in attendance, trade shows offer a good opportunity to conduct working meetings (perhaps meetings where sales are closed) with local prospects or those who have also traveled to the event.
- Meetings with selected media. These should be scheduled weeks before the event. Although it is possible to arrange these meetings at the show itself, editors are so busy it is much more fruitful to pre-plan.

All editors and reporters have something in common with you. They eat and you eat. Take advantage of this fact by inviting editors and reporters (preferably one at a time) to dine with you. Unless you know the individual well, make it a breakfast or lunch meal, not dinner. And yes, you should always pick up the cost, unless the editor has a policy against this.

If the editor or reporter doesn't have time for a meal, suggest a quick cup of coffee. Try to get your senior, chairman or another executive to attend. Then your job is easy. Keep quiet and smile at all the wise and witty things the editor and your boss are saying to each other.

Once you have set these objectives for the trade show, make sure each person who attends from your company is well aware of his or her specific part in making the goals a reality. It is also a good idea to have a post-show meeting to evaluate your success (or lack of success) in reaching the stated objectives.

HOW TO GENERATE HIGH QUALITY TRADE SHOW LEADS

If you are going to spend anywhere from £2,000 to £50,000 to exhibit, you will want to make sure you've done everything possible to generate a large number of high quality leads. As stated earlier, lead quantity and lead quality are often two very different things. Consider this point carefully because the type of programme you develop to attract large numbers of people to your booth is very different from that required to attract quality prospects.

From my perspective, this is a primary reason to forego the booth "giveaway" offer. Giveaways are gifts, games or contests which are designed solely to attract the greatest number of people to your booth, regardless of their need for, or interest in, your product and company.

What makes this type of come-on appealing is the large number of people that seem to crowd around the booths with the best giveaway offers. This is okay as long as quantity is the primary consideration, such as when almost everyone attending is a potential prospect. But this is usually not the case. What you often have are large numbers of "shoppers" who are looking to fill their bags with the largest amount of goodies possible before the exhibit hall closes.

I am not suggesting that it is not important to get people to your booth. I am just suggesting that it is more important to get the "right" people to your booth. The right people are those who have the need for your product or service, and the authority to buy it. Anything you can do to attract more of these people, and fewer "shoppers," will be an investment toward a successful trade show.

One technique that accomplishes this purpose is the pre-show mailing. Contact the organization sponsoring the show. Ask them to send you a list of people registered to attend. Most will provide this list to exhibitors for a nominal fee. The trick is to make the request in plenty of time to get out a mailing before the show, yet not so early that you miss a large number of late registrants.

Most often, these lists will be provided on pressure-sensitive labels, not computer tapes. Unless the list is very large, you should order the pressure-sensitive labels. You will want to delete the delete the obviously unqualified people from your mailing. This is obviously unqualified people from your mailing. This is very easy to do with pressure-sensitive labels.

When you receive the list, send a pre-show mailing to all qualified registrants. I suggest you make it a coupon or gift-certificate which is redeemable only at your booth. The certificate should be for something of reasonable value. If you've selected your audience carefully, you will find it more effective to spend the same amount of money providing decent gifts to smaller numbers of qualified prospects, instead of cheap trinkets for large numbers of unqualified people.

Since you have worked so hard to bring "qualified" prospects to your booth, don't hesitate to sell very hard once you have the individual in front of you. After all, that's why you came to the show in the first place.

An alternative, or addition, to the pre-show mailing is to personally call to invite important prospects to visit your booth. Important prospects should be invited to come by at a time when one or more of your senior managers will be there: "Mr. Smith, our managing director would like to meet you at the show and buy you a cup of coffee." This type of call can be flattering to the prospect and is a very effective way to increase attendance and increase sales.

There are two other keys to making the giveaway programme work. First, the gift item should be something that would make an excellent gift for a spouse or child. This is true because trade shows tend to be very busy. Many people who attend these events have all good intentions of purchasing gifts for their spouses and children before returning home. By providing the prospect with such a gift you are providing a valuable, and long remembered service.

It also doesn't hurt if the gift has some connection with your product or service. At the National Direct Marketing Association Conference in Boston last year, a company that sells flowers by catalogue gave away single long-stemmed roses, pre-packaged to withstand the rigors of travel. This was a great way to highlight the company's services and make friends as well.

The second key is to require something more than the individual's presence in return for the gift. For instance, you can require the prospect to fill out a short questionnaire at your booth, which asks about his use of, and interest in, the type of products or services you offer. The amount of information you can collect is directly proportional to the value of the gift you are offering.

Let's illustrate how this works. Suppose you have £1,000 budgeted for giveaways. You could give away 1,000 cheap trinkets, worth £1.00 each, but prospects will give you little more than a name and mailing address for a £1.000 gift. You could have a prized draw and give away the £1,000 to one lucky winner. For a chance at £1,000, people will give you lots of information about buying habits, etc., but of course you will find most of the contest entrants unqualified. Your third option is to give away £10 gifts to 100 pre-qualified prospects, who will be glad to give you plenty of data in exchange for a £10 gift.

If this is starting to sound to you like a blatant attempt to purchase information on your prospects, you are right on target. The truth is, most exhibitors have little opportunity to do any significant selling at the trade show. However, you can make very good future use of the information you collect at the show. It does you little good to generate a large amount of booth traffic if you have no information on these prospects after you get home from the event.

TYPES OF MATERIALS TO HAVE AT YOUR BOOTH

Imagine for a moment how many beautiful trees have died to make the thick brochures distributed at trade shows, only to end up in dustbins outside the hall. In addition to the printing and shipping costs, many sore backs have been caused by lugging all that extra weight around. Marketing managers, and especially sales managers, have the tendency to bring lots and lots of information to trade shows.

I hope I have made it clear by now that the primary purpose of exhibiting at a trade show is to gather information on your qualified prospects, not to feed them information about you. I realize this goes against the natural instincts of many salespeople, but it is true nonetheless. If you think about it, you'll realize that many prospects ask for product literature only because they feel it is a polite way to extricate themselves from you, not because they have a genuine interest in what you are offering.

So what should you hand out at trade shows? I suggest small brochures or two to three page product descriptions. If someone asks for in-depth product data, tell him you will be glad to mail it or deliver it personally.

WHAT TO DO AFTER THE SHOW

When I was a fresh young marketing director in the software industry, at the end of each trade show, salespeople would descend on the pile of business cards we gathered like a pack of hungry wolves, shouting "This one's mine!" or "Give me this guy. He's in my territory." Naively, I distributed all the leads, on the condition that each salesperson was to inform me of the disposition of each lead.

As you can probably guess, despite repeated urging, I never saw or heard about those leads again. They were swallowed up in the sales reps' own prospect files, lost to me forever. Another lesson learned the hard way.

I soon switched to a system whereby all leads collected were kept in the possession of the marketing manager (me) until we got back to the home office. Leads were then entered directly into our database system, and within 48 hours, a letter signed by the managing director was on its way to the prospect. Then, and only then, were the leads distributed to the salespeople.

Was this a better method of handling trade show leads? Although the salespeople had a little trouble getting used to it, they loved the fact that their prospects were getting a follow-up letter shortly after returning from the show. Plus, they still got their leads within days. And, best of all, identified sales from trade show marketing went up significantly. A winning system for all concerned.

I hope this chapter has given you a fresh perspective on trade show marketing and its value as part of your marketing programme.

15

POWER PACKED
PUBLIC RELATIONS STRATEGIES

*P*ublic relations can be an integral element in a well-planned marketing campaign. Yet, even among PR practitioners, there is a great deal of confusion about what public relations is and how to use it for maximum benefit. This ambiguity causes many organizations to forego public relations altogether and others to waste valuable resources on misguided, or counter-productive efforts.

Funk & Wagnalls Dictionary defines public relations as: "The activities and techniques used by organizations and individuals to establish favorable attitudes and responses in their behalf on the part of the general public or of special groups."

This excellent definition points out why there are only three fundamental components of a public relations programme:

1. The public or special groups you are attempting to influence.
2. The type of favorable attitudes or responses you wish to generate. These can be considered the objectives of the public relations campaign.
3. The specific techniques that can best be used to generate these attitudes and responses among the target groups.

DETERMINING YOUR PUBLIC

In order to do a good job of influencing the "public," you must first determine who it is that comprises your public. Most often, the public is a series of unique groups, each with its own needs. Here are some of the special interest constituencies that may be part of your public:

Employees - Although they are often overlooked, employees should never be taken for granted. They can do more to help you, or hurt you, than any other group. Companies with excellent PR programmes find it easier to attract the most qualified new employees. Your employees can also be excellent barometers of the credibility of your message. Believe me, if it won't sell to your internal audience, it will never sell to the external audience.

Customers - Needless to say, customers are always an important segment of your public. Their opinion of your products and services is paramount because it is only the dollars they spend that allow your continued existence. But you must remember that the message you send to your customers must be accurate because they start with a base of knowledge about your company.

Prospects - Public relations can be a powerful weapon in the effort to turn prospects into customers. Prospects can be divided into subgroups by industry, size, type of products purchased, and other criteria.

Stockholders - Whether you are a public or private company, your investors have a large stake in the success of your organization. Their continued allegiance can never be assumed. Witness the financial losses and plunging stock prices faced by organizations receiving a string of unfavorable publicity. Remember also that investors will always be deeply interested in the message you communicate to all other groups.

Business Press - Included in this category are all the print and broadcast communications media that deal with general business and financial issues. Public relations managers at public companies should get to know these people well.

Trade Press - This segment includes editors and reporters from the industry publications you read and those that your customers and prospects read for professional development and to keep up with industry news. Although the trade press is more influential in some industries than others, coverage by the leading publications can be very helpful in establishing your credibility in the marketplace.

Industry Leaders - Every industry has a small number of individuals who have the capacity to influence large numbers of others. I call these people "opinion leaders" because the opinions they express today often become standard industry dogma tomorrow. Industry leader segments include association leaders, authors, public speakers, editors, known innovators, and heads of large companies. Building relationships with the right industry leaders can do more for you and your organization than a mass mailing of press releases.

Community and Government - Most organizations depend on the loyalty and support of people in the local community. Also, having local, or central government on your side is always a good idea.

OBJECTIVES FOR THE PUBLIC RELATIONS PROGRAMME

Unfortunately, it is still rare to find an organization with well-defined PR objectives. Yet, just as with every other marketing discipline, you will be successful in public relations to the degree that you establish specific objectives and develop programmes to achieve them. Whenever possible, these objectives should be quantifiable and contain a timetable for their accomplishment. Following are some examples of goal ideas:

1. Establish a consistent corporate identity. This is your organizational "BIG IDEA" and should be closely allied with your mission statement. You may have to consolidate several independent divisions or product strategies to accomplish this objective. Kraft Foods and Black & Decker are two corporations which have been able to establish a consistently strong image across multiple brands.

2. Create goodwill with prospects, customers, employees and suppliers. It is always better to appear to the public as a benevolent or even charitable organization, instead of "just another money-hungry corporation."

3. Position your organization as an attractive target for joint ventures, takeovers, and so forth. A good PR program can increase the value of your firm.

4. Promote the image of key company leaders and get

these individuals invited to speak at industry conferences.

5. Attract investors and financial institutions which you
    would like to have a monetary interest in your company.

6. Gain favorable editorial coverage with the trade and
    financial press. This coverage can be monitored by
    clipping services (see Resource Guide) that will send
    you copies of all press mentions.

7. Influence public policy on an issue or issues that affect
    your organization. This is known as "lobbying."

8. Increase name recognition of your organization and its
    products and services. This objective alone will greatly
    aid the entire marketing effort.

The following is an excerpt from our agency's 1992 public
relations plan and is an excellent example of how an organization
can state these types of objectives:

RYAN KING RENNINGER, INC.
PUBLIC RELATIONS OBJECTIVES 1992

I. Corporate Image - In all PR and marketing activities, we
intend to position RKR in the minds of its prospects and clients as
an agency with these characteristics:

a. Integrated media experts. We know each of the media
    and how they can be coordinated for maximum success.
b. Results-driven. Clients can count on us to get the best
    possible results for every promotional dollar.

    c. Creative. RKR is capable of "breakthrough" ideas when appropriate.

    d. Industry leaders. RKR and its managers, account executives and creative staff remain at the forefront of all relevant technology and creative issues.

II. Creating Goodwill - We will show our community spirit and generosity through our pro-bono work for worthy organizations such as Lombardi Cancer Center, Lupus Foundation and Ronald McDonald House. While RKR will not actively promote its involvement with these organizations, we will take advantage of whatever opportunities are available for networking and publicity among the volunteers and professional staff affiliated with these groups.

III. Exposure for RKR and Key Executives - Speaking and writing opportunities will be sought for Christopher Ryan and other senior managers. Specifically, in 1992, RKR managers will speak at least eight times at industry conferences and seminars, and six or more articles written by Christopher Ryan will appear in publications such as <u>Target Marketing Magazine</u>, <u>DMAW Advents</u> and the <u>Washington Business Journal</u>.

Additional exposure for the agency will be gained from the promotion of <u>The Master Marketer</u>, as well as Christopher Ryan's first book, <u>The Direct Marketing Challenge</u>, and his audio-cassette programme, <u>How to Sell the $12 Potato</u>.

IV. Press Mentions - RKR and its executives must be kept in the news to maintain "top-of-mind" awareness among prospects, clients and industry leaders. This will be accomplished through a steady stream of press releases on company activities and personnel changes (at least one per month) and Letters to the Editor of trade and business publications (at least one every six weeks).

As you can see, while these goals aren't as quantifiable as other marketing objectives (revenue, number of leads, etc.), they are much more so than the typical PR goals of "increasing our name recognition" or "getting some exposure." And they are precise enough so that you can evaluate the success of the public relations effort and its contribution in supporting the overall marketing plan.

MEDIA RELATIONS STRATEGIES

Most successful public relations programmes are built on a foundation of media relations. There is no denying that you can influence certain groups, including customers, prospects and investors, through channels such as advertising, direct marketing, personal selling and promotions. However, none of these paid methods carry the weight of the implied endorsement of exposure in the non-paid media. This is the paradox; the least expensive form of promotion is often the most influential to your target audience.

The most important skill you can bring to a media relations programme is the ability to work well with the press. After all, the media and PR professionals operate best in a mutually beneficial and supportive atmosphere. Unfortunately, there is no set of techniques that will always foster such an atmosphere because reporters and editors are human beings just like the rest of us. That is, they are just as unique and unpredictable (and frustrating) as anyone else.

This individuality factor means that you will probably not get along with every editor. Perish the thought, one or more may even dislike you. But this is okay, unless you're dealing with a very small universe of press contacts. You don't need a perfect batting average; any more than you need 100 percent success with any other part of your communications effort.

Keeping these differences in people in mind, here are six rules to follow for effective media relations:

Media Relations Rule One: Don't take it personally. Ultra-sensitive people should not adopt PR as a career. Unless you forego contact with the press altogether, you are bound to experience some or all of the following:

- Editors don't return your phone calls (a frequent occurrence).
- Editors don't answer your query letters (a less frequent occurrence).
- Editors forget who you are.
- Publications don't pick up your press releases.
- Editors edit your releases or article submissions mercilessly. If they only knew how you slaved over every word!
- Editors hint or even promise to use your story and then renege (after you've told the chairman to watch out for the article focused on his leadership skills).

The natural tendency when any of the above occur is to feel angry and disappointed. Don't. Recognize the reality of an editor's existence. Chances are, there was nothing personal in his action. Choose to put the most gracious interpretation on the event ("spin control" as they say in politics). Here are some different ways of looking at the above events:

- Your phone call wasn't returned because the editor was under deadline (an inescapable fact of life).
- Your letter wasn't answered because the editor never saw it. Perhaps a junior editor decided it wasn't relevant.
- The editor forgot who you are because he deals with hundreds of people every week. Or perhaps you failed to make a good impression.
- The publication neglected to pick up your press release

because someone considered it irrelevant to their editorial mission, because it was poorly written (more on this later), or because you were unlucky to have it arrive with 200 others on a day the editorial department was short-staffed.

■ The editor butchered your copy because:
    a. It was too long
    b. It was too weak
    c. It didn't fit in stylistically
    d. That's what editors get paid to do

■ Although the editor may intend to publish your article, he may have omitted it because:
    a. The editor never promised to use the article. Rather he told you he "probably" would use it, which is not the same thing.
    b. A paid advertisement took the space.
    c. When the publication was put together your article didn't fit in editorially.
    d. Final edits on your article weren't completed in time.
    e. You called the editor too many times to "check on the progress" of your article.

As you can see, editors have a number of different reasons for acting in specific ways, most of which have nothing to do with you personally. Accept the fact that they have very difficult positions and that they make occasional mistakes like everyone else. You'll sleep a lot better and chances are, if an editor's actions hurt you, he will make it up to you down the road.

Media Relations Rule Two: If you can't follow rule number one, never call the editor to give him a piece of your mind. This holds true no matter how badly you feel betrayed, or how justified your anger. Such an action will make you feel good for approximately two hours. Then you will spend the rest of your professional career regretting it. How do I know? I've made such a call. Do I still regret making the call? You bet I do.

Media Relations Rule Three: Accept personal responsibility for the relationship. In most cases you will be the party in the weaker position in your dealings with the press. You are the seller and the individual editor or reporter is the buyer. As such, it is incumbent on you to take full responsibility for the success or failure of the relationship.

Media Relations Rule Four: Practice "friendly persistence." If your phone call or query letter isn't answered, call or write again. Editors understand that it is your job to pursue them. If the information you wish to convey is of genuine interest to the readers of the publication, you are doing the editor and yourself a favour by being persistent.

The exception; don't pursue to the point of being a pest. If, after two or three calls it becomes apparent that the editor has no interest in speaking with you, back off. Don't burn your bridges over one article or one press release.

Media Relations Rule Five: Never use the publisher to force editorial coverage. More often than not, such a move will be counter-productive and anger the editor. And from my experience, editors take a long time to forget such slights. There is an ongoing debate over whether companies can influence editorial coverage in the publications where they advertise. The answer is "yes" and "no." Yes, because the editor is more likely to be familiar with your organization, and you probably have established credibility in the industry. This familiarity can only help you since your competitors for non-paid media space may be relatively unknown to the editor.

On the flip side of the coin, editorial integrity is a prime consideration at all credible media. Print and broadcast media realize that their readers can detect biased editorial and will take great pains to eliminate any hints of slanted coverage. Occasionally, this can even work to the detriment of a paid advertiser.

My suggestion is to always handle the contact with editors exactly the same way, regardless of whether or not you are a paid advertiser. Editors aren't stupid. They know who advertises in their publications and don't need you to point this out to them.

Media Relations Rule Six: Be a reliable partner. If there is one thing editors and reporters need, it is reliable industry sources. This is one area where the media need you as much as you need them, and where you have the ability to separate yourself from your less reliable competitors. How do you build a reputation as a reliable source?

- Always keep your promises. Develop a reputation for total reliability. If you tell an editor you will have your material to her at 10:30 Tuesday morning, don't get it there Wednesday. Allow no exceptions to this policy.
- Practice integrity. Make sure the information you provide is not unfairly slanted toward your organization. Do not attack the competition. Be completely accurate with your data and honest about your strengths and weaknesses.

  I have seen this rule violated repeatedly in the computer software industry, where PR managers destroy their credibility with the press by announcing products that do not yet exist (this is where the term "vaporware" originated) or wildly exaggerating the capabilities of a particular product. This type of practice embarrasses the media. As I noted before, editors have good long-term memories and such blatant violations of trust are never forgotten.

■ Don't hide from the press when the news is bad. Whatever the problem; product failure, poor earnings, legal difficulties, falling share prices; the natural tendency is to unplug the phone and go fishing. Keep in mind though, if you refuse to talk to reporters when the news is bad, you have no opportunity to reflect the most favourable light on the subject, and the coverage you receive may be more negative than was necessary. Plus, you will be instantly dropped from that editor's list of "reliable information resources."

HOW TO GET YOUR PRESS RELEASES PUBLISHED

Press releases are a primary means of educating and influencing an organization's various publics. Much of a public relations manager's time is spent on writing, distributing and following-up press releases. The better the job you do of writing relevant, informative press releases, the more often your organization will get its name in print.

As mentioned earlier, editors are extremely busy, especially around deadline time. Add this fact to the incredible number of releases received (one editor friend averages 55 per day) and you can see why it is so difficult to get noticed and published. Given the reality of space limitations, in a sea of competing releases you must find a way to stand out.

The most important section of the press release is your opening paragraph because this is all that may be read. Due to time constraints, editors are more likely to publish releases which contain the essential facts in a minimum of space. Editors like to edit from the bottom-up, so a well-written opening makes the editor's job easier, and improves the odds that the release will be printed.

A good way to evaluate every release is to ask whether the first paragraph can stand alone, without the rest of the copy. To accomplish this, the opening paragraph should always answer the basic questions: WHO, WHAT, WHERE, WHEN and HOW? The remainder of the release offers copy which supports the opening paragraph.

As a general rule, try to keep the release to one page. Always double space to make the publication's editing job easier. Include the subject of the release, the date of the release (or the words "For Immediate Release") and a contact name and number at the top of the page.

Try to keep gross exaggerations, hyperbole, and unproven allegations to a minimum. Editors look for facts, not sales copy. A sentence such as "Chairman Bob Smith stated that the company's new product is the most exciting thing to hit the market in years," will more often than not get your release relegated to the bin (referred to in the PT industry as the "round file").

If you have a suitable photograph, such as a product shot or a picture of the individual mentioned in the release, by all means include it with the release. A 5 x 7 is preferred but 8 x 10s are also acceptable. Make sure the photos are labeled on the back with the subject, your company name and your phone number. Everyone in the picture should be identified.

Although there are several acceptable formats, the following will give you one example of how to format a press release.

NEWS RELEASE

RYAN·KING RENNINGER

PUBLIC RELATIONS

1901 RESEARCH BLVD
SUITE 310
ROCKVILLE, MD 20850
(301) 251-4708

News From:

TOUCHDOWN CLUB

Contact:

(301) 251-4708

R E Q U E S T   F O R   C O V E R A G E

JOIN REDSKINS MARK RYPIEN, ART MONK, GARY CLARK, DARRELL GREEN, RICKY ERVINS, WILBUR MARSHALL, EARNEST BYNER AND RICKY SANDERS BEFORE THE SUPER BOWL AT THE TOUCHDOWN CLUB'S ANNUAL TIMMIE AWARDS BANQUET, SATURDAY, JANUARY 18, 1992 AT THE WASHINGTON SHERATON HOTEL,2660 WOODLEY RD.,N.W. WASHINGTON, D.C. OTHER CELEBS ATTENDING INCLUDE ED McMAHON, SECRETARY OF DEFENSE DICK CHENEY, GENERAL P.X. KELLEY, MAYOR SHARON PRATT (DIXON) KELLY AND GEORGETTE MOSBACHER. REDSKINS AND CELEBS WILL BE AVAILABLE FOR INTERVIEWS IN THE HOTEL'S "MARYLAND SUITE" FROM 4:30-5:45 P.M. EXCELLENT PHOTO OPPORTUNITIES.

THE INTERNATIONALLY-RENOWNED "DIAL AWARDS", PRESENTED BY THE DIAL CORPORATION TO THE TOP MALE AND FEMALE HIGH SCHOOL SCHOLAR/ATHLETE WILL ALSO BE AN EVENING HIGHLIGHT.

PROCEEDS FOR THE EVENING WILL PROVIDE SCHOLARSHIPS TO FIVE WASHINGTON AREA SCHOOL ATHLETES AND ALSO BENEFIT LOCAL CHARITIES. STUDENTS RECEIVING TIMMIE AWARDS WILL ALSO BE AVAILABLE FOR INTERVIEWS.

DATE: Saturday, January 18, 1992

TIME: 4:30-5:45 P.M.   **Press Briefings & Photo Opportunities**
in hotel's "Maryland Suite"(1st floor, off main lobby)

6:00 p.m.   Reception (Cotillion Room)

7:00 p.m.   Dinner (Ballroom)

PLACE: The Sheraton Washington Hotel
2660 Woodley Road, N.W.
Washington, D.C.

COVERAGE INVITED

A standard press release

TYPES OF EVENTS TO PUBLICIZE

While by no means complete, the following is a list of some types of events that routinely receive press attention:

- Introduction of new products or services. These are usually published in a special section of magazines and newspapers. If the product is unique or innovative, it may even warrant its own feature story.
- Significant improvements to existing products or services. The key word here is "significant" because routine upgrades are not considered newsworthy.
- Fresh uses of existing products. Probably the most famous example of this approach is Arm & Hammer's promotion of its baking soda as a refrigerator deodorizer.
- Appointments and promotions of executive personnel. These releases are picked up by the media in almost every industry, as well as community newspapers and the general business press. Certain publications will even list the hiring of junior staff which is a morale-booster for the new employee. If you send a photo with this type of release, make sure it has the subject's name, title and company affiliation on the back. Better yet, tape the subject's business card to the back of the photo.
- Grand openings or significant remodeling. These are particularly important for retail establishments. Inviting local politicians and celebrities will increase the chances of receiving press coverage.
- Awards received by the organization or its key personnel. These are most effective if related to its corporate mission – for instance a car being named "car of the year" or an agency winning a "DADA" award or a "Clio". But do not neglect local awards such as an employee being named

"Young Businessman of the Year" or "leading fund-raiser for the Round Table" Community newspapers love these types of stories:

■ Corporate sponsorship of charitable events.
■ Contracts signed with prestigious clients.
■ Record-breaking financial performances of privately-held and public companies.
■ Unusual advertising campaigns. If your creative idea is unique enough, it is possible to receive more attention from the non-paid media than the paid media.
■ Important company anniversaries.
■ Major predictions by executives. If your media will cover his business forecasts, provided they are intriguing and not outside the realm of possibility.

SHOULD YOU HOLD A PRESS CONFERENCE?

When someone mentions a press conference, what comes to mind? An angry Chairman facing a room full of empty chairs? Or worse, a lone figure from an obscure publication asking the Chairman if he would like to buy advertising space?

If you feel this way, join the crowd. Many PR managers, if asked if they would rather arrange a press conference or have dental surgery, would immediately choose the latter. However, contrary to prevailing wisdom, properly organized press conferences can be well-attended, highly successful events.

When deciding between holding a press conference or spreading the news another way, ask yourself two questions:

1. Does my story contain a compelling news element?
2. Does my story lend itself to the use of a strong visual?

An exception to the need for a strong visual setting is when you are releasing hard news that the media is vitally interested in. For instance, when the Prime Minister announces his plans to run for re-election, coverage is guaranteed whatever the setting.

A great deal of creativity comes into play when deciding on press conference visual themes. The following are some notable examples I have seen used in the past, each of which received extensive print and broadcast coverage:

- A restaurant well known for its hot dogs solicited the help of the Chinese Basketball Team. When he discovered the team would be in town as part of a national tour, the press agent invited the players to the restaurant. Of course he invited loads of press to witness the Chinese players' reaction to one of America's favorite foods. Both the restaurant and the basketball team benefitted from the barrage of media coverage.
- To promote a humane organization's position on a particular issue, a PR professional arranged a press conference during the Easter season. Disney's "Donald Duck" was invited to the group's headquarters in honour of his 50th birthday. Donald Duck dolls were given away to scores of children. The group's message: "Don't buy live chicks and ducks at Easter." This event received extensive press exposure.
- Faced with introducing a new ice cream product to the consumer press, a public relations manager bypassed standard press release distribution and organized a press conference. Her visual: A cavalcade of carts carrying the cool new confection parading down the main street of a major U.S. city. The result: local and national TV and print coverage.

These examples point out the important role visual images can play in the success of a press conference. Here are other factors to consider:

Location - As the above examples illustrate, press conferences can be held in restaurants, city streets, or a thousand other locations. Sometimes, the locale itself can be part of the story. If possible, hold the event at a convenient location for the press. Hotels or conference centres are fine locations, so long as they are accessible to the editors and reporters you most want to attend.

Time - Morning conferences are my favorite but don't schedule before 10:00 a.m. If it has to be in the afternoon, never schedule after 2:00 p.m., since you will be interfering with closing deadlines. Tuesdays through Thursdays are generally the best days for scheduling a press conference.

Set-up - If the conference takes place indoors, there must be a raised platform and podium for the speaker. There should also be a central aisle for the television crews and space between the platform and chairs for photographers. A banner or sign displayed on or behind the podium will assure that the company's name appears in the majority of photographs.

Follow-up - After the event, contact all the press who attended. Make sure they have the information they need. Send out press releases on the event to non-attendees by fax or messenger.

OTHER PUBLICITY TOOLS

Direct Marketing

One image-enhancing direct marketing technique is to send out press releases on your company, products, and personnel to an expanded audience. Although many companies routinely send releases to the press, few have the foresight to share their important company news with customers, prospects, investors and key industry leaders.

While usually considered a direct response medium, direct mail can also be used to increase a company's top-of-mind awareness and name recognition. One of my clients proved this point recently with an in-depth market research study. Over 1,000 individuals in the company's target market were contacted and asked a series of questions to determine if they were aware of the company, and if so, how they became aware of it.

For the list of potential interviewees, a well-known publication's subscriber list was used. The company advertised monthly in this publication and also mailed to its subscribers periodically. The study was conducted blind so that the person being interviewed could not tell which company was the true subject of the survey.

The survey proved that, although the company spent five times as much on print advertising in the publication as mailing to its subscribers, only 32 percent of respondents could remember seeing a print ad for the company's products, while 54 percent remembered a direct mail package. This was true despite the fact that the company had not mailed during the six weeks prior to the survey.

The conclusion; Since the direct mail packages and print advertising had different themes and copy, we can't be entirely sure whether it was the medium or the message which caused the difference in awareness levels. But we can infer, at least in this case, that direct mail was far more cost-effective as an awareness builder than print advertising.

Two lessons can be learned from this study. First, that direct marketing should be considered as a publicity tool. Second, that you should be careful about what your direct mail and other marketing vehicles say because they can help make or break your organization's overall image.

Newsletters

Several important objectives can be achieved by creating a newsletter for your organization. As someone who has used newsletters to great advantage, I can assure you of the image-building power of this type of direct marketing vehicle. A well-written newsletter will establish your expertise in a given area faster than almost any other marketing tool. Of course, the converse is also true. Publish a poorly written newsletter and your organization's credibility will suffer.

Even before you write your first word of newsletter copy, make sure you have a good mailing list. The types of contacts you want to include on your list include customers, prospects, suppliers, key industry contacts, press, shareholders, and anyone else who can have a positive impact on your organization.

Once you develop the initial masthead design, the most difficult task in newsletter creation will be choosing appropriate topics and writing fresh copy for each issue. Keep in mind that it will be more effective if you keep your newsletter informational, and not sales oriented. Try to think of it in terms of a service you are providing to your prospects and customers, to help them run their organizations more effectively. The underlying theme should be that you are an expert and that they should contact you with any questions or problems in your area of expertise.

Always include some type of reply device in your newsletter design. Give your readers an opportunity to request additional information on your products/services, as well as anything they read about in the newsletter. With each of the newsletters I created, we generated enough leads to more than justify the cost of the entire newsletter programme, even though lead generation was only a secondary objective.

SOFTWORKS

Perspective

Volume 5   Number 1   **April 1992**

Four New Releases Give Softworks' Customers More Performance

The Mechanic ™ 5.1

Since its introduction in 1986, VSAM Mechanic ™ has become the industry standard for catalog recovery, repair, and maintenance. VSAM Mechanic's ability to quickly repair catalog and data set problems has made it indispensable in numerous data centers. And because VSAM Mechanic provides the only reliable method of backing up an ICF or VSAM catalog, it is regarded as a true ICFRU replacement. Now, with Version 5.1, several valuable enhancements have made it necessary to change the product's name. VSAM Mechanic is now The Mechanic. The name change is the result of the much requested non-VSAM capabilities that have been added, including eight new diagnostic routines:

- **GENERATE-DEFINE NONVSAM (GDN)**
- **GENERATE-DELETE-NONVSAM (GDLN)**
- **GENERATE-UNCAT-LIST (GUL)**
- **CHECK-VVDS-CATALOGS (CVC)**
- **GENERATE-AMS-DIAG-VVDS (GADV)**
- **GENERATE-AMS-DIAG-BCS (GADB)**
- **CHECK-SPANNED-RECS (CSR)**
- **GENERATE-RECATALOG-CARD (GRC)**

Several additional features make this product better suited to the needs of The Mechanic user community. This includes new support for VVDSs and VVCM records (VVCR Space Map Extension Records). VVCM records, created by the VVDS manager, remove the VVDS size limitation imposed by a fixed length space map structure in the VVCR. VVCM records currently residing in the VVDS are reused during VVDS rebuild processing.

The ability for you to audit the origin of generated control cards is an important addition to the Mechanic. This includes comments for DATE, TIME, JOBNAME, and COMMAND to document The Mechanic's processing. The information is stored at the beginning of each output file produced during DIAGNOSE processing.

We've also updated SCRATCH command processing. New keywords have been added to support the removal of non-cataloged (orphaned) data sets from SMS volumes. An IDCAMS DELETE VVR command is invoked when The Mechanic encounters one of these data sets.

Finally, a security exit has been added to The Mechanic. Module VM$SEC is called during the initialization of each command. This exit verifies that the user has the authority to process the command. The return code from VM$SEC determines whether The Mechanic will continue or terminate its processing.

Capacity Plus ™ for VSAM 1.2

Capacity Plus for VSAM (VCP) is a flexible compression product from Softworks. VCP lets you make the most of your current storage capabilities by compressing existing data up to 85% to make room for new files. By using VCP, your data center will achieve exceptional benefits because the compressed data speeds system throughput and improves response time system wide. Now, with VCP 1.2, several features have been added to enhance flexibility and usability. We are pleased to be able to include enhancements based on customer requests.

First of all, Virtual Storage Constraint Relief (VSCR) allows the base product modules and most work areas to run and reside above the 16 megabyte line. In the past, VCP could not be used with some applications because of region constraints below the 16mb line. This enhancement changes that. The data sets used by those applications can now be compressed because the majority of the storage used by VCP will be obtained above the line.

The VCP control catalog has been converted to a control repository (VSAM KSDS). This eliminates the need for RACF and ACF2 security exits and allows VCP to be installed without an IPL. Additionally, a convert utility has been added so users can quickly and efficiently convert existing VCP or VSAM Data Compressor (VDC) control catalog to the new control repository format.

Beginning with this release, VCP can be enabled in TEST mode from a non-LINKLIST library. With this enhancement, users can now test VCP without altering their current LINKLIST configuration.

Other enhancements include:

- **SMS support without ACS routine changes**
- **Improved compatability with MSA, QUIKJOB, and several other applications**
- **Improved compatability with several backup and recovery products (ie; FAVER, FDR/ABR, DFDSS)**

Like previous releases, VCP 1.2 is totally transparent. It requires no program, JCL, or operating system changes.

VSAM I/O Plus ™ 4.3

VSAM I/O Plus (VIO Plus) is a widely-used performance tool from Softworks. VIO Plus is probably best known for its ability to cut VSAM batch processing time up to 90%. Other notable benefits include automatic adjustments to data and index buffers and the ability to implement Hiperspaces, LSR, and DFR. The recent release of VIO Plus Version 4 Release 3 provides VIO Plus users with even greater benefits. This release of VIO Plus supports DFP Release 4 and is 100% downward compatible with prior releases of DFP.

The Winning Combination for Compression and Tuning

Softworks' High Performance Option

Softworks has the perfect combination for increasing productivity and reducing DASD costs. The High Performance Option (HPO) (which consists of VSAM I/O Plus ™ and Capacity Plus ™ for VSAM) pairs the latest compression technology with proven data set tuning techniques. With HPO, you can approach the theoretical limits of data compression and significantly reduce EXCPs, wall clock time, and CPU time without JCL modifications. HPO helps you save CPU cycles and enables you to achieve great compression.

HPO's ANALYZE utilities automatically select the optimal processing parameters and the best of three available compression strategies. What's more, HPO continually monitors your files and, as processing requirements change, dynamically tunes each VSAM data set to ensure that the most efficient processing parameters are being implemented every time the file is processed.

Continual data set tuning and extraordinary DASD savings are only two of the advantages that HPO provides. HPO also allows you to

back LSR buffer pools with a percentage of Hiperspace, improving performance in an ESA environment. When it's appropriate, HPO defaults to LSR processing so no JCL or program modifications are needed.

Flexibility is another impressive element of HPO. You can implement any parameters by data set name, high-level qualifier, DDNAME, program name, or process. All control information is centrally stored by HPO and can be viewed to determine what parameters have been implemented on each data set.

HPO lets you delay CPU upgrades by maximizing the efficiency of the CPU you already have. Furthermore, because of the high rates of compression, each DASD volume can store as much as 85% more data. You can then delay future spending of tight budget dollars on DASD and the associated extras (i.e., floor space, management, extra controllers, etc.)

HPO, the only option for compression and tuning, is just a phone call away. To examine the High Performance Option from Softworks, call your sales representative at 1-800-638-9254 or 1-301-856-1892. □

Continued on page 4

A sample newsletter

Sales Seminars

Seminars are an outstanding way of combining image-building and lead-generating activities. If you have the type of expertise that a room full of prospects would find interesting, by all means try seminars. Financial institutions and high-technology companies find this vehicle especially effective.

Trade Shows

Trade shows allow you to come in direct contact with your various publics, including the press. Editors and reporters attend almost all trade shows to see what's new and interesting in products and companies.

To get maximum publicity out of any trade show follow these steps:

- Thoroughly brief everyone from your organization who will be attending the event. Make sure they have suitable materials and know where to refer press inquiries.
- If you have an important announcement to make or new products to introduce, contact the press before the show. Send editors briefing materials ahead of time.
- Arrange meetings with editors and reporters at the event. If a product demonstration is necessary, you may need to meet at the exhibit space. Otherwise, I prefer meeting the editor for breakfast or lunch. This way, you get to know each other as individuals, outside the hustle and bustle of the exhibition hall.
- Arrange to have plenty of materials, such as press releases, product literature and spec sheets at the press room. Visit the room occasionally to check on the press who are in attendance.
- Trade publications often exhibit at trade shows. Their stands are excellent places to find editors, or to leave messages for them.

EIGHT QUESTIONS TO EVALUATE
<u>YOUR PUBLIC RELATIONS PROGRAMS</u>

Whatever methods you use to generate publicity, ask yourself the following questions to evaluate the programme:

1. Does the message I am communicating speak to the public's interest or my own?

2. Am I sharing solid information or vague pronouncements?

3. Does my message have the sound of truthfulness?

4. Does my message position my company unmistakably or is it confusing or conflicting?

5. Does the message make the reader want to buy the company's products or services, or invest in its shares?

6. Am I practicing friendly persistence in public relations?

7. Is my message consistent?

8. Are all my public relations activities based on the objectives listed in the PR plan?

If you can answer all of these questions positively, you are using public relations to great advantage in promoting your organization.

OTHER MEDIA
AND SALES PROMOTION

*T*oday's Master Marketer is no longer confined to mass media. There are a wealth of marketing choices available. Sometimes these tools are used in conjunction with broadcast, print and direct mail advertising, and sometimes they are used as stand-alone marketing tools. Although there are literally hundreds of alternate media options (several companies even sell advertising space in *public restrooms*), in this chapter we will discuss the following:

- Sales and trade promotions
- Sampling
- Coupons
- Premiums
- Point-of-purchase displays

- Contests and sweepstakes
- Inserts
- Handbills and flyers
- Co-op mailings
- Card decks
- Directories and yellow-pages
- Outdoor
- Transit
- Advertising specialties

ADVANTAGES OF ALTERNATE MEDIA

Alternative media vehicles offer the marketer two major advantages; cost and targetability. For these reasons they are often the first choice of new businesses. For instance, a new retail store that would find the mass-media prohibitively expensive, can use a combination of yellow-pages, flyers and co-op mailings to generate store traffic and announce its presence to the community.

For those with larger marketing budgets, alternate media also allow excellent reinforcement of mass-media advertising. Alternate media should be considered key components of the coordinated marketing campaign.

Despite these benefits, you should be very careful in choosing your alternate media weapons. I have seen a great deal of money wasted on frivolous and ineffective marketing tools. A healthy dose of skepticism is always advisable.

For example, because of my involvement with business and community activities, I am often asked to sponsor an event or run an ad in a group's directory. I know from experience that these expenditures rarely lead to new business. So if I make a decision to sponsor an event or buy an ad, I do so to help the group, not because I expect a certain return on my marketing investment. If you wish to run such ads or sponsor community groups, set up an extra budget category, but do not use funds that you've designated for cost-effective marketing activities.

SALES PROMOTION

In the UK over £6.5 billion is spent annually on sales promotion activities including coupons, free samples, premiums and contests. Sales promotions can be directed at customers (consumer promotion) or at dealers and retailers (trade promotion). According to Advertising Age, US product marketers are especially fond of trade promotion, as they devote approximately half of all marketing budgets to this marketing medium.

The most effective promotions are targeted at both consumers and trade outlets and are supported by print, broadcast and direct mail advertising.

Sales promotions usually have one of two primary objectives; either generating short-term sales or persuading consumers or retailers to try a sample of the product or service. Unlike image advertising, sales promotions are only successful if they generate immediate sales or trials. This instant feedback helps marketers continually refine their promotional activities for maximum effectiveness.

There are two hazards to beware of in sales promotion. First, promotions can often lead to a burst of short-term sales activity, at the expense of long-term sales. This will be true if you encourage people who use your product at a steady rate to buy a greater quantity now at a discounted price, leading to a slump in future sales. Second, too many promotions can cheapen the image of your product or service. Consumers will become trained to "wait for the next promotion" instead of buying now.

A prime example of the dangers of "over-promotion" is the car industry. Rebates and deep-discounts are probably necessary in times of recession. But these promotions have become so prevalent that car buyers now expect them as a notmal part of the car shopping experience.

SAMPLING

Sampling is an excellent method of generating sales and awareness, provided you have the necessary resources. Companies such
as Kellogg's and Proctor & Gamble have made sampling a key
part of their marketing arsenal for years. Sampling is particularly
effective when introducing a new product in a crowded field. If
you do not have the advertising budget to overcome the brand
awareness of the industry leader(s), sampling may be the only way
to get your product into the hands of its intended audience.

One caveat, however: Your product <u>must</u> prove a demon-
strable point of differentiation to the consumer. Even though the
consumer will probably try the free product you send, he will not
become loyal to your brand just because you sent him a free
sample. If the product is not superior in some way, sampling will
have a meager impact on sales, at best.

As with other marketing techniques, sampling can be conducted on a test basis. Instead of spending large sums distributing
samples to a national audience, consider trying your program in a
local area and then monitoring its effect on sales in that area. If the
program works it can then be expanded on a regional or national
basis.

Sampling has been used successfully in the business-to-business arena. For example, Great American Software, Inc., of
Nashua, New Hampshire, has given away thousands of its $59.95
small business accounting software program called Money Matters. Great American believes the sampling program has greatly
increased awareness of the company and contributed to 40 percent
annual increases in revenues.

The company also knows that many of the firms that accept its
free offer are currently using another company's software. If its
products were not superior, Great American would not be able to

get customers to switch from their existing software and adopt Money Matters. Just as with consumer sampling, business products must have readily identifiable advantages.

What was probably the ultimate sampling program in history was conducted by William Wrigley, Jr. in 1915. Wrigley mailed a free stick of chewing gum to every person listed in a phonebook in the entire United States. Talk about covering the market! While high postage rates make this a prohibitive method of promoting its products today, the Wrigley Company still keeps the sampling spirit alive by handing out free packages of its gum to pedestrians on street corners.

COUPONS

In the age of diminishing brand loyalty, discount coupons will entice many consumers to try a new product or service. As with samples, a customer redeeming a coupon will not necessarily increase future purchases of that product, unless the product is obviously superior. Since coupon offers tend to be most effective in attracting frequent "coupon-shoppers," you may be forced to keep running these programmes to keep sales volume high.

PREMIUMS

Premiums come in two major categories. The first category is free gifts or services which are given to a customer who buys your product. The second category is known as self-liquidating premiums. With self-liquidating premiums the consumer pays some or all of the cost of the item. We all learned about self-liquidating premiums as children from reading the back of cereal boxes. Remember when two dollars and three boxtops could get you a Captain Marvel Decoder Ring or some other valued treasure?

One thing to remember when using premiums to enhance your offer is that it is often better to focus the promotional copy on the premium, rather than on the product or service. The word "Free" is the most powerful word in advertising so use it liberally.

POINT OF SALE

The success of a sales promotion may depend as much on what happens at the retail establishment as on how you advertise to the marketplace. An attractive and compelling point-of-sale display will help entice people to purchase your product, even when they had no intention of buying such a product when they entered the store. However, convincing retailers to give you the necessary floor or counter space to mount an effective point-of-purchase exhibit can be difficult. Retailers will only be receptive to your display if you can demonstrate how it can help them increase sales.

The copy and graphics theme of your display should always closely resemble the advertising that supports the promotion. This consistency will lead to a large boost in results.

COMPETITIONS AND LOTTERIES

As a promotional strategy, competitions and lotteries have their benefits and limitations. Although the two are often confused, there are major differences between competitions and lotteries.

A lottery is basically a game of chance. All participants have an equal chance of winning. Usually, no great effort is required to enter and, in fact, many European countries will not allow you to require participants to make a purchase as a condition of entry. This is why the phrase, "No purchase necessary" is part of most lottery promotions.

By contrast, competitions require some degree of effort from the participant. For instance, contestants may be required to answer a quiz, guess how many marbles are in a jar or write an essay on how they use your product. Competitions can be as much a game of skill as they are a game of chance.

Competitions and lotteries offer the following advantages to the Master Marketer:

- They generate excitement for your product or service.
- They bring your organization greater exposure.
- Tying a lottery to an offer will almost always lead to greater response.
- They are great ways to build your prospect database.
- In the case of competitions, participants must often learn more about your products and organization to enter.

Watch out for these drawbacks:

- They can be very expensive to operate.
- There are complex regulations covering lotteries. You will need to know the rules in each participating jurisdiction. This can be particularly cumbersome for international offers.
- Publishers and fundraisers have demonstrated that many people who buy through lottery promotions will not renew through other marketing efforts. Thus, you must periodically run new offers to keep these customers loyal.
- Since it is necessary to focus on the lottery or competition, the product and your organization may be overshadowed.

INSERTS

Inserts are a "secondary" marketing medium. They usually consist of printed matter that is inserted into some other promotion or communication going to the prospect. Places where inserts can be used include:

- Fulfillment packages. Along with the product or information he ordered, the prospect also receives an insert for an offer promoting a different product or service. These insert programmes are effective because people are most receptive to new offers immediately after a purchase, particularly if the two products are related.
- Catalogues. People who purchase by catalogue are very receptive to other mail offers. The catalogue marketer benefits by having the insert sponsor subsidize the postage costs. Inserts are also a good way for two catalogue companies to build their customer files.
- Bills and invoices. These types of inserts are known as "statement stuffers." They can be found in monthly invoices and credit card bills. Often, the insert found in a credit card statement will feature a special offer that is valid only if purchased with that credit card. American Express has made extensive use of this merchandising method. Both parties benefit from this programme. The credit card company sees increased usage of its card and the insert marketer receives an implied endorsement of its products by the credit card company.

HANDBILLS AND FLYERS

Handbills and flyers are printed sheets that are distributed directly to the consumer, either by handing them out in person, through delivery to the home or office, or by placing the flyer on car windscreens in parking lots. Handbills are an excellent way to introduce a new retail store to the community or to announce new products and services by an existing business.

Since the flyer is usually glanced at and quickly discarded, special time-sensitive offers work well. Needless to say, the offer must be very strong and clear. If you fail to make your point within five to seven seconds, your chance of making the sale is very slim.

CO-OP MAILINGS

Co-op mailings are just what the name implies. Two or more companies "cooperate" by mailing their offers together in the same envelope. Co-op mailings can be sent to consumer or business audiences. The products or services may be related or entirely different. Although response rates for each unique offer will be lower in a co-op package than if each company had mailed alone, the cost to each mailer in a co-op programme is much lower.

As with other types of direct mail, the most important key to success in a co-op package is to ensure that your mailing is being sent to the right audience. To make sure that this happens, ask for verification that similar offers have been mailed to the same list with good results. And although you want to be viewed as unique, I would advise you to stay away from co-op mailings with totally dissimilar products or services.

CARD DECKS

Card decks are very similar to co-op mailings. Card deck mailings are groups of a dozen to over a hundred cards. As with co-ops, card decks are most effective if each advertiser has a somewhat related offer. For instance, card decks featuring computer hardware and software products are mailed to managers who work in computer-related jobs. The same offers mailed to a list of marketing executives would most likely generate little or no response.

Card decks can be used to sell products directly (one-step offers) or to produce leads for later follow-up (two-step offers). Although the cost to generate each lead will be less than with other types of marketing vehicles, you may find the lead quality to be rather poor. Likewise, you probably won't sell a lot of products through a card deck offer, but the cost of advertising in the deck is so low that the acquisition cost for each new customer may be in the acceptable range.

The two keys to an effective card deck promotion are a powerful headline and simple graphics. Because your card may be one of dozens of others in the deck, at best you only have a few seconds to get your message across. State the offer and your most important benefit in the headline. Don't forget to make it crystal clear exactly what you want the person to do. If possible, give the prospect a choice of responding by phone or mail. And finally, create a sense of urgency. You must cause the prospect to react right away; not flip past the card and not file it for later consideration; but take action NOW.

DIRECTORY AND YELLOW-PAGES

Many local and retail companies find the Yellow Pages directories their greatest source of new business. This is because the average consumer uses these directories to locate an appropriate nearby source for goods or services.

Community directories tend to be less effective than regional Yellow Pages directories. Unless the directory gives all companies a free listing, they tend to under-represent the business community. Frustrated consumers soon go back to the trusty Yellow Pages. On the other hand, these local directories are much less expensive than Yellow Pages, so if you get a great rate, they may be worth a try.

There are two important things to remember with Yellow Pages ads. First, people are looking for specific facts when perusing the directory. They have most likely already made up their mind about buying and are now in the investigation stage of their purchase. They want to know basic information such as what products and services you offer, what your hours of operation are, and what forms of payment you accept.

Second, there is a numbing sameness about Yellow-Page advertising. To stand out, study what everyone else is doing and then try to do something different.

How big should your ad be? Consumers will often judge the size and prestige of your firm in relation to others in the yellow pages by the relative sizes of your ads. So the ad should be as large, or larger than, your primary competitor's ad. The optimum ad size is also predicated on the amount of information you have to share with the consumer.

OUTDOOR

Outdoor advertising is that which is seen by consumers when they are out moving about. This medium is popular with many advertisers because people now tend to spend a lot more time in their cars than watching television and reading newspapers. Outdoor advertising currently accounts for about 6 percent of UK expenditure.

Outdoor advertising ranges from billboards and posters, to the signs that adorn almost every retail establishment of the most popular formats are the 48-Sheet "billboard" poster and the "Adshed" bus shelter poster. These and other size billboards are leased for one month or longer terms by companies known as "plants".

Outdoor advertising creativity is limited by the short amount of time you have to reach each prospect. It is hard to craft a compelling selling story in the few seconds a consumer has to read your message while driving down the road. Here are a few ways to make your outdoor advertising more effective:

■ Keep the message simple. A brief headline should be used, preferably a powerful benefit statement. Try to hold your copy to eight words or less.
■ Use a large, colorful graphic. This will attract the consumer's eye, and then he or she will read your eight words or less of copy. Blown-up photographs of people

241

make excellent graphics.

- Use large, bold letters. No script or unusual fonts please. To be seen from the road, letters should be a minimum of six to eight inches high.
- Make your outdoor consistent with other advertising. If possible, use similar themes and graphics.
- If it fits, use humour. Travellers tend to be tense and bored. They will appreciate your advertising if they find it amusing. Heineken's famous "refreshes the parts other beers cannot reach" campaign ran equally well on posters as well as television.

TRANSPORT ADVERTISING

Transport advertising offers several major advantages:

- Since commuters tend to use the same transportation system every weekday, transport advertising offers high frequency (although commuters are very good at "tuning out" unwanted advertising messages).
- In heavily populated urban areas, transport advertising matches its high frequency with large reach as well. London transport or any of the European "metro" systems are prime examples.
- Travellers are something of a captive audience and in some cases spend two or more hours commuting per day.

One disadvantage of transport advertising is the environment in which it is run. Certain marketers simply do not want their company prominently displayed on the outside of a bus or train, particularly since these ads can become soiled and weather beaten.

Transport advertising includes three types of formats:

1. Posters placed inside bus, underground, train and airport facilities. These ads are seen only by the patrons of the transportation system.

2. Advertising placed on the outside of trains, buses, coaches and taxicabs. These are seen by the passengers and outside audiences.

3. Interior posters placed inside the bus, train or taxi, which are seen only by the passengers on that route.

Although there are exceptions, such as affluent commuters in suburbs of cities or cities with a large number of tourists, transport audiences tend to represent a disproportionate share of lower income groups. You will want to carefully research advertising, this means the passengers. For exterior advertising, this means those who live, work or commute along the transportation route.

Ideas to get the most from your transport advertising:

■ Make sure your creative approach matches the audience.
■ Treat exterior transport advertising the same as outdoor advertising, with a very brief message, bold colours and large letters.
■ Use large lettering even on interior posters, since the reader may be sitting or standing several yards from the ad.
■ Commuting is an unpleasant experience for many people. The use of warmth, humor and emotional copy will be appreciated and remembered by the audience.
■ Use transport advertising as a reinforcement of your print

and broadcast promotions.

- Use good taste. Commercial clutter is seen as a problem by a large segment of the population. Don't contribute to the problem by offending community sensibilities.

ADVERTISING SPECIALTIES

Advertising specialties are items given by an organization to its prospects and/or customers. The specialty may be something as simple as a pen or keychain, or as expensive as a leather jacket. There are literally hundreds of thousands of products you can use as ad specialties; in fact, anything that can be imprinted with the advertiser's name and selling message.

Ad specialties are rarely used as primary marketing tools. Rather, they best function as reminders of the organization. The ideal item will relate to the product or service; for instance a car dealer who gives out key chains, reminding the prospect where to go to get his car serviced, or a printer who gives out pads of scratch paper, reminding the prospect where to get her printing done.

It is also a good idea to give something that the prospect will keep for some time. Try to find something that is either highly unusual, or if an everyday item, has good value. Stay away from cheap trinkets, especially if dealing with a business audience. In other words, always match the premium to the audience.

HOW TO GET THE BEST RESULTS
FROM ALTERNATE MEDIA

Follow these guidelines to achieve the best results from your alternate media:

- Start with in-depth knowledge of your target audience. Use only media that contain a high concentration of people from that audience.

■ Make sure the medium matches the message. A high price product should probably not be advertised on the back of a matchbox, nor should a low price, commodity product be promoted in an opera programme.

■ Run the numbers. Subject your alternate media choices to the same critical scrutiny as all other media.

■ Be consistent. Double your effectiveness by using the same creative themes on alternate media as you do on mass media.

■ Be unique. Many of the alternate media are undiscovered by large advertisers. This is an area in which you can really stand out.

SECTION IV

DIRECT MARKETING

THE MASTER MARKETER'S EDGE

THE ART AND SCIENCE OF FINDING
GOOD MAILING LISTS

*C*hances are, whatever your product or service, you face the daunting task of finding a steady stream of new prospects to fuel your marketing engine. You are not alone. Many organizations are challenged by the necessity of finding new list sources and choosing from the thousands of available mailing lists.

Just how important are mailing lists to marketing success? In the direct marketing industry there is a saying, "The three most important factors in a direct marketing campaign are the list, the list, and the list." Not only do I agree, I would go so far as to say you can accomplish more by sending a mediocre direct mail package to a good list than you can by mailing the most clever and expensive package to a poor mailing list.

DEFINING A QUALITY MAILING LIST

While many people know how to define their best prospects, they may not understand how to evaluate mailing lists. Following are eight characteristics you should always look for in a mailing list:

1. The list should contain individuals who match the profile of your existing customers.

2. It should be available in sufficient quantities.

3. It should contain recent names (those who have purchased or responded in the past six months) and be well maintained.

4. It should allow for segmentation through selection options.

5. The list should be available on the media you require (e.g. nine-track tape or labels).

6. It should be available for testing in small quantities (usually 5,000 names).

7. It has been used successfully for similar offers.

8. The rental price should be reasonable.

Although each of these characteristics will be discussed in some detail, I would like to point out that characteristic eight, the cost of the list, is probably the one that novice direct marketers focus on the most. Yet, in fact, it is the least important factor. Differences in the response rates of direct mail lists are so great (particularly in business-to-business marketing) that a cost differential of 10 pounds, 20 pounds, or even 30 pounds per-thousand names is not likely to make or break a programme. The only time these slight differences in price should be a factor is when you are comparing marginal lists.

FOCUSING ON OBJECTIVES

Before beginning the process of selecting lists, you should review the overall objectives for the programme. Since direct marketing is a quantifiable marketing tool, it helps to express your obectives in numerical terms. The three basic formulas used in direct marketing are cost-per-thousand (CPM) prospects reached, cost-per-lead (CPL), and cost-per-sale (CPS). Fund-raisers rate their programmes in terms of CPM, average gift, cost-per-donor (CPD) and cost-per-pound of contribution (CPC). Membership associations calculate CPM and cost-per-new-member (CNM).

Don't make the mistake of focusing on CPM. If CPM is your priority, you can miss the larger and more important picture. The fact is, every organization survives, and hopefully thrives, to the degree it can attract new customers, donors or members. And while it is important to communicate with large numbers of prospects, without a good handle on your cost-per-sale (CPS) or cost-per-lead (CPL), your cost-per-thousand (CPM) will be an inaccurate gauge of the success of your marketing programme.

Too many direct marketers carefully track the cost to reach each prospect but neglect to figure in the costs of converting raw leads into customers. The problem is that many lists will produce large numbers of responses but few sales. Conversely, there are mailing lists which generate few responses, but a large percentage of the people who respond will become customers. On a comparison basis, the latter type of list is much more valuable.

To illustrate, let's look at a segment of an actual list test our agency conducted for a bank. The offer was a money market account and the mailing package sent to each list was identical. All lists were tested with 5,000 names. To simplify the example, we have only included the cost of the list when computing CPM, CPL and CPS, even though we would normally use the entire package costs to compute these figures in actual application. Note also that we have simplified the formula by stopping our analysis at cost per sale, when we would usually be interested in computing the total sales generated from each list.

	CPM	# Response	% Response	CPL	#Sales	CPS
List A	£65	50	1.00	6.50	5	65.00
List B	£50	35	.70	7.15	2	125.00
List C	£80	25	.50	16.00	7	57.15

Each of the figures used in this chart was computed as follows:

CPM (cost per thousand) was the price we paid the list owner for every 1,000 names we rented.

 # Response is the total number of leads we generated from mailing to a particular list of 5,000 names.

% Response is computed by dividing the number of responses by the 5,000 names we mailed from each list.

CPL is the cost per lead. As stated earlier, we only counted the list costs in this example. For List A, the rental fee is £65 per thousand. We rented 5,000 names, so our total cost for the list is £65 × 5 = £325. £325 divided by the number of leads generated (50) gives us our cost per lead of £6.50.

# of Sales is the total number of new orders received from our mailing to that list.

CPS is the cost of acquiring each new sale. It is computed by dividing the total cost of mailing each list by the number of sales to that list. For example, rental of the 5,000 names on List A costs £325. We made five sales to List A so the cost of each sale (CPS) is £325 divided by five, or £65. This small test illustrates very clearly why it is so important to look at all the relevant numbers when deciding which lists are most effective. If we based our list decisions solely on the basis of cost per thousand names (CPM),

List B, with a CPM of £50 would be chosen. However, if we choose on the basis of cost per each lead (CPL), List A, with a CPL of £6.50 is the clear winner. This is where the decision making process ends for many mailers.

The Master Marketer focuses on where the real payoff lies: the cost per sale (CPS). In this example, although List C has the highest cost per thousand contacts at £80, and by far the highest cost per lead at £16.00, its cost per sale at £57.15 makes it, in my opinion, the winner for purposes of this test. This is not to say that lists A and B are bad lists. List A shows characteristics that make it worth a second consideration. But always keep in mind the number one priority, which is generating new sales.

PROFILING YOUR MARKET

After you have a good handle on your specific objectives, you must then decide on the size and breadth of your marketplace (the universe). If you are a business-to-business marketer, answer these questions to help define your universe:

- What industries do you now service, and which do you intend to service in the future?
- Who are the specific individuals within these industries making the decisions to buy your type of products or services?
- What are the functional titles of these decision makers? Note that "functional title" refers to a generic title for a position (e.g. Chief Financial Officer), not the title listed on that person's business card. Mailing lists are often segmented by functional titles, not actual titles.
- What is your geographic market area?
- Are there other factors that define your market? For instance, do you work with companies of a certain size, as defined by sales revenue or number of employees?

For consumer offers, analyze the following demographic attributes of your ideal prospects:

- Age
- Sex
- Family size
- Income
- Educational level
- Homeowners or renters
- Previous purchase or donation history

When you ask these types of questions you are profiling your current customers. Profiling is important because chances are, the individuals most likely to purchase from you in the future probably have a lot in common with those who purchased from you in the past. Asking the questions necessary for you to develop a customer profile (or multiple profiles), can be an eye-opening experience. You may not know your customers as well as you think.

THE IN-HOUSE MAILING LIST -
YOUR PERSONAL "GOLD MINE"

When setting a value on the in-house database of customer and prospect information, the closest I can come is that of a "gold mine." Because that is exactly what your prospect and customer database can turn out to be. This is true because generating additional business from existing customers is much easier than searching for new buyers. On a pure cost-efficiency scale, selling to a repeat customer can cost as little as one tenth as much as converting a new customer.

But don't make the mistake of taking it for granted that your customers will always come to you when they want new products and services. You have to ask, and ask again. For instance, studies of banking customers have shown that the reason they do not use their main bank (where they hold their personal current account) for a new banking service is that they were never asked and had no idea their bank offered the service.

Many organizations fail to promote to their in-house file often enough because they don't want to irritate customers. Yet, the most successful direct marketers mail as often as once a month to their customer or donor files. A few mail even more often. Frequent mailings, if targeted properly and based on genuine needs, will not annoy, but rather help build the relationship between you and your customers.

Another mistake is to treat existing customers the same as prospects. A high frequency of mailings to your house file must be balanced with a sensitivity to the fact that you are dealing with your most important assets. Do not send your customers anything that does not acknowledge this special relationship. And by all means, run your house file against the outside lists you rent (this is known as "file suppression") to prevent your customers from getting the same mail as prospects.

A great deal of effort will be required to prepare your in-house file for maximum return. Remember, a gold mine doesn't produce gold without hard work. The same is true of building and crafting your in-house list.

You should first decide which information you are going to maintain on each customer, donor or member on your house-file. A cardinal rule is that it is better to compile too much data than not enough, because it is easier to delete information than add it later. Some examples of the type of information that you may want to maintain:

- Full names, including gender and prefix titles (Mr., Ms., Dr., etc.).
- Complete mailing addresses, including postcodes if you have access to them. These postcodes are useful for segmenting your file and adding demographic information.

graphic information.
- Telephone numbers. There are several good reasons to collect phone numbers, even if you have no current intention of calling these people. Telephone numbers are handy tools to segment files. For example, when I was director of marketing for a national software company, we used area codes to assign sales territories when more than one representative worked within a county. Also, if you ever decide to rent your list to other organizations, you will find its value enhanced if it contains phone numbers.
- Industry designation codes such as Standard Industrial Classification (SIC). SIC codes identify the general type of business activity a firm is engaged in, (e.g. manufacturing), as well as its specialty (e.g. electrical equipment manufacturer). This type of code allows you to send out mailings targeted by industry. These mailings are usually more effective than generic efforts.
- Buying history or account potential. This data is important for target marketing purposes. And while all marketers can benefit, fund-raisers find this type of information especially helpful, as they often base a request for donations today on the size of an individual's largest past gift and frequency of contributions. This is important because you don't want to ask a frequent £100 giver for the same amount as a one-time £10 giver Commercial organizations can use buying history to tailor special marketing programmes to their largest customers.
- Response history. This is similar to buying history but tracks what initially caused the prospect to become a customer, member or donor, and what motivates them to continue. For example, a fund-raising organization may find that a particular issue was the catalyst for

many donations. A business mailer may discover that a large portion of its customers may only respond to discount offers. This type of data can be invaluable in designing future campaigns.

■ Contact information, including all communications with the customer by mail, telephone and in-person, and the results of these contacts.

■ Demographic/psychographic data that can be important in designing future targeted campaigns. For instance, a life/health insurance company would be very interested in the age distribution of its prospects and customers, and which of them are smokers or nonsmokers.

A PERSONAL EXAMPLE

We went through the above steps when profiling our ideal prospects and setting up the in-house file for our agency. In defining the market potential, we realized that our prospect base could be segmented by several factors, including:

■ Geography - Although our clients market all over the U.S., Canada and Europe, they are primarily headquartered in the Mid-Atlantic region, with 85% in the Washington, DC area. With occasional exceptions, outside-the-area prospects come to us through word of mouth, or prior personal contact, not through our marketing efforts.

■ Industry - We have worked with firms in many industries but the bulk of our customer base is comprised of banks, hospitals, insurance companies, software companies, and professional associations.

■ Size of firm - We prefer to work with medium to large firms, not small companies and retail establishments.

■ Titles - With some exceptions, our average prospect

257

> company contains three individuals we want to get to
> know better - the president of the company, the person
> who heads up the marketing function, and the person
> responsible for public relations.

Once we established this customer profile, we set out to discover every individual and company that fits the above criteria and then enter these people into our in-house database. On an ongoing basis we then contact our prospects by mail, telephone and person-to-person. We maintain this contact until a prospect becomes a client, is disqualified or changes jobs (in which case we attempt to establish contact with them at their new company).

While we built our database company-by-company and name-by-name, and have no need to mail to large, general lists, there are many organizations that are better served by taking a mass-marketing approach to building their in-house lists. For example, one client mails to various outside lists totaling 40,000 potential prospects. If the mailing achieves a response rate of two percent, that company has now identified 800 individuals who have demonstrated interest in its products.

Instead of merely sending literature to each of these respondents (like many of its competitors), the company enters each into its in-house database, along with all information that the prospect filled in on the response card. These individuals will then be tracked through the system until they either purchase or are disqualified on some basis. This process may take months or years. In the meantime, the company will not lose contact with these people, and will have many more chances to persuade them to buy its products.

This is how you build your house-file. Contact-by-contact, mailing-by-mailing, day-by-day. Your database can soon become a solid foundation upon which your entire marketing programme is built.

USING OUTSIDE MAILING LISTS

No matter how good you are at building and using your in-house file, chances are you will need to supplement your mailings with outside mailing lists. Much of the preparatory work for selecting outside lists has been accomplished by the construction of your prospect profile(s). Now the trick is to find the best match between your prospect profile and **individuals** available on outside mailing lists.

Keep in mind that your job is not to communicate with mailing lists, it is to communicate with human beings. The fact is, a mailing list never purchased anything from anyone. You are not selling to mailing lists, you are selling to individuals who could be your mother, brother, friend or next door neighbour.

Although lists come in thousands of varieties, there are two general categories: "response lists" and "compiled lists."

Response lists, as the name implies, are comprised of individuals who have responded to a previous offer of some type, whether that offer was generated by mail, telephone, broadcast or personal contact. People on response lists have taken specific action that shows they are interested in the product or service represented by that list. Examples of response lists include:

- Magazine subscribers
- Mail order product buyers
- Donors to charities or political causes
- Trade show attendees
- Lottery entrants
- Leads generated from direct mail or other marketing programmes

COMPILED LISTS

Compiled lists, by contrast, contain individuals that have been grouped according to shared characteristics. These lists are often compiled (built) from multiple sources. Sources of compiled lists include:

- Members of trade or professional associations
- Directories
- Telephone and utility subscribers
- Homeowners
- Business owners
- Credit reports

Compiled lists can be far more extensive than a simple collection of mailing address information. Compiled consumer lists can be overlaid with demographic and psychographic information to enhance their versatility. In the business-to-business arena, the primary demographics used are SIC codes, industry categories, functional titles, geography, annual revenue and number of employees. Demographic data overlays for consumer lists include income, age, sex, home value, presence of children, ethnic background and educational level.

Psychographic data is based on a person's lifestyle characteristics and segments individuals into groups that share common traits and buying habits. Psychographics also deal with individuals' values and attitudes and can be used to help predict future purchasing behavior.

One application of demographic and psychographic overlays is called cluster-coding. Researchers have identified some 40 different lifestyle segments, ranging from the super affluent to the urban poor. Utilizing demographic data obtained from the census bureau and other sources, these clusters of people with similar lifestyle characteristics can be pinpointed down to the neighborhood level.

In other words, while the list compiler does not know that Mr. Jim Smith has all the characteristics of a particular lifestyle group, they do know that he lives in a neighbourhood populated by such people. Thus, they lump Mr. Smith in with all the others in that group, figuring that like people congregate.

But the fact is that similar people do not always congregate, particularly where housing is concerned. A typical scenario may find a mid-thirties baby-boomer couple with small children living between a retired couple on one side and an early twenties child-less couple on the other. In my opinion, this lack of homogeneity is one of the major drawbacks of cluster-coding and why it is out of favour with many direct marketing experts.

Response lists and compiled lists each have their own benefits and liabilities. Review the following to determine which is better for your mailing programme.

ADVANTAGES OF RESPONSE LISTS

- Not always, but generally, response lists pull better than compiled lists. This is because individuals on response lists have one characteristic that separates them in a positive way from compiled lists; they have responded. And the single greatest predictor of a person's likelihood of responding to your offer is whether he has responded to a similar offer in the past.
- Response lists are available in infinite varieties. Chances are good that you can find one or more that match your prospect profile.
- It has been my experience that response list owners and managers have a more in-depth knowledge about the individuals on their lists. The response list owner is often a magazine publisher, association manager, mail order operator; or a professional who has a need to know a great deal about his customers.
- By renting a number of response lists, you have the ability to track multiple responders. This is important because multiple responders are much more likely to

261

respond to your offer than single responders. By contrast, a person appearing on more than one compiled list usually has no more likelihood of responding than a person appearing once.

■ Response lists are often cleaner and more up-to-date than compiled lists. With most response lists, approximately 95 percent of the addresses will be deliverable. Many compiled lists are only about 85 percent deliverable.

ADVANTAGES OF COMPILED LISTS

■ Compiled lists are usually less expensive than response lists. On average, compiled lists rent for £60–£100 per thousand, versus £100–£150 per thousand for response lists. Some of the pricing difference is no doubt caused by economies of scale, since compiled files are usually much larger than respondent databases.

Another reason is that you get what you pay for. Since compiled lists don't pull as well, mailers are not willing to pay as much for compiled lists. And it bears repeating that the lower cost of compiled lists, in itself, should not be a reason to use them, unless the total cost-per-lead or cost-per-sale compares favorably to that of packages mailed to response lists.

■ Since compiled databases are so large, there are more names to choose from. This can be important to large national mailers who need new sources of prospects, or regional mailers who need complete market coverage. For example, we recently mailed a seminar invitation to Chicago area architects. We found virtually all of them on a compiled list while a response list would have left us far short of the names we needed.

■ Not only are there more compiled names, these names tend to be fresher. In the list industry, "fresher" means they haven't been mailed as often. Much of the cream of buyers, donors and other mail responders has been skimmed long ago. Optimistic direct marketers believe there is a great untapped wealth of prospects on compiled lists which can be converted into responders.

■ Demographics and psychographics play a major role in compiled lists. This information can be overlaid onto response lists, but as a practical matter may not be cost-effective. Compiled lists can often be rented with exactly the demographic criteria or cluster codes you specify, and you pay only for the names you rent. If you apply demographics to a response list after rental, and thereby disqualify part of the list, you will usually have to pay for all of the original rental names.

■ Compiled list owners are more flexible in two important ways. First, they will often sell you the list for unlimited use. This can give you an instant prospect house-file. Second, the compiler will be less strict about seeing a sample mailing package before approving the rental (often requiring no sample). This can be especially important if the only good response lists available are owned by your competitors, who will not rent you their lists.

HOW TO SELECT THE RIGHT MAILING LISTS

Choosing a mailing list is as much art as science. As noted earlier, it all begins with a profile of existing customers. And while it is wise to go outside the circle for new prospect sources, you must start with a firm grasp of your foundation.

Generally, when conducting research for a mailing programme, I will look for list sources in this priority order:

1. House lists - your house file will usually generate the best response.

2. Competitor lists - If you can talk a competitor into renting his list to you, it should work very well. However, most will not cooperate. One solution is to trade (or exchange) the names on your own house file for a similar number of names from your competitor's file. If the competitor will not rent or exchange his list with you, he can be just as helpful if he'll tell you which outside lists have worked well for his mailings. But, since this is unlikely, a better course is to ask your list broker to investigate which lists the competitor has used.

3. Purchaser response lists - First I look for lists that were generated from similar products and services, then other lists of known responders who share similar characteristics.

4. Subscriber lists - Magazine and book-club subscribers are very good prospects for most offers.

5. Members of trade associations, consumer associations and trade show attendees.

6. Compiled lists - If I can't find enough names to mail from the first five categories, I will then try compiled lists.

There are three major sources of data on mailing lists:

■ BRAD Direct Marketing, published by British Rates and Data (BRAD). This is a directory containing in-depth information on virtually every business and consumer mailing list available for rental.

■ List compilers, which are companies that collect large

databases of consumer or business records. You will find these listed in BRAD Direct Marketing.

■ List brokers. Perhaps the best advice I can give about selecting mailing lists is to work with a list broker. A list broker's function is to recommend mailing lists for its clients and handle the resulting rental agreements. Best of all, a list broker receives its commissions directly from the list owner, list manager, or compiler. Its clients pay nothing for the broker's services.

To illustrate: If the rental price of a list is £60 per thousand names (about average for business-to-business lists) and you placed your order directly with the list owner, your cost would be £60 per thousand, unless you are a recognized agency or list broker. This is the same price you would pay the list broker for the rental, who in turn would remit £50 per thousand names to the list owner. The difference, £10 per thousand, is the list rental commission. And believe me, list brokers work very hard for their list commissions.

Brokers and list managers supply their recommendations to clients on list cards. List cards contain information about mailing lists, including:

■ Full description of the list, including a profile of the individuals contained on the list.
■ Total quantity of names available.
■ All selection options.
■ Rental fees, including base rate and selection charges.
■ Terms and conditions.
■ Types of mailers who have used the list recently.

WALL STREET JOURNAL ACTIVE SUBSCRIBERS   C1900015330

1,403,167   Active U.S. Subscribers $125/M

Note: Active subscribers now available to Non-
Political Fundraisers @ $95/M.

The Wall Street Journal, the only national
business daily, is edited for men and women
needing news of and affecting business.

Can select the following @ $5/M extra:
     767,578   Men Subscribers
     148,445   Women Subscribers
     676,740   Individuals At Home
     538,726   4-Line Business Address
     121,201   3-Line Business Address

Profile:
 51 Median Age
 94% College Educated
 49% Top Management
 24% Mid-Management
 $127,700 Average Personal Income
 $169,500 Average Household Income
 $1,141,500 Average Household Net Worth
 $1,000,800 Average Value of Investments
 81% Married

Updated monthly.

Delivery: 10 working days after order is
approved.

DMA Preference Names removed.

List owner requires a list rental agreement and
all orders must be accompanied by a guarantee of
payment 30 days from mail date.

Net Names: Gross Billing Only.

BUSINESS
BUS/PROFESSNL PUBS
SIZE:1 MIL-4,999,999
STATE $5.00M
SCF $5.00M
ZIP $5.00M
P/S LABELS $10.00M
KEYING $3.00M
HOME ADDRESS $5.00M
BUSINESS ADDRESS $5.00M
SEX $5.00M
MAG TAPE NON RETURN $20.00M
MOSTLY MALE
DIRECT RESPONSE
10% COMMISSION
HIGH TICKET - $100+
FUNDRAISING/SPEC PR
PUBLICATIONS

        NON-RETURNABLE
        MAG TAPE FEE
           $20.00

1901 Research Boulevard
Suite 310
Rockville, MD 20850   ideaLists
(301) 294-8133 FAX: (301) 762-8049

Standard data card.

QUESTIONS TO ASK A LIST BROKER

Ask the following questions when considering whether to work with a particular list broker:

1. Does the broker have expertise in your industry? You would definitely not want to use a broker specializing in fund-raising lists if you are a commercial mailer, or vice versa.

2. Is the broker recognized by the industry? The simplest way to find out is to pick up a copy of <u>BRAD Direct Marketing</u> and see if the prospective broker is listed. If not, be careful.

3. Would your account be important to the broker? If you consider 20,000 packages a large mailing and your broker generally handles clients who mail millions, you probably won't get the attention you deserve.

4. Will the broker allow you to build credit? Unless you are a large mailer who is known to be financially stable, you can probably expect to prepay the first order or two. But, this should not be a permanent situation and your broker should soon start working with you on a credit basis.

5. How hard does the broker work for your business? One indicator is the speed in which the broker makes list recommendations to you. Good list selection is a painstaking research process. You don't want a broker who simply rattles off the first couple of lists that pop into mind. In the list business, creativity and hard work go hand-in-hand.

A FEW MORE TIPS ON LIST SELECTION

Follow these suggestions to get better results from your list selection efforts:

- Test, test, test. No matter how good a list looks on paper, test it before purchasing the entire list. Experts differ on the minimum number of names to test, but my preference is to test at least 5,000 for consumer offers and 2,500 for business-to-business offers.

- Look for clean lists. By "clean" I mean the list has been updated and run through MPS (Mailing Preference Service) within the past six months or so. Remember, when the housing market is healthy, a list which hasn't been updated in the past year will include an unacceptable number of bad addresses.

- Ask the list owner/broker who else has used the list in the past year, and how many times each organization has mailed the list. If mailers with offers similar to yours have rented the list in small quantities, but declined to use the list in larger quantities, this is a strong signal for caution on your part. The list probably didn't pull well enough for that mailer to invest in the remainder of the names.

- If mailing to several lists with similar characteristics, consider merging the lists and eliminating duplicates (known in the industry as merge/purge). On multiple list mailings of over 100,000 names, duplication can run as high as 20 to 30 percent.

- Make sure you order your list in the correct format. Your

choice will probably be limited to 9-track tape or pressure sensitive labels. If you are using personalization, make sure you order on 9-track tape. If you order mailing labels, make sure the labels are run in postcode order.

■ Ask the list owner if he can give you a net-name arrangement for the list. This means that you pay only for the names you mail after eliminating duplicates in the merge/purge process.

■ If you are interested in exploring the benefits of appending demographic information, consider sending your existing customer file to a major compiler to have the demographic data applied. This is a fast method of customer profiling that will benefit you greatly when selecting mailing lists, particularly compiled lists.

■ Despite everything I have stated about matching your existing customer profile when choosing outside lists — please don't be afraid to go outside the circle and try new lists. The greatest successes in direct marketing are achieved by those not afraid to take a chance.

ONE LAST EXAMPLE

One of our clients, a large mainframe software company, wanted to send a new product mailing to application development managers. We offered to handle the list transaction, as we always do for this client. However, the client decided to handle the list themselves because they had been promised 20,000 FREE names by a publication in which they advertised.

To help out, we sent the client a memo listing exactly what they should request from the publication, in terms of title selections, computer hardware, and so forth. We also asked for one contact per site. The client then called the publication and ordered the list by telephone, with no written confirmation.

Luckily, the list owner sent a "partial dump" with the mailing tape. A "partial dump" is a computer printout of the first 25-100 records on the file. While many people ignore the dump, we read them carefully as a quality control check. Perhaps 10 percent of the time we find errors by checking the tape dump. This was one of those cases. Instead of "applications" staff, the list owner sent "systems" staff, a very different thing. To top this off, instead of one contact per site, we found up to seven per site.

By discovering these errors and re-ordering the list, we were able to prevent a catastrophe. At stake was more than the cost of the list. Most of the cost of the entire mailing would have been wasted. Instead of a tiny response, we were able to achieve a large response, and a successful campaign.

This example contains several important lessons:

- A "free" list can be very expensive. It is not worth jeopardizing an entire campaign to save a few dollars.
- Never order a list by phone unless you follow-up with a written confirmation.
- Always check to see that what you ordered is what you get. If you order the list on magnetic media, always request a tape dump.
- If you are not sure about what you're doing, use a competent list broker.

18

HOW TO USE THE POWER OF DIRECT MAIL

*D*irect mail is the fastest growing advertising medium for a very good reason – it works. In Europe, direct mail accounts for 20–30 percent of total advertising expenditures. From 1985 through 1991, European direct mail grew at an annual European rate.

Direct mail is mostly (but not exclusively) a direct response tool; you are asking the person who receives your mail package to take some specific action, such as sending in a reply card or calling a free phone number to place an order. Some frequent uses for direct mail include:

■ Direct sale of products or services. Items sold successfully by mail include books, food, computer hardware,

software, clothing, auto accessories, electronic equipment, toys, sporting goods, investments and insurance.
- Lead generation. Half of the companies utilizing direct mail use it to generate leads which are later followed up by mail, telephone or personal sales calls.
- Cross-selling and upgrading customers. Organizations ranging from banks to mail order companies use mail to sell additional products and services and upgrade existing customers.
- Prospecting for new customers. Even organizations with large databases must continuously replace customers and prospects lost through attrition.
- Acquiring new members. Trade associations and special interest groups use direct mail to solicit new members.
- Acquiring donors. Political and charitable non-profit groups use direct mail to build their donor files and to solicit new contributions from existing donors.
- Creating awareness. Private organizations, associations and political groups use direct mail to distribute information to their customers, members and the general public.

ADVANTAGES OF DIRECT MAIL

As noted above, direct mail has been growing as a marketing medium because it works. Other advantages of direct mail include:

- It is a highly personal form of communication.
- It is a target-marketing tool offering many selection options.
- It has the potential to capture the prospect's complete attention (since he chooses when to open and read his mail).

- It offers an almost unlimited choice of formats without the space and copy limitations of other advertising.
- It is a highly quantifiable advertising medium.
- It offers a low cost-per-lead or cost-per-order when compared with other advertising methods.

DISADVANTAGES OF DIRECT MAIL

Despite its advantages, direct mail has a number of drawbacks that must be considered:

- Thanks primarily to high postal rates, direct mail is becoming increasingly expensive.
- Mailbox clutter has led to declining response rates in many industries.
- Good mailing lists are being overused and fresh new lists are hard to come by.
- Due to poorly conceived and poorly targeted offers, much of the public perceives all advertising mail to be "junk -mail".
- Environmental and privacy concerns are increasing the likelihood of restrictive legislation on mailings and list usage.

ELEMENTS OF A DIRECT MAIL PROGRAM

While every direct mail campaign is unique, most of the time you will go through similar steps in developing and implementing your direct mail program. Here are the basic elements of a direct mail program:

Element One: Determining the Need

Direct mail, like many other types of promotion, is not conducted in a vacuum. First there must be a need, either in terms of a problem to be solved or an opportunity to be pursued. The need must be one that lends itself to a mail solution. Remember, direct mail can accomplish a great deal but it does have limitations.

An example of a need that can be met with direct mail is, "The quantity of leads for our sales reps has declined." A need that probably would not lend itself to a mail solution is, "Our stores can't keep enough of Product X stocked to meet demand."

Element Two: Stating the Objectives

After defining a need, the next step is to get down to the specifics of identifying the solution. How exactly do you want the end result to look? Your desired goals could be framed in terms of the number of leads to be generated, members to be acquired, customers to be upgraded, seminar seats to be filled, or dozens of other possible objectives.

Always ask the following questions about your objectives:

A. Are they measurable?
B. Are they precise? Instead of setting a goal of "bringing in more leads," state it as "bring in 1,250 leads by August 31st."
C. Are they achievable? Dreaming big is one thing, but unless your goals are realistic, the letdown from consistently falling short of your target will produce more harm than good.
D. Are they time specific?
E. Have they been agreed on by all concerned parties?
F. Are they in writing? It has been my experience that goals that are not written are seldom achieved. There is something about putting pen to paper (or more likely putting fingers to computer keyboard) that signifies a much deeper commitment to an objective.

Element Three: Setting Campaign Strategy

The third element in a direct mail campaign deals with five important strategic considerations.

A. Audience - The audience will have been suggested in a general way by your needs and objectives, but now it is time for you to get specific. Make sure you read the previous chapter to learn more about the important subject of selecting mailing lists.

B. Offer - Many a would-be direct mail winner fails because it lacks an enticing offer. The offer is the "what's in it for me" part of your direct mail programme. An offer could be a special sale, an invitation or information that helps the prospect do his job better. Remember that no one will ever be as interested in your product or service as you. We all have our own priorities and interests. This is why a strong offer is necessary; it cuts through the preoccupation of your prospect like a hot knife cuts through butter.

C. Programme Format – This is where you begin to choose the direct marketing weapons you will use to achieve your objectives, including the general structure of the direct mail package (and the outline of the telemarketing programme if you are following up the mailing by phone).

D. Timetable – Set a schedule for the entire programme including creative development, production coordination, fulfillment and back-end analysis.

E. Budget - Assuming all the above issues have been decided, you should have enough information to budget the entire program. To allow some flexibility for later changes, you may want to leave a contingency of plus or minus 10 percent in your budget numbers.

Element Four: Developing Creative Tactics

Just as with strategies, creative tactics require consideration of several elements:

A. Package format - This is where you specify the components of your mailing package, such as whether you want to use a window envelope, closed-face envelope, or self-mailer; whether to use personalization, and if so, on what components; what type of reply device to use; what type of lift note, if any, to use; and dozens of other decisions which need to be made regarding format.

B. Copy - In my opinion, copy is the heart and soul of any direct mail programme. Never sit down to write copy until you have an offer and thorough knowledge of the individuals who comprise your marketplace.

C. Graphic Design - Because of the flood of direct mail received by the consumer today, the impact of design on the success of direct mail campaigns is growing. But I would add (with occasional exceptions) that graphic design should be driven by copy, not the other way around.

Probably the most important criteria for a direct mail designer is knowledge of the production process. There is nothing more disappointing than a brilliantly designed mailing piece that won't fit in the envelope or a reply form that can't be personalized.

Element Five: Producing the Package

Element five deals with the mechanical aspects of the direct mail campaign. The production coordinator should be involved early in the programme so that all elements are designed for maximum efficiency. In a smaller operation, the production person and creative manager may be one and the same.

A production coordinator will have responsibility for the following areas:

A. Offset printing of package components such as letterhead, envelopes, and reply forms;

B. Data processing and list management such as merge/purge and postal presort processing;

C. Personalized printing such as laser, impact or ink-jet;

D. Mail processing including inserting, stamping, sealing and preparation of postal reports.

Element Six: Fulfilling the Offer

A key to any successful mailing programme is the speed and accuracy at which orders, leads or donations are followed up and acknowledged. All the creativity in the world won't save a campaign with a poorly designed or poorly executed fulfilment programme.

Element Seven: Tracking and Back-End Analysis

The final element in a direct mail programme is lead tracking and analysis. Tracking and analysis are necessary to achieve constant improvement in your direct mail activities. Without proper backend analysis, you are at best making your decisions based on intuition, and at worst, by total guesswork.

BUDGETING FOR A DIRECT MAIL PROGRAMME

Direct mail costs can vary widely. For instance, our agency has produced packages for as little as 25 cents and for as much as 12 dollars per package. Variables affecting the cost of a direct mail programme include:

- Quantity of the mailing. Direct mail pricing is highly volume sensitive.
- Mailing list(s) used.
- Printing specifications and paper stock.
- Number of ink colors.
- Number of components in the package.
- Graphic costs such as photography and illustrations.
- Creative charges for concept, copy and artwork.

To give you an idea of the total cost of a mailing project, I have taken the following figures from a recent programme we completed for a national trade association. This mailing was sent to middle managers. The paper stock used was a medium-grade laid paper and all components were printed two-colour, except the brochure, which was four-colour process and contained six photographs. Total mailing quantity was 50,000 packages.

A. CREATIVE

Copywriting all components	£2500
Design, layout & typesetting	£2000
Color separations (6)	£1000
Photography (one day shoot)	£750
Model fees	£300
TOTAL CREATIVE	£6550

B. MAILING LIST

30,000 names @ £0.085 each	£2550
27,000 names @ £0.105 each	£2835
TOTAL LISTS	£5385

C. PRINTING

Carrier envelope	£1800
Reply envelope	£1250
Letter (2 pages)	£3200
Reply certificate	£1750
Lift-note	£650
Brochure (four fold)	£3500
TOTAL PRINTING	£12,150

D. DATA PROCESSING

List conversion	
Post Code correction	
Merge/purge	
Postal presorting	
TOTAL DATA PROCESSING	£1060

E. PERSONALIZATION

Auto-type envelopes	£1925
Laser letter page one	£2250
Laser reply certificate	£2175
TOTAL PERSONALIZATION	£6350

F. MAILING HOUSE

Fold components
Match 3 personalized components
Insert components into envelope
Affix stamps
Sort
Tie, bag and mail
Deliver to Post Office

TOTAL LETTERSHOP	£4250

G. POSTAGE

50,000 @ avg. of .186	£9300
TOTAL PROJECT BUDGET	£45,045

Direct mail costs are often broken down either as a per thousand rate (Per M) or as a per-package rate. For the 50,000 packages mailed, the above mailing would have a per-package rate of £0.90 or a Per M rate of £900.

If you compare the cost-per-thousand (CPM) of this and other direct mail programmes against the CPM of mass marketing mediums such as newspaper or television, you will quickly see that direct mail is an expensive way to reach prospects. The good news is that direct mail is a very efficient method of generating leads and sales if you have targeted your audience correctly, because there is virtually no waste. Despite its relatively high initial cost, it will often bring in orders, members or donors at a lower cost per sale (CPS).

You will see this point repeated elsewhere in <u>The Master Marketer</u>. Each marketing method, including direct mail, should be evaluated on its ability to achieve the best possible results at the lowest possible cost. The cheapest marketing medium is often not the most cost-effective marketing medium. Although this is a hard lesson to learn for marketing managers faced with tight budgets, many of us have discovered through painful experience that the most important question is not "what will it cost?" but rather, "what will it produce?"

WHEN TO MAIL FOR BEST RESULTS

While response rates vary widely by product and audience, the following table should give you an idea of the better months to mail. It is based on a three year consumer test showing the comparative monthly mailing response for a nonseasonal product. I believe this study was first reported in <u>Successful Direct Marketing Methods</u> by Bob Stone, although I have also seen it elsewhere. The mailing was sent to an equal quantity of names from the same mailing list each month. January, the best month, is rated at 100 percent, with all other months rated in comparison to January.

January	100.0
February	96.3
March	71.0
April	71.5
May	71.5
June	67.0
July	73.3
August	87.0
September	79.0
October	89.9
November	81.0
December	79.0

DIRECT MAIL FOR THE RETAIL MARKETER

Of all the groups that could use mail marketing to its advantage, retailers are perhaps the least sophisticated in their use of this medium. I believe this is true because retailers are unfamiliar with the many benefits direct marketing can bring to them. Direct mail can not only bring in many new customers, it can increase the size of your effective market area. If you have a unique product, direct mail marketing is the quickest way expand your company on a regional or national basis.

Local retailers such as dry cleaners and chemists find that most of their customers come from a radius of one mile or less. Certain types of specialty shops serve a wider area with customers driving ten miles or more. The challenge is to increase the distance that consumers are willing to drive to patronize your business.

Most retail establishments depend heavily on repeat customers. Not only is it less expensive to sell existing customers, their orders tend to be larger and have fewer returns. For these reasons, it is important to build a database of information about your customers and mail to them on a regular basis.

Any retailer who has kept good records of his customers (you'd be surprised how many don't) has an excellent prospecting list to begin with. It is also important for the retailer to learn the characteristics of his "typical" customer. Much of this investigation can be accomplished by the retailer's own observations, and the rest can be completed with standard market research tools, such as person-to-person interviewing, postal questionnaires and telephone surveys.

In addition to your own list of customers, there are always mailing lists of local residents or businesses available through companies which compile this information.

Here are a few of the direct mail offers the retailer can make to customers and prospects:

1. Sale of specialized or discontinued merchandise.
2. Customer-only sales.
3. "Co-op" or "syndicated" mailings, where a product manufacturer pays all or part of the mailing costs.
4. Mailings outside the normal market area.
5. Testing of new product/service ideas before making an investment.
6. Catalogue or other direct sales.

Many retailers open their businesses, hang a sign on the door, perhaps take out a few ads in the local community newspaper, and wait for the customers to come pouring in. Don't make this mistake. Increase your chances of success by judicious use of direct mail. And whatever the objectives of your direct mail programme, remember to start small, test continuously to refine your approaches, and tie your direct mail into the rest of your marketing strategies.

CHOOSING THE BEST PACKAGE FORMAT

"Format" refers to the structure of a direct mail package, including the components contained inside the envelope (printed or otherwise), as well as the outer envelope. Format also refers to the way the components are put together, including issues such as how and where specific components are to be personalized.

The decision on which format to use is based on numerous tangible and intangible factors, including:

- Your audience - Who are the recipients of your mailing?
- The message - What are you planning to say?
- Length of message - How much room will you need to express your message?
- Your organization's image - Do you want to preserve an

existing image or promote a new one?

■ Size of the mailing - Certain formats lend themselves to large volumes and others to small volumes.

■ Action requested - Format choice can be dictated by the type of response you request of the mail recipient.

■ Budget - Our last, but certainly not least, format consideration.

Although direct mail experts may argue that no two packages are alike, there are formats used so often they become almost standard. One of the most commonly used package formats consists of the following elements:

1) Outer envelope, either closed-face or window.

2) A4 sales letter.

3) Response device to be filled in and returned by the recipient.

4) Business reply envelope, imprinted with the mailer's address and reply paid licence.

5) A brochure or flyer of some type, with copy that reinforces the letter's message.

Let's take a close look at each package element, define its purpose, and discuss the options.

Outer Envelope

The outer envelope is always a key component of the package. It alone will not cause anyone to take action on your offer, because unless your prospect opens the envelope, you have a zero percent chance of selling him. Thus, the envelope has one primary purpose; to prompt your prospect to open it and read what is inside.

Outer envelopes come in dozens of sizes, with the most common being the standard D 9 ×12. The D envelope is used frequently because it is the standard size for business-to-business correspondence and is recognized as such, especially to business audiences. Also, a standard size envelope is much less expensive to print than non-standard sizes.

Larger envelopes are useful when you need a slightly more personal touch. As an example, we used a special size package to send a letter from the president of a Virginia-based software company from the company's Paris Office to Fortune 1000 companies in the United States. The sales staff was having a great deal of difficulty reaching decision makers at these companies and we needed a vehicle to break through the secretarial screens.

To enhance the personal touch, we had the letters auto-typed and hand-signed, and used artistic French postage stamps. The return address listed no company name, only the president's name and a Paris street address. Although the package was expensive to produce, it accomplished its mission. Few, if any, packages were screened, and the software company substantially increased its name recognition among senior decision makers.

Here are several reasons you may want to consider using a larger carrier envelope (6 x 9 or 9 x 12):

- You want to make a bold graphic statement on the outer envelope.
- The size and/or shape of the components to be inserted requires a larger envelope.
- The volume or weight of the components requires a larger envelope.
- A test has shown that for your offer, a larger outer envelope pulls more responses than a standard size.

There are three basic choices on how to address the outer envelope:

1) Imprint the address information on the envelope.

2) Apply a pressure-sensitive mailing label to the envelope.
3) Affix a label or imprint the address information on an inner component, and let that personalized component show through a window in the envelope.

Although there are exceptions, the closer the package looks to personally-typed correspondence, the higher response it will generate. This is true for both closed-face and window packages. Studies show that the average person takes only four to seven seconds to decide whether to open an envelope or toss it away. You have very little time to entice the reader inside the package. Use these techniques to get your packages opened and read:

- Use commemorative stamps or multiple postage stamps.
- Don't be too predictable. If you always mail in white DL envelopes, switch to a different size or colour, or try a self-mailer.
- Use a curiosity provoker, such as a quiz that starts on the envelope and carries through to the internal package copy.
- Place copy and graphics on the back, as well as front, of the envelope.
- Write a strong benefit statement on the envelope.
- Offer a glimpse of your key visual or product through a window in the envelope.

Sales Letter

Letters are the most important components in direct mail packages. If possible, your mailing should contain a letter of some type. The letter is a standard form of communication which has stood the test of time and can be used with virtually any format, even the self-mailer. The most frequently used letter size is A4 combined with the D envelope. Usually the mailer's own business letterhead serves as the artwork for the letter, but alternate mast-heads can be designed as well. Smaller letters connote a more personal message.

A format which can be very effective is the extended letter, where the top 10 ½ to 11 inches is used for letter copy, and the bottom three to three and one-half inches is used as a tear-off reply device. This format is particularly useful when it is necessary to capture vital information on the reply form such as the recipient's computer record number, name and address, or mailing source code.

Whether your package contains an 11 inch, 14 inch or small letter, personalization will almost always increase your response rate, usually enough to justify the increased production costs.

Try these additional tips for a more effective direct mail letter:

- Use a P.S. Studies show that the postscript is often read before the body copy of the letter. Try to keep the P.S. to 25 words or less.
- Have a credible individual (with legible handwriting) sign the letter. After reading the salutation, readers usually look to see who signed the letter.
- A two-color letterhead out-pulls one-color.
- Illustrations or photos on letters can increase response.
- Use, but don't overdo, underlining, bold type and handwriting in the margins.
- Use subheads to break up long text.

Response Device and Reply Envelope

Each prospect has a preferred method of responding to a direct mail offer. While many prefer the convenience of a free phone 0800 number, a majority of individuals like to respond by post. On average, when both options are offered, approximately one-third respond by phone and two-thirds by post.

For post-responders, a reply device of some type is necessary. Tests show that a package with a write-in response option will almost always pull better than a package with only a call-in option. Since it adds only a small incremental cost to the mailing, it is usually wise to include a reply device in the package.

If your objective is lead generation, and you do not require the responder to send a check or supply sensitive information (such as credit card numbers), then a Business Reply Card (BRC) should work. A BRC is a self-contained response device, with space for the respondent to fill in his return address and other pertinent information on one side and the mailer's address and business reply paid licence on the other side.

Business Reply Card

Business Reply Cards must be printed on stock at least seven points in thickness and must conform to size and other restrictions. Contact your local Post Office customer service representative for further information on how to open a business reply account and for Business Reply regulations.

Another postage-paid option is to use a lighter weight paper stock for the fill-in reply and include a Reply Paid Envelope. Regulations for these are very similar to those for Business Reply Cards, and can also be obtained at any Post Office.

In most cases, failure to provide a reply-paid envelope will decrease response. This is particularly true if you are mailing to prospects, and not previous buyers. However, there are circumstances where it is better to require responders to pay their own postage.

For instance, if you are receiving a large number of leads from unqualified prospects, forcing the responder to supply postage will separate the truly interested from the merely curious. Anyone who has mailed packages containing postage-paid cards or envelopes to large numbers of people knows the frustration of sifting through dozens of blank or partially completed cards to discover the wheat among the chaff. Yet with this in mind, for most mailings, the postage-paid reply vehicle will be worth the extra cost.

Reply devices are not limited to simple response cards and envelopes. Coupons, surveys, mock-invoices, certificates, competition entry forms, and a hundred other formats have been used successfully. Each of these formats can be personalized with all or part of the information contained in the prospect's computer record. The most common data to be inserted on a reply device is the name and address, mailing source code and computer record number.

Try these suggestions to make your response cards and envelopes more effective:

- ■ If possible, fill in the prospect's name and address.

This will boost response.

■ Repeat the offer on the reply form or re-state the major benefit.

■ Include a tear-off stub which repeats the offer and/or serves as the customer's receipt.

■ Show an illustration or photo of the product on the reply form.

■ Use a separate response form, not one that must be torn from another component.

■ Make sure your ordering instructions are crystal clear. And leave plenty of room for the person to fill in his name, address and credit card information.

Brochures and Other Inserts

A guiding principle in direct mail is to say only as much as you have to say to accomplish your mission. This means that you must overcome your natural tendency to stuff as many components as you can fit in the envelope. Too much information can actually hurt response rates.

This principle is most important in two-step mailings. In a two-step mailing you attempt to get the recipient to make some lesser commitment, such as sending in a reply card requesting additional information, before you ask for a greater commitment, such as purchasing your product. Since you are not going to sell the prospect with the first package, and presumably want a follow-up opportunity to convince him of the merits of your offer, do not supply so much information that the decision to purchase (or not purchase) can be made solely from the first mailing.

Remember that curiosity is a major human motivator. In a lead generation package, consider the power of a short sales letter highlighting the two or three primary benefits of your product or service, followed up with a compelling call-to-action. If you include a brochure in the package, thereby satisfying the prospect's curiosity for more information, the prospect may talk himself out of responding.

If your package is a one-step offer, and you are asking the prospect to make a major decision, based solely on the package you have put in his hands, add all the information he will need to make a positive decision regarding your offer. The greater the level of commitment you require, the more information you are likely to need to make the prospect feel comfortable with the buying decision.

How can you tell when you've got too much, or too little information? The best way is to test. Test a package with a brochure against the identical package without the brochure. Or try a "lift note." A lift-note is a short note, usually folded, with a message printed on the outside such as "Read this only if you've decided not to respond," or "One last reason you should consider responding today." The lift-note got its name because it usually "lifts" response. Whatever the message or format, the lift-note is a proven, low-cost method of boosting direct mail response.

Self-Mailer Format

Self-mailers are inexpensive formats that can be very effective for certain types of offers. The term "self-mailer" is used because this format needs no outer envelope to carry its message. Usually, the self-mailer also contains its own response vehicle, in the form of an attached or bound-in Business Reply Card (BRC).

In a six-panel brochure, one panel can serve as the headline or billboard which states the major benefit; three more panels can be devoted to supporting copy and a call-to-action and one panel can be used for the respondent to fill-in return address information. The final panel is used for the mailer's reply-paid licence information.

Double-Postcard Format

Double-postcards are even less expensive than self-mailers. Double-postcards use two panels for headlines and supporting copy, one panel for the responder to fill in his name and address information, and the final panel for the mailer's business reply permit information. I have found double-postcards very effective for promoting registrations at sales seminars, for generating leads and for other applications where the message is concise.

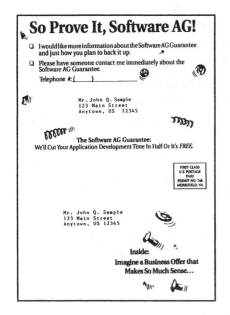

Double postcard

Specialty Formats

Unique or unusual format packages serve a purpose when you are communicating to a very important or highly targeted audience. Examples of specialty formats include die-cut brochures, pop-up devices, boxes, cassette tapes, records, advertising specialties (such as pens, key chains, etc.), and telegrams. Many specialty formats are also known as "dimensional" mailers because they have greater depth and substance than traditional packages.

USING PERSONALIZATION TO
INCREASE YOUR RESULTS

Personalization is a hot topic in direct mail for a very good reason; it is the one technique which can have the strongest impact on results. On test after test, we have found that personalizing a mailing leads to a 15 to 60 percent increase in response rates, depending on the type of product or service being marketed. This means that you can mail fewer pieces and achieve greater results.

The typical organization must maintain contact with a myriad of groups such as current customers, past customers, prospects, professional associations and the press. In most industries, 60 to 80 percent of a company's sales come from its existing customers. This means that there are two important objectives — mining the gold from the existing customer base, while aggressively pursuing new customers from the prospect universe.

Since these two objectives often conflict due to time constraints, technology can be used in the form of personalized communications to stay in touch with those you don't have time to contact in person. And while not a substitute for face-to-face or telephone contact, personalized mail allows you to maintain high quality contact with prospects and customers. Personalization also helps improve your company's image and can be used to differentiate your organization from the competition. But it's not just the fact that you personalize but how you do it that is important. Most mailers use personalization to some degree today. To be successful, you must be creative to stand out from the crowd in your prospect's post.

Your decision as to the degree you will make use of personalization depends on a number of factors including the audience you are mailing to, the frequency of mailings, the amount of information you maintain on each prospect in your database, and the type of personalization equipment available.

The technology that has meant the most to the ability to get personal in communications is laser printing. Laser printing allows you to produce documents on a mass scale with the quality formerly seen only with one-on-one correspondence, and it also permits an unlimited amount of variable data to be inserted into these documents.

Laser printers come in two varieties: sheet-fed and continuous-form. As the name suggests, sheet-fed laser printers utilize cut sheets (most often A4). This makes sheet-fed lasers the preferred choice for printing on letterhead. The fastest sheet-fed lasers output up to 7,200 personalized forms per hour.

Continuous-form machines print on fan-folded forms and feed the forms with pin-feed holes on both sides of the paper. Continuous-form lasers work well with large volume runs, for jobs with unusual formats, and when more than one item in the package is personalized. For example, you can print a personalized letter, lift-note and reply form all in one pass through the continuous-form machine. High volume continuous-form laser printers operate at even faster speeds than sheet-fed - up to 9,000 forms per hour This is equivalent to two personalized forms per second.

Those with modest requirements may be able to meet all their needs with desktop laser printers. At an output speed of eight to 20-plus pages per minute, you can easily produce personalized mailings of 1,000 pieces or less right in your own office.

Impact printing is another type of direct marketing personalization. Impact printing provides letter quality personalization, much like a typewriter and is widely used to address envelopes. Letter quality printers are useful for personalizing envelopes in any size from invitation up to 10 x 13.

Ink-jet printers, as the name implies, spray ink directly on the paper in the dot pattern specified by the computer. As with line printers, ink-jet printers are often used for matched fill-ins, where the variable information will be ink-jet printed and the remainder of the form (or envelope) will be offset printed.

USING AN OUTSIDE SERVICE BUREAU

If you don't have the in-house capability to produce personalization in the quantities and quality needed, then an outside service bureau can help. Here are some factors you should take into consideration when evaluating a personalization supplier.

1. **Capability.** Can the supplier handle the complexity of your projects? Can your laser printing vendor also handle the data processing steps necessary to clean and manipulate the data on your mailing list(s)?

2. **Cost.** Service bureaus usually price either at a per-image or per-thousand images rate. As with everything else in life you receive a discount for higher volumes. Lower volume jobs are priced at a premium because it may take the vendor longer to do the preliminary set-up than it does to actually run the job.

3. **Timeliness.** Can the service bureau meet your turn-around requirements? If you are a relatively small mailer and one of the supplier's best customers sends him a large volume job while your project is still in the shop, will your project get delayed? Some suppliers routinely meet deadlines while others take a week to put even simple jobs into the production process.

4. **Sensitivity of Data.** There is a great deal of variance among service bureaus in the level of security they provide. Remember it is your data, your prospects, and your customers. Mailing tapes have been known to be duplicated, and labels to disappear. Choose a reliable supplier so this won't happen to your important data.

SIX RULES FOR DIRECT MAIL SUCCESS

Following these six rules on every direct mail programme will virtually ensure your success:

1. Always test your programme on smaller quantities before attacking the prospect universe.

2. Make sure you thoroughly understand the characteristics of your target audience and what motivates them to take action.

3. Never undertake a direct mail programme without specific and measurable objectives.

4. Spend a lot of time developing a unique and compelling offer. The only thing more important than the offer is the mailing list.

5. Make sure your direct mail reinforces the rest of your marketing activities.

6. Work with direct mail experts. Unless you are sure about what you are doing there are many costly pitfalls. Also, watch out for general advertising agencies since many of them know little about direct mail and much of what they do know is wrong or out of date.

19

TELEMARKETING

The Unappreciated Marketing Weapon

*D*espite reams of bad publicity, telemarketing will
continue to play an important role in marketing. The telephone can
be used as a stand-alone marketing tool, as well as in partnership
with other media, for applications such as:

- ■ Direct sale of products and services - Telemarketing has
  been successfully used to sell products ranging from
  magazine subscriptions costing a few pounds to financial
  investments in the hundred thousand pound range. One of
  our computer software clients sells virtually all of its products
  (costing up to £60,000 each) by telephone.
- ■ Acquiring donors or members - Fund-raisers have used
  telemarketing (often in conjunction with direct mail) to

find new contributors and increase the size of donations from existing donors. Trade, professional and consumer organizations have used the telephone to build their membership bases and to renew inactive members.

- Upgrading current customers - Telemarketing is an excellent way to keep in touch with existing customers, cross-sell new products and services, and increase the average order size for products now being purchased.
- Generating leads - Telemarketing can be used to contact raw leads on outside mailing lists and convert these suspects into bona-fide prospects. These new prospects are then followed up with other marketing methods such as direct mail or personal selling.
- Reactivating stagnant accounts - Commercial marketers refer to these accounts as "inactive" customers while fund-raising and membership organizations refer to them as "lapsed" donors or members. These former customers, members and donors are often totally neglected. This is unfortunate because they are an excellent source of business. It is easier and far more cost-effective to revive an inactive account than to gain a new one.
- Generating attendance at trade shows and seminars - Telemarketing is a good method of filling free and fee-based seminars and can also help you sell exhibit space and registrations at trade shows and conferences.
- Setting appointments for sales reps - Cold calling is an expensive and frustrating way of making initial contact with prospects. Sometimes it makes more sense to use telemarketers to phone ahead to schedule appointments for sales reps.
- Following up other media - We will show you later in this chapter how campaigns using telemarketing to follow up other marketing activities achieve substantially better

results.

■ Pre-qualifying leads - Leads generated from most sources can range from worthless to extremely valuable. If leads are turned over to sales personnel without pre-qualification, sales representatives may ignore most or all of the leads. But if you qualify your leads by telephone before they are given to the sales force and pass on only those that are qualified, you can achieve a significant improvement in the closing percentage.

■ Testing new lists - Telemarketing can be used to test outside mailing lists before their use in direct mail. Those marketers who test lists only by mail are missing a good opportunity to use the telephone as a test tool.

■ Researching the market - Telemarketing has been used extensively as a market research tool. No doubt you have received a call from someone conducting a marketing research survey (sometimes these are legitimate research and sometimes disguised sales pitches). Telemarketing can also be used to pre-test new products, services, offers, benefits and market areas.

ADVANTAGES OF USING TELEMARKETING

Telemarketing has several advantages that recommend its use as an important part of the marketing mix:

Telemarketing works - Organizations that use telemarketing once (assuming it is implemented properly) tend to continue its use, because it works.

Telemarketing is measurable - As with direct mail, it is easy to determine an exact cost-per-contact, cost-per-lead and cost-per-sale. With this information, you not only know where you stand on the current project, you also receive a steady stream of response data that helps improve future programmes.

Telemarketing is fast - All you need to get started with telemarketing is a telephone, someone to make the calls and a list of people to call. If you have the necessary resources at hand, it is possible to design the programme and write the script in the morning, and begin calling in the afternoon. No other medium can be set up and executed as quickly as telemarketing.

Telemarketing is flexible - Telemarketing expenses are primarily based on equipment and personnel costs. Once a programme begins, the product, offer and script can be changed at any time, with little or no increase in cost. The degree of flexibility on a telemarketing campaign is greater than with any other marketing activity, with the exception of personal selling.

Telemarketing is cost-effective - While it is not cheap, a telemarketing contact costs only a small fraction of the average cost of a personal sales call (approximately £200). Granted, a larger percentage of person-to-person calls will result in a sale; but in terms of cost-effectiveness, telemarketing can prove to be a much better investment.

DISADVANTAGES OF TELEMARKETING

The telephone medium does have its drawbacks, including the following:

Telemarketing has a negative reputation among the press and public - Although this does not prevent companies from using the medium today, restrictive legislation could lead to future restrictions.

Telemarketing is an intrusive medium - Every other promotional activity gives the prospect a greater deal of control, but he or she has no choice as to the timing of your telephone sales call. With direct mail, the mail may arrive the same time every day, but the prospect can choose to read it immediately, or at his leisure. This is also true of print and broadcast advertising.

Telemarketing can be an annoyance - Many people react negatively to telephone sales calls. While procedures are available to remove such people from mailing lists, there is nothing that will stop the automatic calling machines that dial numbers randomly. And even those of us who make our living in marketing are annoyed by inappropriate offers or calls that arrive during dinner.

Telemarketing doesn't work well with complex offers - With direct mail, we can increase the amount of copy to explain complex or detailed offers. This may not be possible with telemarketing since it is very difficult to keep someone on the telephone more than a few minutes.

Telemarketing is not a visual medium - Products and services requiring visual demonstration do not lend themselves well to telephone marketing.

Good lists may be hard to find - Many mail-generated lists do not include phone numbers. While lists can be appended with phone numbers, it is an expensive process that will, at best, find phone numbers for only 50 to 70 percent of your list. Another option is to use compiled lists, which often contain phone numbers. However, compiled lists may not work as well for you as response lists.

Telemarketing personnel are difficult to hire and retain - The reason for this is obvious. If five to 10 percent of prospects take advantage of a telephone offer (a very good response rate), this means 90 to 95 percent are responding negatively. This is a great deal of rejection for anyone to take, and a primary reason telephone sales representatives burn out so quickly.

Also, because of the fact that many consumers work during weekdays, telemarketing schedules tend to run in the evening hours and weekends. Some people find these schedules very difficult. The best telemarketing agencies have learned to overcome these limitations and attract long-term motivated employees.

USING TELEMARKETING WITH
OTHER MARKETING VEHICLES

Telemarketing can achieve impressive results by itself. But when combined with other marketing tools, the results can be fantastic. And of all the possible combinations of marketing vehicles, no two work better together than direct mail and telemarketing. Instead of considering these two mediums as rivals for the same marketing budget, smart organizations are using them together in new and powerful ways.

For example, as reported by Jeff Deaner in DM News, by adding telemarketing to its existing direct mail programs, Hewlett-Packard increased its response rate from 1.5 percent to 12 percent, AT&T increased from 1 percent to 11 percent and IBM jumped from 1 percent to 19.9 percent.

While most marketers will not achieve response boosts of this magnitude, they will almost always find that the increased results more than justify the incremental cost of adding telemarketing to the marketing mix. Studies show that on average, a mail/telemarketing combination will increase the response rate over that of mail only from 200 to 500 percent.

A typical example is that of one of our mainframe software clients. In a recent split-test, the portion of the list receiving only direct mail achieved a 1.2 percent response. The portion of the list receiving the identical mailing package followed by a phone call achieved a 4.6 percent response, an increase of almost 300 percent.

Keep the following tips in mind when you develop a coordinated direct mail/telemarketing campaign:

- Consider cutting back on the amount of packages you mail since you will be following up with calls. Count on being able to contact about half of the list by telephone, since you may not have phone numbers for some prospects and could have difficulty reaching a large percentage of the prospects.

- Plan to start follow-up calls two to three days after you expect the mail to arrive and try to complete all calls within two weeks. People forget their mail quickly so keep the time between mail and phone calls as short as possible.
- Reference the fact that you will be calling in your letter. If the list is small enough, mention a specific morning or afternoon that you plan to call. You will earn a lot of points from the prospect for keeping your promise (since so many people don't). However, if there is any doubt that you will be able to meet the commitment, don't promise a specific time.
- When you call, mention the mailing. Assume that your prospect has read your letter and will respond positively to the offer.

FINDING MAILING LISTS FOR TELEMARKETING

In an earlier chapter we covered the importance of selecting and using mailing lists. These ideas apply equally to telephone lists, except that telephone marketers face one challenge not shared by mailers; finding suitable lists that contain telephone numbers. A large percentage of response lists do not have phone numbers available. This may be true because numbers were never collected by the list owner or because he doesn't want list renters to call his customers.

By contrast, most compiled lists do contain phone numbers. Owners of compiled lists are usually happy to provide you with phone numbers provided you pay them for each time you call the names on the list.

Despite the number of compiled lists with phone numbers available, there is still a problem. As we mentioned earlier, compiled lists usually do not perform as well as response lists. Also, keep in mind that, in the same way previous direct mail responders are most likely to respond to a new direct mail offer, previous telephone responders are most likely to respond to a phone call. So your best bet is to look for lists containing people who have purchased a similar product or service by telephone. For example, if you wanted to sell a small business software programme with a direct mail offer followed-up by telephone, you should look for a list with the following characteristics:

- Previous business software purchasers.
- Purchase prices in same range as your product.
- Orders generated by phone and mail.
- Title selects available to match your customer profile.
- Telephone numbers available.

If you find suitable response lists that do not contain phone numbers, there is one solution; telephone matching. For a fee, telephone matching companies will run your mailing list through a process that adds telephone numbers onto the records. This option is much more effective for consumer lists than business lists. With reasonably clean consumer lists you will probably be able to find numbers for 40 to 65 percent of the records.

Many list owners will not allow you to "telematch" and phone their files. You must ask permission first. Most who do allow phoning will require compensation for this extra use of the list and will also require you to submit a calling script for approval.

Once you have built your own list of telephone generated customers, finding lists becomes much easier, because now you have something of great value; telephone responsive names. If you want access to a valuable list, simply offer to trade a portion of your file for an equivalent quantity of the other list owner's names. This is known in the industry as "list exchanging" or "list swapping." Most list brokers will be happy to find suitable exchange candidates and handle the details for a small fee.

This brings up an interesting question - should you rent your telemarketing house file to other organizations? While this can be a source of considerable revenue, there are some pitfalls to avoid. Catherine Lincoln, Regional Manager of Database America and one of the country's leading experts on mailing lists, offers five suggestions to ensure the integrity of your important data:

1. Establish a written policy on which rentals you will permit and which you will not (such as competitive offers).

2. To prevent abuse, insist that all renters provide a telephone script for your approval, BEFORE you agree to the rental. Periodically check to make sure that the telephone reps are not deviating from this script.

3. Prepare a standard agreement to be signed by the telemarketing agency and include the principles listed in the Direct Marketing Association's Guidelines on Ethical Business Practices. The agreement should also state that you will not allow high-pressure tactics, obscene or offensive material, scams, or anything else that you deem inappropriate. Never ship your list to anyone who hasn't signed the agreement.

4. Put dummy names into your list (this is known as "seeding" the list). You should do this in greater quantities than with lists that are only mailed because a telephone call doesn't leave the physical record that a direct mail package does. Another solution is to hire a telephone monitor service which will track authorized and unauthorized calls to your list.

5. Protect your customers' privacy wishes by allowing them to remove themselves from the list when you rent it for

telemarketing (or mailing) purposes. There are moves to set up a register of people who have expressed a desire to receive no unsolicited phone calls.

If you follow these five rules, you will have adequately pro-tected your data and your customers from misuse. The only suggestion I would add is to find a list manager who specializes in handling lists in your industry. List managers know every trick in the trade and the best ones will protect your information with as much diligence as you would yourself.

HOW TO MAKE YOUR TELEPHONE CALLS COUNT

Most telephone sales reps use a prepared script. The script can be as basic as an outline of key selling points, or it can be an exact listing of the words you want the operator to say, including his or her response to objections and questions. Generally, the more experienced the operator, the less reliance on a detailed script is necessary. My advice is to make the script as detailed as possible but give your operators maximum leeway to change the wording to fit their unique personalities.

Always remember the context in which the telephone call is made. You are likely disrupting some activity, since few people are sitting by their telephones hoping to receive a sales call. So you must grab the prospect's attention immediately and open with a compelling benefit. In other words, you must always get to the point quickly.

A good example is the call I received from a department store the day before writing this chapter. Within seconds of saying hello, the operator informed me that the store was holding a credit card in my name, that the card was pre-approved, and that there was absolutely no charge or annual fee associated with the card. Before I had time to say no, the operator threw in the special bonus; the new card would come with a 10 percent discount on my first order. This was a very good offer combined with an excellent sales presentation.

Other tips for making the most of your telephone selling program:

- Don't open the conversation by asking the prospect how he's doing or about the weather at his location. The person called knows such questions are just useless banter. Instead of serving as effective ice-breakers, these questions merely irritate the caller and tell him you have little respect for his time.
- Don't become overly familiar with the prospect. I don't know about you, but I react poorly when someone I've never talked to opens a conversation with me by saying, "Hello Chris. How's the weather out there, my friend?" Not only am I not the person's friend, I become annoyed when he addresses me by my first name.
- Introduce yourself and your company immediately. Don't leave the prospect in suspense about who you are. The prospect can't concentrate on what you are saying until his curiosity about who you are is satisfied.
- State the purpose of your call. "I am following up on information I sent you about ABC last week."
- Lead with your biggest benefit. Quickly tell your prospect how he will benefit from your product or service.
- Continue with secondary benefits. If your prospect does not show positive response to benefit number one, continue sharing benefits until you hit the person's hot button.
- Be pleasantly persistent. Don't be curt, rude or overly aggressive. If you must use pressure, remember Mark Twain's definition of tact: "Tact is the ability to tell a man to go to hell, and make him glad to be on his way."

INBOUND TELEMARKETING

So far we have been referring to "outbound" telephone selling, where a representative takes the initiative by placing either a cold call (unanticipated by the prospect) or a warm call (promised in a direct mail letter) to the prospect. By contrast, with "inbound" telemarketing, the prospect places a call to your organization, usually in response to a print, direct mail or broadcast ad featuring a freephone number. It is important to have a freephone number because a large percentage of your orders will come by telephone and you want to make it as easy as possible for prospects to respond.

Inbound telemarketing can be used for direct sales or lead generation, running the gamut from simply answering the call and taking an order to the beginning of a complex selling process. Make sure that you adequately prepare for the type and quantity of expected calls. For instance, a television ad promoting a simple product may generate a great many calls in a short time period, virtually all of which can be handled by relatively inexperienced operators.

Alternately, a magazine ad for a high-technology product may generate a small number of calls over an extended time period, most of which should be answered by experienced, technically sophisticated operators. Just as with outbound telephone selling, it may benefit you to hire a professional service bureau to handle your inbound needs.

One key to a successful inbound telephone operation is to gather as much information as possible from each prospect who calls. If you are selling directly, this data will make your in-house customer file much more valuable and if you are capturing leads, the extra information will increase the likelihood of converting these leads into sales. Asking the questions will often help the qualification process since a prospect who is reluctant to provide your operators with information is probably not a very good candidate for your product or service.

IN-HOUSE VERSUS SERVICE BUREAU

When you decide to begin a telemarketing program, you will have to answer a very important question; whether to manage and implement your program in-house, or hire an outside service bureau to do it for you. This decision should be based on a number of factors including:

- Complexity of your product or service.
- Number of inbound and/or outbound calls expected.
- Availability of trained management and telephone reps.
- In-house expertise in telemarketing.
- Size of budget allocated to the project.
- Physical space restrictions.
- Length of the telemarketing campaign.

Generally, the following are circumstances favoring the use of an outside service bureau:

- When you need to get started right away. A good service bureau can have your program underway much faster than you can allocate necessary resources to the project.
- When you don't have the initial investment needed for equipment, space and personnel. Telemarketing start-up costs are high. A service bureau charges only for the specific services provided, although you and other clients will also pay a proportion of the bureau's equipment, space and personnel costs.
- When the flow of incoming and outgoing calls can be expected to fluctuate greatly. As an employer, you need to provide your telephone reps with some degree of job security. On the other hand, you certainly don't want to pay people to stare at telephones that aren't ringing, or

to pay people who don't have anyone to call. A service bureau solves this problem because you are only charged for the time its personnel are making (or receiving) calls on your behalf.

■ When the campaign is of short duration. If you plan to make an ongoing commitment to the telemarketing medium, consider an in-house programme. Otherwise, work with a service bureau.

■ When you lack the necessary expertise. Service bureaus get paid to provide telemarketing services. It isn't a game for the fainthearted or inexperienced. If you are willing to make the commitment to the training that this medium requires, bring your programme in-house. If not, use a service bureau.

The following are reasons to consider bringing your telemarketing programme in-house:

■ Saving money. Unless your programme is completely inefficient, you should be able to run an in-house programme at less cost than using an outside service bureau.

■ Faster feedback. Your in-house personnel will be able to react very rapidly to any changes in the market since they are receiving up-to-the-minute feedback from prospects.

■ Close coordination with other marketing activities. If you manage your print advertising, direct mail and other activities in-house, it may be a good idea to handle the telemarketing programme this way as well.

■ Exercising greater control over the programme. No matter how flexible an outside service bureau is, you lose some degree of control by delegating the programme. Hands-on means maximum control.

While I have provided you with both sides of the in-house versus outside service bureau argument, my policy is: when in doubt, use the professionals. Until you've managed an in-house telemarketing programme you can't believe how many details and problems there are to worry about. At least test your programme using a service bureau. You will learn a great deal and can always bring your programme in-house later.

HOW A BUSINESS-TO-BUSINESS MARKETER
USES TELEMARKETING

Bruce McBrearty, president of TransAmerica Marketing (a telephone marketing company located in Vienna, Virginia), shared the following case history of one of his company's campaigns. It contains a number of valuable lessons.

Group Health Association is the third largest health maintenance organization in the Washington, DC area. In 1991, Group Health approached TransAmerica because sales were not as strong as the organization needed to remain a leader in the competitive marketplace.

Prior to the telemarketing test, Group Health believed its target market consisted of companies having 100 or more employees, so its sales staff spent little time pursuing smaller prospects. Group Health relied on direct mail, television and radio to generate leads and had not used telemarketing in the past.

TransAmerica recommended segmenting the market by employee size to better define the company's market. Segments tested were:

- a. five to 19 employees
- b. 20 to 49 employees
- c. 50 to 99 employees
- d. 100 plus employees

After many calls to each segment, TransAmerica found that the best prospects were not in the 100 plus employees segment as Group Health suspected, but rather in the segments with 20 to 49 and 50 to 99 employees. To the surprise of Group Health, both of these segments responded twice as favorably as the 100 plus segment.

In order to create a sophisticated database for Group Health, TransAmerica captured the following information from each call:

314

- ■ decision maker's name and title.
- ■ name of current health insurance provider.
- ■ current policy expiration date.
- ■ timing of insurance decisions.
- ■ level of interest.

All data captured was used by Group Health to contact the right person at the appropriate time to maximize its sales closing percentage. After the test, Group Health dramatically increased its sales to companies with fewer employees and a new market niche was created. Sales people no longer had to make "cold" calls since they were dealing with "pre-qualified" prospects. Thanks to the successful campaign, telemarketing is now used as a key component of the company's marketing programme, along with print, television, radio and direct mail.

20

DATABASE MARKETING AND
LEAD TRACKING SYSTEMS

"**D**atabase Marketing" is an often used but little under-stood marketing concept. The name implies a blend of technology (database) with traditional marketing techniques. If you think of a database as a "collection of related information," then you will see that databases have been around for years in the form of financial databases, product purchase databases, statistical databases, cus-tomer information files (CIFs), and so forth.

But how can you determine whether you simply have a collec-tion of related information or something that qualifies as a "mar-keting database?" For starters, every marketing database should meet these criteria:

■ The marketing database allows easy entry of names and addresses of customers and/or prospects. This is the simplest of criteria and why many mailing list mainte-nance systems are referred to as databases.

- The marketing database contains all other known relevant information about customers and prospects, including demographics, response history, purchasing history and contact history. When you have a means for collecting and storing such information, you are building a "knowledge base." And the larger your reservoir of knowledge, the greater the potential for your marketing programmes.

- The information contained in the database can be used to construct a profile of customers and prospects. Again, you are building the knowledge base which will make your marketing efforts much more effective.

- The database can be segmented for target marketing purposes. Without this ability to select subsets of the database, you will be severely handicapped. Almost all new database systems offer this segmenting ability, but many older systems require large amounts of computer programming to accomplish simple selection tasks. Even though such systems have lots of horsepower with the ability to handle tens of thousands of records, their clumsiness and lack of flexibility will constantly frustrate you.

- The database facilitates communications between your organization and its prospects and customers. These communications can then be used to gather more relevant information, in a continual cycle of renewal.

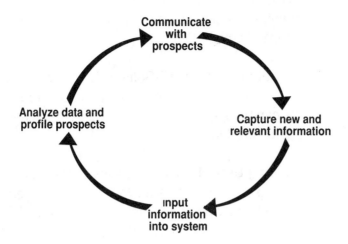

TEN PROFITABLE WAYS TO USE
A DATABASE MARKETING SYSTEM

Database marketing systems can be used to increase your marketing effectiveness in the following areas:

1. **Target Marketing** - Information contained on the database can be used to include those prospects and customers most likely to purchase a particular product and exclude those unlikely to purchase.

2. **Test Marketing** - By strictly defining and controlling those who are exposed to a promotional message in small quantities (at low cost), inferences can be made about the effect of that message on larger quantities.

3. **Marketing Research** - Provided you enter an adequate quality and quantity of information into your database, you can use it to learn a great deal about the character-

istics, needs and interests of your marketplace. Remember the old expression however, "Garbage In Equals Garbage Out."

4. **Upgrading and Cross-Selling Customers** - Once patterns of purchase behavior are discovered, customers can be upgraded to new products, and cross-sold add-on products.

5. **Deleting Unprofitable Customers** - By maintaining full purchasing history data on your customers, you can delete those who prove consistently unprofitable. Likewise, unresponsive prospect segments can be identified and deleted.

6. **Keeping in Touch** - A database allows you to maintain mail contact with your customers and prospects, even when you don't have the time to stay in touch personally.

7. **Personalizing Your Communications** - Variable information contained in the database allows you to easily send out correspondence directly relating to the customer and his past purchasing behavior.

8. **Building the Relationship** - I have likened entering a prospect/customer into our database to "bringing him into our circle" (see chapter on relationship marketing). Databases can be used to create, build and maintain ongoing two-way communications with prospects and customers.

9. **Improving Your Image** - In addition to prospects and customers, your database can be used to maintain contact with other groups important to your success,

including press, industry leaders, trade and professional association leaders, suppliers and employees.

10. **Earning Extra Income** - A well-developed database is a valuable commodity. If you build a large, accurate database, other organizations will want to rent it from you. This can serve as a considerable revenue source. Of course, you should never rent your list to competitors (unless they will trade their list with you), and only rent name and address information, not response or buying history.

LEAD TRACKING AND RESPONSE ANALYSIS SYSTEMS

Today's Master Marketers use the power of database marketing, demographics and psychographics to selectively target prospects most likely to respond to their offers. Yet those who devote a great deal of time and effort to the front-end of their marketing programmes give scant attention to the all-important back-end. Thus, in many instances, the results of these carefully planned marketing campaigns are not monitored precisely.

It is the combination of careful targeting in the front-end, and precise analysis in the back-end that will allow you to remain successful in the highly competitive world of marketing. And one of the most useful tools at your disposal is the "Lead Tracking System," or "Enquiry Management System."

Lead tracking and enquiry management systems can be defined as, "decision support tools to aid marketing management in evaluating the true effectiveness of generating sales and prospect inquiries."

USES FOR LEAD TRACKING/ENQUIRY MANAGEMENT SYSTEMS

With the above definition in mind, let's explore some of the specialized and important uses of lead tracking/enquiry management systems. A good system will help you:

■ Force continual improvement in marketing programmes.
■ Develop the most effective prospecting strategies.
■ Convert the maximum number of leads to purchasers.
■ Analyze the effectiveness of each media and mailing list used.
■ Budget for and analyze the proper utilization of every marketing pound.
■ Feed the database marketing system by collecting vital information on prospects/customers.
■ Increase cross-sell opportunities and increase the average amount of sales to each customer.
■ Pre-qualify leads before further sales activities.
■ Monitor the movement of leads/enquiries through the database system.

SEVEN STEPS TO DEVELOP A
LEAD TRACKING SYSTEM

The following steps will help you design a lead tracking and enquiry management system:

1. **Define your objectives.**
2. **Develop your methodology.**
3. **Collect the data.**
4. **Pre-qualify enquiries (optional).**
5. **Fulfill your inquiries.**
6. **Follow-up to convert leads to sales.**
7. **Report the results.**

1. Defining Your Objectives is the first and most important step. You must decide exactly what you want the

system to accomplish. Although there is no generic set of standards for all applications, the above list of uses for enquiry management systems should give you a good start.

2. Step two is developing the specific methodology you will use to accomplish your objectives. Whatever system you use, and whether it is automated or manual, make sure that all enquiries coming into the system are identifiable as to their original source (e.g. from what media, list of marketing activity they originated).

Incoming post should be coded with the media, list source and date of posting. Telephone responders should be asked for the same information as you get from postal enquiries. All leads should flow through one input area for precise h tracking.

3. Step three is managing the collection of data. Incoming data can be recorded on lead sheets or entered directly into a computerized database system. Although the data required will vary from company to company, common items include: date the lead is received; type of lead (e.g. media, direct mail or telephone); source of lead (which specific media or mailing list); name and address; company size; buying time-frame; and level of interest.

A key point: Remember to ensure that every qualified lead is entered into the database management system as soon as possible. Many companies that operate telemarketing centers routinely enter the lead information into the system as it is being received over the phone. If you can't do it this promptly, never distribute leads to sales reps before they are entered into the system.

4. Step four is to pre-qualify your leads. If the leads generated by any marketing activity are to be turned over to a sales force for follow-up, you may wish to pre-qualify them. The purpose of this optional step is to weed out the unqualified and uninterested before the sales department contacts these people. With the average cost of a personal sales call now reaching over £250, any step you take to prevent salespeople from making calls on unqualified prospects is money well spent. If your selling is done entirely by post or telephone, then prequalification is probably not justified.

Pre-qualification is usually accomplished by telephone. Telephone qualifying differs from typical telemarketing because it is information or research oriented, rather than sales oriented. Telequalifying can be described as an "image building conversation with an individual who has a possible interest in your product or service, designed to elicit a specific degree of interest and buying time-frame."

Pre-qualification can range from simply disqualifying leads based on the information contained on their response card, to an in-depth telephone survey of relevant information on the prospect and his or her company.

5. Step five in the enquiry management programme is fulfilment. The first thing you need is an honest appraisal of whether your leads are currently being followed up at all. In a surprising number of industries, less than half of all enquirers are ever contacted by the company which received the lead. For instance, on average, respondents to newspaper "reader service" ads are contacted by high technology companies less than 50 percent of the time.

To test these numbers, several months ago I responded to ten companies advertising in a postcard deck going to sales and marketing executives and ten other companies that advertised in a marketing industry trade publication. In all cases I provided full information, including my phone number. Further, I only responded to companies which would not automatically disqualify me on the basis of my company's name or my title. The results:

A.. Postcard Deck - 10 Enquiries

Five never followed up.

Three followed-up by phone (one also sent written information).

Two followed-up by post (one within 10 days, the other took over 30 days).

B. Trade Publication - 10 Enquiries

Six never followed-up.

Two followed-up by post.

Two followed-up by phone (one of these two later sent information by post).

In the above instances, each of the companies that failed to contact me wasted every penny of the money they used to get me to respond to their advertisement. Please make sure that your company isn't operating in a similar fashion. Treat every lead as a precious commodity, because that's exactly what it is.

Besides the basic necessity of responding to the lead in the first place, speed of response and quality of response are the critical factors in your chances of converting a lead into a sale. A worthwhile goal is to respond to all enquiries, by telephone or mail, within 48 hours of your receipt of the lead.

Quality of response refers to sending the prospect materials that are relevant to his needs, as discovered on the prospect's own enquiry or in the pre-qualification process. The specific information you should send depends on a number of factors, including the cost of your product or service. For instance, you would not want to send a £5 brochure to sell a £20 product.

Another important consideration is whether you should stop at sending one fulfillment package to convert leads, or whether sending out a second, third, or even fourth package is warranted. For the most part, this should be an economic decision. Find out if the additional revenue brought in by subsequent fulfillment mailing(s) covers the costs associated with those mailings.

6. The next action step is to follow-up the enquiry and to pursue the sale by post, telephone or in-person. This may be a one-step process where you only send out information as a follow-up to an enquiry. Or, you may have a two- or three-step process where you follow up both with a telephone call and/or in-person visit by a salesperson.

No matter what specific follow-up techniques you use, without a strong effort at this stage, all the previous work will mean nothing. Also consider that implementing the pre-qualification process mentioned earlier should yield a greater sales conversion percentage than before you installed the system.

7. The final stage in the lead tracking system is reporting important information captured by the system. A key is

to develop reports that are clear, concise and easy to use. It should be a simple process to transfer the information needed from the in-house database onto those reports used most often.

Two of the more commonly used reports are the Source Analysis, which is used to track the totals of leads produced by every marketing source you are using, and the Enquiry Summary Report, which goes into greater detail, and lists every lead source by its cost per lead (CPL) and cost per sale (CPS). This is the report that will tell you where to put your marketing budget in the future.

Other types of useful reports include enquiries by sales rep, division, product requested, and type of lead source (e.g. media, telephone or direct mail). Although these and many other types of reports can be helpful, I would urge you to keep things simple when you first develop the system.

Designing and implementing a database marketing and lead tracking/enquiry management system is not easy. However, major benefits accrue to the marketer who establishes these systems, as they remain well ahead of competitors who believe marketing is a game of numbers, and not precision.

21

HOW TO USE THE COMPUTER TO
IMPROVE YOUR DIRECT MARKETING RESULTS

Two of the most important innovations in our ability to communicate through direct marketing have been the computer and the Post Code. Computers allow the direct marketer to compile large amounts of data and use this data to selectively target prospects who are most likely to purchase. Post Codes offer a practical means of segmenting the country and make postal delivery more efficient for the large quantities of direct mail generated by the new technology.

Computers can be used to improve the effectiveness of direct marketing in five important ways:

1. Offering an efficient way to maintain lists and target mailings.

2. Cleaning your mailing lists to increase deliverability.
3. Applying presort discounts to obtain major savings on postage.
4. Personalizing mailings to increase the response rate.
5. Tracking response and managing fulfillment.

MAILING LIST MAINTENANCE

Mailing files can be maintained in several ways. Ideally, your in-house list should be maintained in a database format consisting of far more than name and address information. Optional data to be kept on business-to-business files includes classifications such as company size, title/function information, Standard Industrial Codes (SIC) and purchasing history.

For consumer offers, demographic data such as age, income, and homeownership, and psychographic data such as established needs, likes and dislikes, and purchasing/response history should be maintained. The purpose of all this information is to allow the mailer to segment the file and target individuals who have the greatest statistical likelihood of responding to a particular offer. The bottom line objective is to achieve a greater number of responses from a smaller number of packages mailed.

Marketers who have regular additions, deletions and corrections to their customer or prospect file usually prefer maintaining these files in an on-line mode. This is true because on-line systems allow the user to have instant access to the data on the file through mainframe or micro computer terminals. By contrast, a "batch" process requires you to batch database updates together and perform them only at certain times.

MICRO COMPUTER LIST MAINTENANCE

Due to the increases in the processing speed of micro computers, as well as the sophisticated mailing list software now available for micros, very large databases can be maintained on small desktop computers. For instance, Group 1 Software's ArcList program allows the mailer to keep over 125,000 records on an IBM compatible computer with a 40 megabyte hard drive. Also, processes such as merge/purge, postal presorting, and Post Code correction, which were previously available only on mainframe computers, can now be accomplished on micro systems.

Not only is the cost of hardware and software much lower if you maintain your files on a micro computer, you will also receive these benefits:

- Greater control over the mailing list.
- Shorter training cycle for operators and data entry personnel. Micro software is usually much easier to learn and use than mainframe software.
- Micro software often has built-in features such as duplicate detection and Post Code correction that are very expensive and difficult to use on mainframes.
- Mailings can be processed much faster. List selection, duplicate elimination, label printing and personalization can be implemented quickly using micro computers and desktop printers.

The only potential disadvantage to a micro-based maintenance program is that the output may have to be converted to a 9-track tape format in order for it to be merged with other 9-track lists, or for the output to be laser printed. Technology does exist to solve these communication problems but it is expensive and cumbersome to use. Computer service bureaus can handle the conversion process or you can purchase a 9-track tape drive which can be attached to the micro computer.

Marketers can also use off-line methods of list management, primarily consisting of storage on 9-track tapes or floppy disks. These methods are appropriate when mailers have very large files, or do not have the hardware capacity or software available on their in-house systems to store and process these files.

Another alternative is to utilize a computer service bureau for file maintenance. An advantage to using outside services is that the supplier probably has a great deal of mailing list management software. You only pay for the computer time and use of the software, not for the expensive software itself.

CLEANING THE MAILING LIST

If you are mailing to more than one rented or purchased list, it will be necessary to run these lists through a process called "list conversion." List conversion, as the name implies, changes every list from its original format into a standard format. This allows the computer to manipulate the data consistently across files, and match records more accurately.

During the list conversion process you can also perform other important functions such as changing the data from all upper case to a combination of upper/lower case, and assigning gender codes such as Mr. and Ms. to the records that do not have these codes. Both of these steps are important if you intend to personalize the mailing.

POST CODE CORRECTION

Post Code correction is a process that can reap large benefits to direct marketers. It should be performed as early as possible because many other programmes, such as merge/purge and postal presorting, depend on clean Post Codes. Post correction should be run on all new lists, and periodically on in-house lists, especially if your file has frequent additions, deletions and updates.

Many mailers are unaware that a significant percent of the Post Codes on the average mailing list are inaccurate (I have seen files with errors as high as 15%). This is true, not only because

Post Codes are entered improperly, but also because the Post Office sometimes changes Post Code boundaries, particularly in fast growing areas. Remember that mailings can be delayed or weakened for a number of reasons:

- Failure to conclude a Post Code
- Incorrect addressing
- Failure to include a return address.

The four biggest causes for non-delivered mail are:

1. Incorrect Post Codes
2. Missing house numbers
3. Address changes

All four of these problems can be solved with existing computer technology. Post Codes can be cleaned and added with software programmes. Mailers should not accept consumer lists without house and flat numbers.

Since a significant number move each year, mailing lists can go out of date quickly. This problem is not easily solved and may require time-consuming comparison with the Electoral Register.

You can standardize your mailing lists by passing your records against the Post Office's Postal Address File (PAF) database and changing the records to match the Post Office preferred method of addressing, as well as adding house and flat numbers.

THE MERGE/PURGE PROCESS

Merge/purge, which is also known as duplicate elimination, is very important to list hygiene. If you are renting multiple outside mailing lists of a similar nature (such as donor lists or subscriber lists) there will almost certainly be duplicate names on these lists (running as high as 30 percent between certain lists). In fact, the greater the similarity between the two lists, the higher the percentage of duplicates will be.

In addition to the large wasted postage, printing, and mailing expenses, there is a psychological cost to duplicates as well. The person who receives two or more identical packages may question your company's professionalism, particularly if the mailing is personalized.

Major differences exist among merge/purge software programs. For instance, consumer merge/purge programs usually use a process called a "match code." This type of system extracts data from each record and builds a code, which is then matched against other codes to determine if a duplicate record exists. To give you an example, look at the following address:

Mr. Christopher Ryan
123 Main Street
Vienna, VA 22180

A match code would be constructed as follows:
22180RYC123VIVA

22180	From the Post Code
Ry	First two letters of the last name
C	First letter of the first name
123	First three digits of street address
VI	First two letters of city name
VA	County

Using this system, any other record that produced an identical, or almost identical, match code would be flagged as a duplicate. Remember that the most important part of the match code is the Post Code. Without an accurate Post Code the merge/purge system cannot find a duplicate.

A more accurate method, and the one recommended for business records, is a procedure that looks at each record, field by field, and evaluates the likelihood that the record is a duplicate. Such systems can be adjusted for the degree of accuracy required in the match process. For example, you may run a "tight" duplicate elimination program, where the record is not considered a duplicate unless it matches exactly. Or you can run a "loose" program, where the matching criteria is less rigid. A loose merge/purge will find far more duplicates than a tight merge/purge.

You can request your merge/purge file output three ways - individual, household or residential. An individual merge/purge will only eliminate duplicate records containing the same full name. Thus, if a husband and wife were on the file at the same address, each would receive a copy of the mailing.

A household merge/purge eliminates all duplicate records which contain identical last names at the same address. Either the husband or wife would be eliminated, and only one would receive the mailing (unless they had different last names, in which case both would get the package).

A residential merge/purge eliminates all but one individual at a mailing address, regardless of the last names of people at that address. For this reason, you must be very careful when running a residence merge/purge program on files that contain large numbers of apartments. If the program looks at only the street address, or if the file contains no house or flat numbers, only one person in the entire building will receive the mailing.

Although merge/purge is primarily thought of as a duplicate elimination system, it serves an equally important function by identifying multiple buyers or donors. For example, if you rent three outside mailing lists of buyers of products similar to yours, and the same individual appears on two or more of these lists, she is known as a "multi-buyer." This multi-buyer is usually more likely to respond to your offer than buyers appearing on only one list. Multi-buyers can be so important that some organizations send them a different promotional package than single-buyers.

POSTAL PRESORTING

Postal presorting discounts were created because the Post Office decided to reward mailers who made its job easier. Since the Post Office is a labour-intensive institution, and the majority of its costs are personnel-related, saving labour hours is a paramount objective in the effort to hold down costs.

From the time you drop a letter into your corner postbox to the time it is delivered across the country to another person's home or office, that piece of mail is handled by a large number of Post Office employees and goes through many steps. Postal presorting bypasses certain of these steps, saving the Post Office labour costs.

In addition to the enormous savings that you can achieve on postage, another important benefit to postal presorting is that applying presort codes will speed the accuracy and speed of your mail delivery. This is true for the same reason that discounts are given; there are fewer steps to slow the post down and fewer humans to possibly misdirect it. Equally important, postal presorting software analyzes the mailing addresses for accuracy and will reject those with undeliverable addresses, saving mailing and postage costs.

In the UK, the postal presort system is known as "Mailsort" and there are a number of options available on bulk mailings above 4000 items. The variables include:

- Speed of delivery.
- Cost of postage.
- The level of presorting that can be carried out.

■ A service for magazine and newspaper publishers under the name "Presstream".

Given the large number of variables and the changes in postal duty, it is difficult to provide practical examples of mailing costs. It is best to contact your local Post Office customer service representative to obtain a copy of the current regulations.

SECTION V

MARKETING STRATEGIES FOR UNIQUE CIRCUMSTANCES

BUSINESS-TO-BUSINESS MARKETING

*M*any people use the same techniques in business-to-business marketing as they do for marketing to consumers. This is not surprising because consumer advertising has been the primary focus of traditional marketing courses. But Master Marketers know better. They know that copying consumer techniques in the business-to-business arena is a sure recipe for disaster. Although there are similarities, let's first address the major differences between the two disciplines:

- The prospect universe for most consumer offers is much larger. This is why consumer marketers make greater use of mass-media advertising channels such as newspapers, radio and television. By contrast, a potential

341

business universe may consist of a few thousand, or in some cases, just a few hundred prospects. This is why business-to-business calls for a targeted, "direct" marketing approach.

■ With a smaller universe, testing is more difficult. Sometimes there aren't enough prospects to thoroughly test offers, media and copy themes.

■ People change jobs even more often than they move (on average every two years), making accurate list maintenance difficult.

■ Sales cycles for business purchases are usually much longer than consumer purchases. For example, capital goods such as new plant or computer systems may have a purchase cycle of three to five years.

■ Instead of a one-layer decision making process, the business sale may have to go through multiple layers and departments.

■ Impulse buying is less of a factor in business-to-business marketing. Since purchases must often be reviewed by others, some cost-analysis justification is necessary. This is especially true with high value products.

■ Good business lists are hard to come by. In consumer marketing there is a large body of response lists, donor lists and buyer lists for almost any type of offer. This is not always true in business marketing.

■ Although others may dispute this (and the situation is changing), there is more expertise available in consumer marketing than in business-to-business. Consumer marketing has attracted the attention of large advertising agencies because national consumer media campaigns are very lucrative.

BUSINESS AND CONSUMER SIMILARITIES

Despite the important differences noted above, there are several similarities between marketing to businesses and consumers:

- Certain time-tested advertising rules apply to both groups equally.
- Business and consumer advertising is read by exactly the same people. Some of the purchasing motivations may be different, but the human qualities of an individual do not change depending on whether she is viewing the promotion as a Purchasing Officer at the office, or as a mother at home.
- Busy people now do more work-related reading at home, where they supposedly have fewer distractions (although I don't know how anyone with children can say this). This means they are open to items such as subscriptions to business journals and trade magazines, and self-development materials of all kinds.
- As people in the marketing services industries become cross-trained in both disciplines, more creativity and ideas will be shared between the business and consumer marketing communities.

FINDING BUSINESS PROSPECTS

I can't overemphasize the importance of targeting the right audience in business-to-business marketing. As much as 50 percent of the success of the campaign can depend on your skill in this area. Industries are becoming highly specialized, and if you don't get your mail package into the right hands, or if you call the wrong person, or run your ads in the wrong trade publication, your effort and money will be wasted.

An informal survey of marketing managers showed that they spend only five to 10 percent of their time in prospect identification activities. And while most marketers devote little effort to this area, the Master Marketer knows the value of proper targeting and spends a great deal of time researching and pinpointing the prospect base. The techniques involved in finding business prospects are covered extensively in the chapters on media and mailing lists.

PROGRAMME OBJECTIVES

You must start with a clear purpose of your objectives for the programme. You can have more than one objective but your primary objective must be cast in stone, and all secondary objectives must be subordinate to this primary objective in terms of the offer, creative concept, copy and media plan.

Your list of primary objectives might include: Selling a product or service, increasing awareness, generating qualified leads, building your in-house database, imparting useful information about your organization, improving your company image and cross-selling existing customers. Many other objectives are possible but this list will give you a starting point.

DEVELOPING THE OFFER

After your primary objective has been determined, and you have a good understanding of the composition of your prospect universe, you will then want to develop your offer. In simple terms, an offer is what you are asking from the prospect, and what you will give him in return. The offer is the "What's in it for me?" part of the marketing equation.

How do you know if you have an effective offer? Here are the five criteria that every business-to-business offer should meet:

  1.   It works. Unless the offer achieves the results you

intended, it was not a good offer.

2. It is compatible with your organization's positioning statement.

3. It is compelling enough to cut through the advertising clutter and your prospect's preoccupation.

4. It is targeted at exactly the right audience. For instance, employees are motivated by offers that help them get promoted, build their work spheres of influence, and make their jobs easier or faster. Senior management is motivated by increasing sales, lowering costs and saving time.

5. It is powerful enough to demand immediate attention from the prospect.

Although by no means inclusive, here are some examples of offers that work for business-to-business products and services:

A. **Straight Sale** - A client said to me, "What do you mean offer? I give people my product and they give me money. That's my offer!" Obviously, this person believes in the straight sale offer.

B. **Special Pricing** - This offer works well with prospects who already know about your product/service. The special pricing offer could be a discount for prompt action or an urge to "buy now before the price goes up."

C. **Introductory Offer** - This offer is used to introduce new prospects to your company. It will have the greatest effect when the discount is significant. You have to be careful, however, not to offend existing customers who just purchased the same product for more money than you charge introductory buyers.

D. Multiple Product - Buyers get the second product for free or at a large discount.

E. Premium - Something extra is given away to spur the prospect to purchase now. Premiums range from advertising specialties such as desk calendars and pens, to expensive items such as trips and electronic equipment.

F. Free Information - Similar to the premium offer but you give away information instead of a product. This is especially effective with a business audience since people are always interested in ways to save money and perform their jobs better.

G. Trade-in Offer - The prospect trades in an old item and gets a discount off the new item. For example, a computer manufacturer can give businesses that trade in a competitor's equipment a £500 credit toward the purchase of a new computer.

H. Free Trial - If you have confidence in your product, let potential customers try it out in their office for 30 days. One large micro software company built a £30 million business by using the 30-day free trial offer.

I. Satisfaction Guarantee - While a guarantee should be part of every offer, an extra-strong guarantee can serve as its own offer. An example would be "double your money back if not completely satisfied."

J. Send a Salesperson - This works for only the most qualified leads; those who are ready, willing and able to buy. You must be careful with this offer (or offer a less threatening alternative as well) since it will scare off many lukewarm prospects.

K. Cash Discount - A special price can be given to help force the purchase decision. This offer works well with free trial offers. The prospect has the option to try the product and pay full price if he decides to keep it, or pay for the product now and receive a substantial discount.

L. Special Terms - This can work as well as a cash discount. For instance, "receive the item now and take up to six months to pay with no interest."

M. Prizedraw – With this offer, any prospect who replies to your offer is automatically entered into a prize draw. Due to prize regulations you will probably not be able to restrict the draw to purchasers only, but the offer still works because many people think they have a better chance of winning if they order something.

N. Demo/Trial Offer - A smaller, trial version of the product is sent (sometimes for a fee, sometimes for free). If the prospect likes the demo, he orders the full product. This offer works well for computer software products and publications.

O. Free Samples - Free samples are an effective way to highlight your product. For instance, an office product manufacturer can offer day planners or desk lamps as a bonus for purchasing a desk set.

P. Performance Guarantee - The customer gets to use the product for a period of time. If it does not live up to the specified criteria, he can return it for a full refund. This offer works well if your product is clearly superior to its competition.

Q. Special Inducement - Something extra is given to the prospect if he acts immediately. The inducement could be extra product, better terms, free training or extended maintenance.

The type of offer you use should be based on the objectives of your programme. If you are selling a high-ticket or complex item, or a personal sales call is needed to finalize a transaction, you should choose an offer that is geared to generating leads. Conversely, if you are promoting a low value, non-complex item, direct selling by post or phone may be the only practical alternative and will call for a different type of offer.

OVERCOMING THE THREE RESPONSE ROADBLOCKS

In a business environment, there are three things that will prevent a prospect from taking action on your offer. We refer to these as the "three response roadblocks." Roadblock one is the cost of the offer. Roadblock two is the effort required from the prospect to respond. Roadblock three is the risk involved in the prospect making a bad decision.

Make sure that every promotion is designed to overcome the three response roadblocks. Prove the value of the offer to minimize cost concerns. Do everything you can to make your offer easy to respond to. And decrease the prospect's fear of risk with testimonials from satisfied users and with rock solid, money back guarantees.

INFLUENCE OF THE GATEKEEPER

A recent study reported in <u>Target Marketing</u> magazine found that over 85 percent of executive secretaries screen telephone calls and incoming mail for their bosses, acting in effect as official "gatekeepers." Because of these gatekeepers, while senior managers receive an average of 20 mailing packages a day, only half of this mail ever reaches the executive's desk.

The study also showed that secretaries spend up to 65 minutes a day screening mail; double the time their bosses spend reading mail. How does this make you feel as the mailer; to know that someone else gives your communication far more attention than your prospect? And if you think getting mail through is tough, getting an executive to answer your phone call is even more difficult.

Fortunately, the farther down the organization chart you go, the less influence screeners have over what is read or listened to. Except in large bureaucracies that have post rooms willing and eager to throw away mail to keep it away from its intended audience, most people at the middle manager and lower level still open their own post and most will accept your phone call.

Even if you aim high in the organization, there are media that do not fall under the gatekeeper's jurisdiction. For instance, since senior managers do a great deal of reading to keep up with their industries and occupations, most subscribe to relevant publications.

Some of these magazines even target a senior audience. Four examples are <u>Information Management Journal</u> for data processing managers, <u>Management Today</u> for general managers, <u>Agenda</u> for local authority department heads, and <u>Marketing</u> for sales and marketing managers. Advertising in these and other occupation and industry specific publications can be an effective way to reach a senior audience.

HOW TO GET YOUR MAIL PAST THE GATEKEEPER

Despite the influence of the screener, you can be successful mailing to the executive suite. But if your task is to storm the castle walls, it helps to have an understanding of your adversary — the gatekeeper.

The first thing to realize is that this adversary can become your greatest ally. Because it stands to reason that, if a large part of each day's mail is discarded before it reaches the executive's desk, the lesser amount that does reach his desk will receive greater attention. In effect, by putting a stamp of approval on your package, or more accurately, by not putting a stamp of disapproval on it, the gatekeeper greatly increases the likelihood that the boss will take advantage of your offer.

What criteria do gatekeepers use to decide whether your package reaches the boss's desk or the nearest waste bin? Basically, the screener wants to know three things:

1. Is it a credible organization and credible offer?

2. Is the subject matter of the mailing relevant to the company, and most important, relevant to the boss?

3. Is the mailing personal or is it advertising mail (or as some call it, "junk mail")?

Given these three criteria, it stands to reason that the key to getting your mail passed on is to make it credible, relevant and personal. Obviously, almost anything that looks like typical advertising mail will be discarded. This rules out most self-mailer formats and envelopes with pressure-sensitive labels.

Instead, use an auto-typed envelope, which looks exactly like an envelope addressed by your typewriter, but is produced in volume. Also consider including a personalized letter, to match the carrier envelope. The preferred method of personalizing the letter is laser-printing, a technology that works well in small and large quantities, and produces excellent print quality.

A reply-device should also be included in your closed-face package. Examples of reply devices are given in the chapter on direct mail. Although there is a large variety of reply format options, the important thing to remember is to make it as easy as possible for the reader of the package to respond to your offer.

One way to make it easier on your prospect is to print his name, address, etc. on the reply device, so all he has to do is check off and sign the card if necessary, and drop it in the post. While this will increase your production costs for the package, the increase in response rates may be worth it. Also, don't forget to prominently feature the firm's telephone number (especially free phone 0800 numbers) on the reply device with a reminder such as "Call 0800-124-4567 for even faster response."

Another option in format design is whether or not to include brochures and other collateral sales materials in the package. Two questions should be asked before you include any components other than the letter in your package. First, what is the cost of including the extra information? Second, will this extra information increase or decrease response?

The answer to the second question may be different than you might suspect. It is true that when you are selling a product or service through the post, you must include all the information that would be necessary for the prospect to make an informed decision. But this is not true when you are mailing to generate leads or inquiries.

Sometimes this is the hardest sale I make to my clients - convincing them to maximize response by sending less, not more information. Everyone wants to believe that prospects are sitting at their desks, eager to read every word about their fantastic product or service. But this just isn't so. This point is so important, I've created Ryan's Law of Direct Marketing:

"If you are selling through the mail, send lots of information. If you are generating leads, send only as much information as it takes to get the prospect to respond. No more, no less."

MORE TIPS FOR DIRECT MARKETING TO BUSINESSES

Here are some additional methods to get your business direct mail opened and responded to:

- Try a "blind" package. This means that there is nothing on the outside of the envelope (other than a street address) to identify the source of the mailing; no logo, no advertising message (teaser) and no company name.
- Make the mailing look like important information. You can do this by creating a newsletter format, or by including a relevant article or cassette tape in the package.
- The higher in the organization you are mailing, the shorter your letter copy should be. I have successfully used letters that have only two or three paragraphs and end with something like the following: "I know your time is busy. Just initial the letter below and return it in the envelope provided and I'll get right back to you with information."
- The higher in the organization you are mailing, the more impressive the title of the person signing the letter should be. A letter addressed to Main Board Directors which is signed by a sales manager or account executive will not be taken seriously.
- Odd-size packages (dimensionals) work well. If you have the budget and are mailing to senior executives, consider an odd-size package. Better yet, send your information in a box since very few people can resist opening a box.

■ If the post won't go through, try another procedure. Alternative delivery methods such as parcel or courier have much greater impact than the normal post. And if you are mailing something heavy, it can be cost-effective.

Copy for your business-to-business offer should be concise and to the point. You should also target the copy as much as possible to the needs and hot-buttons of the prospects on your list. For instance, a finance director responds well to the promise of saving money, while a sales and marketing manager is much more concerned with increasing sales.

Follow-up is a key in all business-to-business marketing. Follow-up should be prompt and it should be relevant. Use a telephone follow-up to further qualify the prospect, identify "hot" leads, and make sure you are responding with the information most appropriate for that particular individual's needs.

Once you identify an individual or company as qualified for your product or service, maintain that prospect in your database. In business-to-business, sometimes it takes time to convert even the best prospects into customers. Be patient, and be in the game for the long haul. This is what the nation's most successful business marketers do, and if you want to include yourself in this category, follow these important rules.

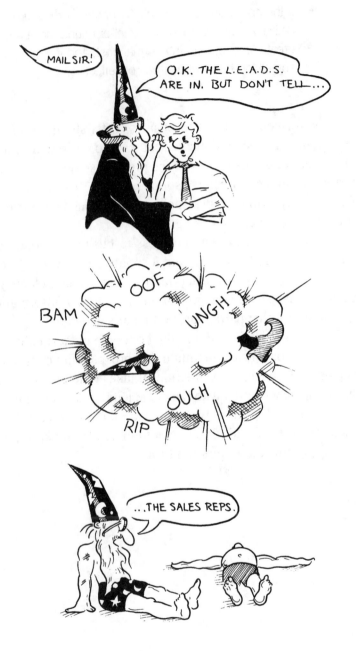

23

LEAD GENERATION

*How to Generate Enough Leads to
Feed a Hungry Sales Force*

L ead generation can be defined as "the process of identifying individuals who have an interest in your product or service."
Lead quality can range from curiosity-seekers to those ready and
willing to make an immediate purchase decision. And since it
costs the average business £100–£200 to generate a lead, it helps to
know how to recognize a good lead. I agree with the definition
Bernie Goldberg, author of <u>The Lead Generation Handbook</u>, uses
to describe a viable lead. Bernie uses the acronym M.A.N.D. (or
D.A.M.N. if you prefer):

M = Means   The prospect has sufficient financial re-
                              sources to purchase your product or service.

A = Authority	The prospect is a decision maker or decision influencer.
N = Need	The prospect has a genuine need for your product or service.
D = Desire	The prospect has the desire to learn more about your product or service.

A prospect with two or three of these characteristics is not a viable lead. For instance, someone with the authority, need and desire for your product is not viable if they lack the means to pay for or finance the purchase. And someone with the means, need and desire is not a good lead if he lacks the authority to make or influence the decision.

Most business-to-business marketers and some consumer marketers build their entire promotional programmes around lead generation. In some companies a marketing manager may be evaluated solely on the basis of his ability to generate an adequate flow of leads.

There are two types of marketing situations in which the lack of leads can be fatal. The first situation occurs when an organization relies primarily on an outside sales force for revenue. Although some industries require sales personnel to generate their own leads, in most companies this is considered a marketing function.

Sales reps depend on leads because they know that no sale can be made until a lead is generated. They need leads as much as a fish needs water (maybe more if the rep is behind quota). Unless you supply the sales force with enough leads, revenues dry up and your salespeople leave for greener pastures.

Situation two occurs when your revenues depend on a two-step sales process. First, a prospect responds to your advertisement, direct mail or sales call, thus identifying himself as interested in your product or service. You then provide the prospect with additional information by post, telephone or personal contact until he is comfortable making a buying decision about your product or service.

Several basic decisions have to be made when designing a lead generation programme. First, ask yourself if lead generation is the best possible use of your marketing budget, or if a one-step direct-sale approach would work better. Let's take a look at some of the types of offers that lend themselves to a one-step programme:

- Selling inexpensive products.
- Non-complicated offers.
- Information offers, including newsletter and magazine subscriptions.
- Office supplies.
- Microcomputer software.
- Low-ticket financial offers (credit cards, money market funds, etc.).
- Most fund-raising programmes.

By contrast, there are applications in which a two-step, lead generation marketing programme would be more effective. The following are just a few:

- Expensive offers.
- Complex or technical products.
- Selling to a limited prospect base.
- Mainframe computer software.
- Most services (including legal, accounting, medical and advertising services).
- High-value financial offers (investments, mortgages, etc.).
- High-value fund-raising programmes.

If you choose the two-step approach, you need to decide the quality of the leads to be generated. This can be a tough balancing act. The sales department will be looking for large numbers of leads and if the quality of the leads is poor, you will hear about it. Worse yet, the leads you give to sales reps may be totally ignored.

For example, at one client's company, salespeople routinely ignored their print advertising reader service leads (often called "bingo cards"). In general, these inquirers were less qualified, even though research proved that a small percentage of them were high quality. However, the sales personnel would not be persuaded and continued to ignore all bingo card leads.

To solve the problem, we instituted a pre-qualification step, where all respondents were phoned and asked a series of qualifying questions. Only qualified leads were passed on to the sales department. The results: happier sales reps and a much higher conversion of bingo card leads to sales.

WORKING WITH THE SALES DEPARTMENT

Despite good intentions, many lead generation programmes fail due to a lack of cooperation between the marketing and sales departments. The sales manager says, "Our marketing people are generating lousy leads," or "Those marketing people don't know the difference between a good lead and a bad lead." The marketing director responds, "If salespeople would only follow up the leads we give them, we'd have a lot more sales," or "Sales doesn't realize how hard we are working for them."

The easiest course of action is to simply design and implement the system that works best for the marketing department. In the short term, this will save you many hours of frustration but you may be setting up your lead generation programme for certain long-term failure. My experience in setting up lead generation programmes in a number of industries has proven the following steps to be essential in establishing a productive working relationship between marketing and sales departments:

1. As a marketing manager, you must take full responsibility for the success or failure of the programme. Although sales is an integral part of the process, lead generation is rightfully considered a marketing function.

2. Sales managers, and preferably sales reps as well, should be brought into the design phase of the programme. They must feel that their input received full consideration and they must "buy off" on the system before it is implemented.

3. Salespeople should feel that the system rewards them for their cooperation. The best reward is for them to be able to make more sales with no extra effort. Show them how the system rewards them for working smarter, not harder. Never institute a new lead system at the same time you take any negative action (such as cutting sales territories) or you will permanently link the two events in the minds of the sales department. You must keep everything positive.

4. Feedback loops should be put in place. Sales reps must always be kept abreast of changes and upgrades in the system. Likewise, their input on how the system is working should be solicited on a regular basis.

5. You must get agreement on the technical aspects of the system. The ideal structure will combine a great deal of flexibility for field sales reps with maximum control by the marketing department (not the other way around) and ensure that relevant information about all prospects will be captured. You must always remember that all prospect and customer data belongs to the company, and not to the individual sales rep.

6. Sales and marketing must agree on what constitutes a "good lead," because this definition will drive much of the marketing department's efforts. For a large mainframe software company, we used the acronym M.A.N.D. (see the beginning of this chapter) as a starting point and further defined a "hot lead" as follows:

   a. Prospect had the proper hardware in place to install our software product.

   b. Prospect's company had the problem our software was designed to solve.

   c. Prospect was interested in implementing a solution within six months.

   d. Prospect was willing to take the next step in the selling cycle (either a trial evaluation or a visit from the sales rep).

ENSURING AN ADEQUATE FLOW OF LEADS

Your objective in setting the proper lead flow is to generate enough leads to keep your salespeople and fulfillment personnel busy without wasting time on unqualified prospects. You also do not want to generate so many inquiries that some of your leads fall through cracks in the system.

When determining the optimal number of leads, you must consider the caliber of your sales reps and their willingness to pursue marginal leads. I have worked with salespeople who want to pursue every lead personally, because they don't trust the marketing department to make decisions about the quality of leads in their territory. Others want only qualified leads and are insulted if you pass along anyone who is not ready to buy today.

You can adjust the number of leads coming into the system by tailoring your advertising messages. For example, the following two headlines are for the same product but will produce vastly different numbers of leads:

"Free Information for Everyone Who Wants
to Save on Taxes"
"A Tax Benefit Programme for Those Making
Over £60,000 Per Year"

Obviously, headline number one will produce more leads. But if you are selling an investment that is useful only to those with high incomes, headline two is the better choice. Although it costs more to generate each lead using headline two, your closing percentage should be much greater.

HOW TO TRACK PROSPECTS THROUGH THE SALES PROCESS

Responses you generate will flow through the marketing system and fall into the following categories:

Raw Lead - Any inquiry that comes to your organization from any source, whether qualified or not.

Suspect - An inquiry that has passed your initial screening and is deemed to have some potential to become a customer.

Prospect - A lead that has gone through a more in-depth qualification process, such as being asked a series of questions by a telemarketing rep. At this point the lead may be classified as a "hot" prospect (one ready to make a decision), a warm prospect (one with the capacity to become a hot prospect), a suspect or a dead lead.

Inactive Lead - This is a person who will not buy now, but has potential for the future. You should enter such leads into your database system for future action.

Dead Lead - This lead has little or no chance of becoming a customer. But be careful in assigning leads to the "dead" file. So-called dead leads can often be resurrected and become purchasers. In fact, some companies assign new salespeople to work the dead lead file, often with surprising success.

Customer - If you have done your job properly, a fair percentage of raw inquiries have been worked through the system and have become customers.

Repeat Customer - The lifeblood of any business. Most companies devote too few resources to increasing revenues from existing customers, even though the cost to bring in an additional pound of revenue from an existing client is far less than the cost of generating a dollar from a new customer.

HOW TO TURN A HIGH PERCENTAGE OF LEADS INTO CUSTOMERS

Every step of the sales process, from generating raw inquiries through building repeat clients, should be monitored carefully. We use formulas called "conversion ratios" to measure what percentage of leads survive each step and move closer to becoming customers.

For example, if 100 raw leads are generated by the marketing program, and 50 survive the initial screening step, the conversion ratio of raw leads to suspects is 50 percent. Likewise, if 20 of these 50 suspects are turned into prospects, the conversion ratio of suspects to prospects is 40 percent. And if five of these 20 prospects become customers, the conversion ratio of prospects to customers is 25 percent.

Conversion ratios will differ depending on your industry, the product or service offered, the type of prospects you are working with, and such factors as seasonality and the economy. The important point is to work and rework these numbers to increase the conversion ratio at each step. After you have a handle on your realistic ratios, you will know exactly how many raw leads have to be fed into the system on an ongoing basis to achieve your sales objectives.

By using conversion ratios, it is easy to demonstrate that a company can use its lead generation system to increase the number of new customers two ways:

1. By funneling a larger number of "raw leads" into the system, while maintaining the same conversion ratios.
2. By improving any one of the conversion ratios, while maintaining the same number of "raw leads" entering the system.

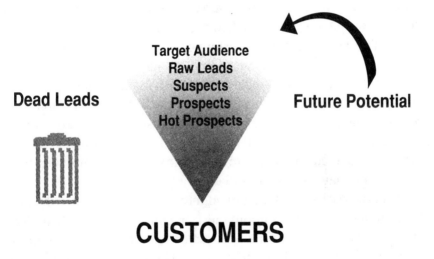

Dead Leads   **Future Potential**

Target Audience
Raw Leads
Suspects
Prospects
Hot Prospects

CUSTOMERS

How your target audience becomes your customers.

<u>SOURCES OF LEADS</u>

While many lead generation efforts rely heavily on direct marketing methods, it is important to remember that leads can come from anywhere. Generally, the following sources will produce the majority of your inquiries:

Direct Mail - In most business-to-business, and many consumer applications, direct mail has proven to be the most cost-effective method of generating high quality inquiries. When using direct mail to generate leads, keep in mind the power of personalization, and the extra response you will achieve by offering a freephone 0800 number response option.

Telemarketing - Telemarketing is another of the direct response disciplines. As a follow-up to a direct mail campaign it can double or triple response rates (or more). The telephone can be used effectively for calls to existing customers and prospects.

Print Advertising - Image advertising in magazines and newspapers is not as effective on a cost-per-lead basis as direct response methods. However, image advertising will improve the pulling power of direct mail. One useful business-to-business technique is to advertise in a trade publication, then follow up with mail to that magazine's subscribers.

Print advertising can be turned into a lead generation vehicle with the addition of a coupon and a freephone number. I would go so far as to say that no advertisement should be run without a prominently displayed phone number. The guiding principle is to do everything possible to make it easy for the reader to get in touch with you.

Consider taking advantage of the publication's reader response offer, whereby the magazine will forward to you the names and addresses of those who indicate interest in your ad. Such responses are known as reader inquiries or "bingo cards." Because the reader has to take so little action to respond to your advertisement (merely circling a number on the reply card), the common perception is that bingo cards are not as qualified as other types of leads. If lead quality is a priority, either pre-qualify all reader response inquiries or forget the bingo card option.

Another print advertising response tool is the bound-in response card. As the name implies, these cards are bound in between the pages of a magazine. If you have the good fortune (or clout) to have your card inserted next to editorial copy which is related to your offer, your response will be greatly boosted.

Television - Television has always been the quickest way to reach large numbers of people, particularly if your product appeals to a general audience. The proliferation of local and cable stations has now made this medium available to promoters of narrow, tightly defined products and services.

Much of the advertising seen on network television is non-direct response and image-oriented in structure because it does not urge viewers to take action now. Rather, it sets us up to purchase a product at some later time, which could be as soon as tomorrow when we visit the soft drink aisle at our local supermarket or next winter when we are making holiday plans and consider the prospects of a Club Med break.

Using this definition of image advertising, it is obvious that most of the car manufacturers' ads are image-oriented, not direct response. Examples include Rover's long-running, "Different because it's a Rover" campaign, and Ford's different variations of "Everything we do is driven by you". By contrast, when the local car dealer advertises a sale on television, he is practising direct response advertising. He is not so interested in your future transportation plans as he is in enticing you into his showroom right away.

A click of your TV remote control will provide many examples of direct-response television advertising. The list of products and

Television has proven very effective for two-step offers, where you are asking for an action other than a direct purchase (such as generating leads for an insurance offer).

Radio - This medium allows almost pinpoint targeting of audiences. Most independent local radio stations serve local markets of listeners with similar characteristics. Examples of unique audience formats include: talk radio, classical, country, rock, gospel, ethnic programming and easy listening. Radio time can be purchased relatively inexpensively and the production costs are small compared to television ads.

A problem with radio as a direct-response tool is that most people will not take time to find a pencil, paper and envelope to respond and, in fact, they may not be in a position to phone, particularly if they are listening to the offer while in a car. Also, people treat radio as a passive medium, using it as background noise while engaging in other activities such as driving, working or housework.

For these reasons, you will have to run radio spots with more frequency than other media to achieve the same level of attention. Two keys to keep in mind are to make your promotion easy to respond to (for example, with a memorable freephone number, such as 0800-FOR-INFO) or to repeat your message often enough to catch the prospect at a time when it is convenient for him to respond.

Exhibitions – Exhibitions are a relatively expensive way to generate leads and, unfortunately, many organizations have had bad experiences with them. However, there are many reasons for an organization to exhibit which are discussed in the earlier chapter on exhibition marketing. And if you do a good job of generating and following up trade show leads, you can convert many of these people into buyers.

Public Relations - Don't make the mistake of ignoring public relations as a lead generation tool. While it is true that PR's primary purpose should be promoting your organization's image, don't discount its lead pulling power. Public relations leads come from three primary sources: newsletters, press releases and trade media articles.

Newsletters are more effective if presented as information vehicles as opposed to hard-sell product or company propaganda. This is particularly true in the early stages of a newsletter programme. Once you have published several issues you can subtly begin to weave more specific product information into the editorial content. I recommend that you always include a response device or coupon in your newsletter for those who want more information about something they read or about your products or services.

By adding a tear-off response form and a freephone 0800 number, one of our clients increased response to their company newsletter 2,000 percent. A response form can also be used to give the reader the opportunity to remove himself from your mailing list or to add interested colleagues to your list.

All other public relations activities, including product press releases, articles and user stories can also support your lead generation goals. Even though you probably won't receive many inquiries as a direct result of these activities, their positive influence on direct marketing tools such as direct mail and telemarketing can be substantial.

Personal Contacts - Never discount the power of personal influence to generate leads. These methods include referrals, networking and cold calls by sales reps. Most people seem to think that successful networking involves meeting as many people as possible and handing out dozens of business cards. Actually, the real secret is not what the people you meet learn about you, it is what you learn about them.

The key is to take personal responsibility for developing ongoing contact with prospects. By all means, give out your business cards, but always in exchange for the prospect's card. If you have a free moment, write down any observations you made about the prospect on the back of his business card. This data can be valuable in future conversations.

As soon as you get back to your office, enter all information from the business cards you collected (front and back) into your database. By following this procedure, you have permanently captured the prospect in your system, and will have many future opportunities to turn that prospect into a customer.

BUDGETING FOR LEAD GENERATION

Every organization has unique objectives for its marketing programmes and therefore, different budget considerations. The following budget ratios are generalized examples that our agency uses for clients. You can adapt these ratios to your unique circumstances.

MARKETING BUDGET RATIOS

A. Start-up companies (under £3M annual sales), require 9–15% of gross sales for effective marketing
B. Sustaining companies (£3M to £10M sales), require 8–10% of gross sales
C. Growth companies (£10–25M sales), require 5–9%
D. Large companies (£25–50M sales), require 4–6%

E. Mature companies (over £50M sales), require 3–5%

The following breakdown figures provide a sample of how a business-to-business client allocates its budget for lead-generation marketing activities:

MARKETING BUDGET BREAKDOWN

<u>Marketing Activity</u>	<u>% of Total Budget</u>
Print/Broadcast Advertising	50%
Brochures and Sales Materials	15%
Direct Mail and Telemarketing	20%
Public Relations	8%
Exhibitions and Seminars	<u>7%</u>
TOTAL	100%

These seven guidelines can help you develop your marketing budget:

1. Greater amounts must be spent to market aggressively, either to increase market share or to compete with large, established firms.

2. Organizations with large sales forces will need larger budgets to generate more leads for their salespeople.

3. Broad-base, general interest products require larger promotional budgets than technical, narrowly focused products.

4. It requires more marketing budget to launch new products than to maintain the market share of existing products.

5. Entry-level companies need to spend a larger percent-

age of their revenue on marketing than established companies. Older firms benefit from previous marketing expenditures and name recognition built up over the years and will usually generate a larger proportion of their revenues from existing customers at a much lower cost.

6. Independent companies must spend more than divisions of nationally known firms. This is true because a parent company often provides a division with leads (from its own customer base) or may purchase much of the division's output itself.

7. Product-driven companies must spend a much larger share of their revenues on marketing than service companies.

CRITERIA OF A SUCCESSFUL LEAD GENERATION PROGRAMME

You should periodically evaluate your lead generation program to ensure that it meets these criteria:

- Conversion ratios are used to continually monitor results and to refine the lead programme to produce greater results.
- The system produces a high percentage of qualified leads.
- All leads are followed up, except those that are obviously unqualified.
- New leads are contacted by phone, post, or a personal visit in a timely manner.
- The lead flow is balanced by territory, sales reps, and

product line.
- Leads are produced at a reasonable cost-per-lead.
- All information generated from inquiries and subsequent follow-up is captured in a database system.

Whatever your company's product or service, never underestimate the importance of a well-tuned lead generating programme. Since three out of every four business-to-business marketing communications are for lead generating purposes, this effort should not be wasted with half-hearted, unprofessional efforts in an area so vital to your success.

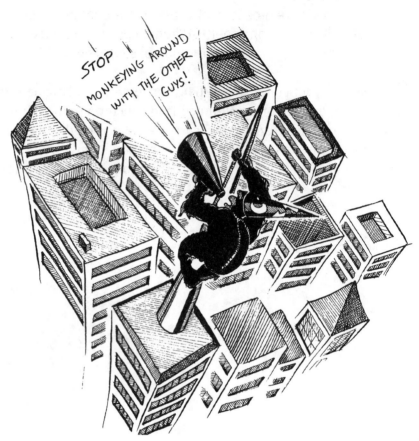

KNOW THE DIFFERENCE BETWEEN CUTTING YOUR BUDGET
AND CUTTING CORNERS.

HOW TO ACHIEVE BIG IMPACT
WITH A SMALL MARKETING BUDGET

*M*any small businesses fail due to a lack of an effective marketing programme. There are many reasons why this is true, including:

1. Entrepreneurs may be very good at their core business, but know very little about marketing. I have found this to be particularly true for high-technology companies, where the founder may be a genius at designing complex software products but lacks even a cursory knowledge about the marketing process.

2. Certain small business people suffer from the better mousetrap theory - "If you build a better mousetrap, the world will beat a path to your door." They are innocently caught up in a love for their own products or services

and believe the world will indeed beat a path to their door when it hears about their fantastic new product. This attitude is wrong and dangerous.

3. An effective marketing campaign is disciplined, hard work. Since marketing is probably not what motivated the entrepreneur to open his or her business, it receives lesser priority than product development and other tasks.

4. Marketing often comes up short when scarce funds are allocated. Sadly, I have seen start-up companies spend thousands of dollars on extravagant furniture and equipment, while complaining that "there is nothing left for marketing."

5. New companies often hire expensive advertising agencies which are incapable of cost-effective, low-budget marketing. Many of these agencies don't recommend direct marketing methods, which are often the best way for a small company to compete with larger firms. Plus, print and broadcast advertising (and designing four-colour brochures) are much more lucrative sources of revenue for the agency than direct marketing. It is very difficult for a small business to survive a relationship with this type of agency.

Small businesses and start-up companies face two major obstacles. First, if you happen to be a small fish in a large pond, you will be confronted by competitors who have much larger advertising and marketing budgets. Second, just to stay even, new and small companies must spend a larger percentage of revenues on marketing than older, established organizations.

Given the reality of this situation, it is imperative, as a Master Marketer, that you learn to squeeze as much efficiency as possible out of every pound. Be assured that much can be done on a limited budget. Expensive is not necessarily better. Your "guerilla marketing" strategies can often beat the big players and will be valuable lessons that will serve you well no matter how successful you become, or how far your marketing budget expands. One thing you must do is find reasonably-priced (but not cheap) experts to assist you. There are a thousand pitfalls in marketing and it helps to have the advice of people who have learned to avoid most of them. And once you find these experts, you must also learn to trust their judgments. If you feel the need to second-guess the advice of your marketing consultant, you need to find a new consultant.

Of course, you pay the bills, and yes, it is your company at stake. But the last thing you want is a "yes man" relationship with your marketing advisor or advertising agency. You may get what you want this way, but it very likely will not be what you need.

HOW TO TAKE ON LARGE COMPETITORS

First the good news. When faced with one or more large competitors, you have one advantage - you have little to lose and everything to gain. For instance, if you are a start-up company in a field where three large firms control over 90 percent of the market, any market share you gain will probably come at the expense of one of these companies. You are playing a game of offense, while the large companies are forced to play defense. This will be true until you begin to hurt the larger company, at which time they may turn into an offensive opponent, a very dangerous situation for the smaller company.

Instead of confronting a much larger competitor directly, I recommend the "unique market niche" approach. Even the largest companies leave pockets of opportunity for clever entrepreneurs to exploit. For example, mighty IBM was slow to attack the market for personal computers, choosing instead to concentrate its energies on its bread and butter mainframe computer market. Whether this was wise business strategy can be debated but the fact remains, many smaller companies benefitted from IBM's reticence in going after what it then considered a small market niche.

Large companies tend to spend a large portion of their budget on image advertising. This gives the small company two advantages. One, your opponent is well known and will have great difficulty escaping the image it has spent so much time and money cultivating. Two, you can effectively counter your competitor's image campaigns with highly-focused target marketing, at a lower cost.

SMALL BUDGET PRINT AD STRATEGIES

Print advertising can be a cost-effective medium for the organization with a small budget. First, make sure your choice of publications is based on sound target marketing principles. Then follow these important rules:

- Always include a coupon in your ads. Tear-out coupons can boost print ad response by 20 percent.
- Offer a telephone call-in option. If possible, use a freephone number. The combination of a coupon and an 0800 number can increase results up to 35 percent.
- Always include a strong call-to-action in your ad.
- Instead of large ads, consider running smaller ads more frequently.
- Don't give up on a successful ad too soon. Let it run longer, build recognition with frequency, and save the cost of creating a new ad.
- Test "type only" ads. They are less expensive to produce, and sometimes pull better than ads with graphics. If you must use a graphic, remember that photographs gain 15 to 30 percent readership increase over illustrations.

■ Negotiate with publications. They are often flexible with new advertisers since they want your future business. For monthly publications, try to negotiate the 12 times rate, even if you are only committing to two or three issues. This can result in a considerable savings.

■ Consider running in regional editions of national publications. This can give you the stature of the national advertiser, at far less cost.

■ Become a "standby" advertiser. If the publication has space which opens up at the last minute, it will often sell that space to you for one-third to one-half the published rate.

SMALL BUDGET DIRECT MARKETING STRATEGIES

Probably the most important step you can take to improve the cost-effectiveness of your direct marketing program is to find good suppliers to work with. Unless your general purpose advertising agency is one of the small percentage which actually has direct marketing expertise, consider finding specialists to produce your mailing projects. Not only will you get better response but your costs should go down.

Another thing to keep in mind is that cost can be measured two ways, as a front-end expense and as a back-end measurement of results. Using the key analyses of cost-per-lead (CPL) and cost-per-sale (CPS), the definition of cost-effectiveness can be more precisely honed. For instance, by using the principles of "coordinated marketing," discussed in other chapters, the marketer may spend an identical amount of money as with typical methods, but will have a much lower cost-per-lead or cost-per-sale.

Following is a collection of ideas on how to spend less and achieve more in your direct marketing programs:

■ Target your lists more effectively by using demographics, psychographics, and some of the other list segmenting tools available. The object is to mail fewer pieces and achieve greater response.

■ Test your mailing and telemarketing in small quantities before committing large sums to full programmes. Equally important, use the information you learn on every programme to make the next work better.

■ Cut back on four-colour process direct mail packages. Unless you sell food, magazines, holiday properties or other products requiring excellent graphic reproduction, you can probably pull as much response using two-colour printing.

■ Closed-face personalized packages are necessary for certain offers, but we've tested many types of offers where window envelopes work as well, at far lower cost.

■ Consider mailing second-class instead of first-class. This will save you money on each package and most prospects won't notice the difference. The exception is with time-sensitive offers because second-class post takes longer than first-class to arrive.

■ If you mail to large numbers on a national basis, or send highly concentrated mailings into local or regional areas, use postal pre-sorting.

OTHER COST-CUTTING IDEAS

■ Read the chapter on public relations carefully and begin carrying out its advice. PR is a low-effort, high-reward promotional vehicle and I urge you to use it.

■ Shift some of your TV ad budget to radio. Radio is far less expensive for both time and production costs, and can be targeted more precisely.

■ Be persistent. Remember the "eight times" rule: You don't have to spend a lot of money on each communication but you must repeat your message up to eight times to gain prospect awareness.

■ Utilize experts. It will cost you something in the short-term but can save you money and aggravation in the long-term.

■ Learn all you can about the production process. Read publications such as those mentioned in the Resource Guide. Go visit your printer, computer service bureau and mailing house. Most importantly, ask a lot of questions.

Last but not least, since consistency is vital for those with small budgets, make sure every one of your marketing efforts supports and reinforces your unique selling proposition (USP).

25

HOW TO BRING A NEW
PRODUCT TO MARKET

*L*ess than one out of five new products ever make it from the concept stage to introduction. Out of this number, less than half survive with any degree of success. While many of these failures can be attributed to inadequate product development, lack of capital and other factors, the majority fail because of poorly conceived, poorly executed marketing.

The Master Marketer knows that successful new product launches are important for a number of reasons:

- ■ In some cases, especially in start-up companies, the new product can be the difference between prosperity and bankruptcy.
- ■ New products drain budgets from marketing, sales and development, leaving existing products vulnerable to

competitive attack.
- ■ If a new product fails, it may cost you more than the direct sales revenue from that product. Revenue can also be lost from accessory sales, warranty work, and future cross-sell opportunities.
- ■ New products can be your introduction into important new market areas and customer niches.
- ■ Successful new product launches create considerable excitement among employees, customers and suppliers. Conversely, failures can lead to pessimism and decreased productivity.
- ■ In some industries, especially high-technology, new product strategies are imperative to survival. Many companies in these industries spend 20 to 40 percent of their total budgets on new product development.

DETERMINING THE VIABILITY OF A NEW PRODUCT

To develop a successful marketing campaign for a new product, you must be able to answer the following questions:

What is the unfulfilled need for the product?
Who (specifically) will buy and use the product?
When will someone buy and use the product?
Where will the product be purchased and used?
Why would someone spend money on the product?
How will the product be used?

To answer these questions, market research should be conducted. Research methods that can be utilized include focus groups, written questionnaires, telephone interviews, and one-to-one interviews (in the home, shopping centres, etc.).

"Consumer use" tests are an excellent method of determining how the product works in real-life situations. In the software industry, these trials are referred to as "beta tests." Beta tests are valuable to consumers because they are among the first to benefit from the new technology. In return for helping the supplier evaluate and fine-tune the product, they often receive it for free, or at a large discount.

Software companies like the beta testing process because they receive important data that helps them refine the product before the programme is released for general sale. As a bonus, the beta-site will also serve as a much needed customer reference.

Unless you are operating on a shoestring, try to rely mainly on primary research, rather than secondary research (e.g. data available from government or industry sources). To get the most value from research, you must talk to the individuals who will make the decision to buy your product.

But when you talk to potential buyers, be careful not to rely on answers to hypothetical questions. For instance, in a focus group or one-to-one interview, the prospect is often asked, "Would you buy a product such as the one we described to you?" If the individual answers yes, he may then be asked, "What is the most you would pay for a product such as this?"

While these questions have some validity, the only thing that matters is what the consumer does when he actually has the ability to make the purchase. This is the only test that matters in the end; the test of reality. Don't skip the reality test because of assumptions about what consumers want. You can't be sure unless you ask (and sometimes you still can't be sure).

Several years ago, I was involved in the introduction of a word processing software package for mainframe computers. No hard data existed on the market potential for such a product but the software developer was convinced he had a blockbuster. I suggested that we contact prospective users of the product to find out if they would have any interest in the product, and if so, what product features they would find most useful.

The developer declined to fund this research because he

claimed to already know the answers to these questions. Instead he pressed on, spending tens of thousands of dollars to get the product ready for market. You can guess what happened; the product was introduced and prospective users said, "So what." Of the few products sold, almost all were returned because the software lacked useful features that could be found on micro word processing software costing 1/20th as much.

COMPETITIVE RESEARCH

Unless you are extremely fortunate, you will have competitors. If you don't have them at the beginning, any success you have will surely attract imitators. The more you know about these companies, the better you will be able to counter their moves.

Where do you find information about competitors? Try these sources to start: government publications, annual reports, corporate directories, trade and professional associations, Registrar public companies, on-line databases, media stories, libraries, patent and trademark offices, universities, legal proceedings, advertisements and published speeches and articles.

You can also learn a great deal from the competitor's suppliers and customers. And surprisingly, you can often receive useful information simply by calling the company directly. There's no telling what you can learn from a talkative and undisciplined sales rep. I am not saying that you should be deliberately deceptive, but I do suggest that you take advantage of people's tendency to want to prove how much they know.

If your competitor is a public company, you should also buy time shares. This is an easy way to receive basic financial data, plus information about the company's plans.

What might your competitors do in response to your new product introduction? The techniques competitors can use to hurt you include:

- Lowering their prices.
- Freezing the market with promises of new technologies (in the computer software industry, this is known as introducing "vaporware").
- Offering irresistible deals to your customers (such as a vastly reduced price when a customer trades in your product).
- Adapting or outright stealing your product advantages.
- Denigrating your company/products to your prospects and customers.
- Attacking you in their advertising campaigns.

All of these techniques can be countered, provided you have adequate time. And some, such as the competitor making a public attack on you, can hurt the competitor more than you. But if you don't keep up with the competition, you run the risk of being blind-sided.

The flip side of researching your competitors is making sure it is hard for your competitors to research you. If you are a small company entering a marketplace dominated by bigger players, time can be your most valuable ally. The longer you can keep your plans to yourself, the greater your competitive edge. By the time the industry giants find out you are around, you can be safe and secure in your own market niche.

TEST MARKETING

It is always a good idea to pre-test a new product. Test marketing has a number of advantages:

- It can often be conducted before large sums are spent on production runs and national marketing. For instance, in the publishing industry, it often costs much more to market a book, video programme or audio programme than it does to produce the material in the first place. Trying to sell such products without test marketing can be disastrous and costly.

■ Initial test markets often point out the need for additional features and upgrades to the product, which if not made, can lead to failure.

■ Not only the product, but the marketing process itself can be refined during the test marketing phase. Sometimes it is impossible to tell which approach will work best for a particular product. This is why we often utilize two or more creative strategies during testing, with the winning strategy used for the marketing roll-out.

■ If successful, the test market can generate revenues to fund a larger-scale marketing effort. This may be the only choice for small start-ups with limited capital.

WHAT CAN KILL A NEW PRODUCT INTRODUCTION

Sometimes, a product introduction is doomed from the start. Make sure your product and marketing plan do not suffer from any of these fatal flaws:

No discernible difference - It is very difficult to achieve success with a me-too, commodity product. Unless you can show a unique and saleable advantage, you will be forced to rely on a low-price strategy. And this is a tough game to win.

Product weakened by committee - The best products are usually the result of the vision of one individual, or at most, a small, tightly-knit group of fervent believers. Once a product gets tied up in a corporate bureaucracy, its chances of success are greatly diminished. It is best to have a product champion, or small group of champions, who feels personal responsibility for the success or failure of "their baby."

Product that is poorly timed - As every surfer knows, it is better to ride the crest of the wave. Likewise, a product's timing is critically important. If introduced prematurely, the prospect base may not be ready for you; too late, and the competition may have passed you by.

Product that bucks the tide - A good example of this is Sony's experience with Beta tape for VCRs. The world was moving to VHS because of its cost benefits. Only Sony held out and continued to produce Beta VCRs and tapes. Eventually, even mighty Sony gave up and joined the VHS revolution. But not before learning an expensive lesson.

Poor pricing strategy - Occasionally, an excellent product cannot be priced at a level acceptable to the consumer. For instance, my agency was involved in marketing a product called Computer Focus, a newsletter covering the computer industry and technology issues. Every business morning, the company would FAX a four page newsletter to its customers' offices. Each newsletter was custom designed and would contain only articles on subjects in which the customer had indicated interest.

Sounds like a great product right? A newsletter, 100% relevant to your needs, with no wasted information. Unfortunately, because of the large investment in technology necessary to create and deliver the newsletters, the newsletter was offered at a price of £1000 per year. As the marketing tests proved, no matter how much they loved the newsletter, prospects would not subscribe at £1000 per year, and the company went out of business. The lesson: even breakthrough products must be affordable.

Good product but small prospect universe - Companies must be able to amortize their initial investments in technology and marketing among a number of customers. For instance, a product that costs £100,000 to develop and sells for £10 would need sales of 10,000 units just to amortize its start-up expenses. And this does not consider all subsequent selling and distribution costs. This is why one of the first steps to take in new product research is to identify the size of the prospect universe as precisely as possible. Make sure you identify all sources, because you want to define the largest potential market.

You don't do this so that your head can swell with all the money you're going to make, but rather, because you know that certain prospect segments will not prove fruitful and your market is likely to be somewhat less than the potential universe. Obviously, it is better to find out this information as early as possible.

PRICING ISSUES

Perhaps the most perplexing issue to decide about the new product is how to price it. While it is beyond the scope of this book to delve into the myriad of pricing strategies, there are a couple of basics:

First, remember that the objective when pricing is not to maximize sales but to maximize profits. So the bottom-line is to sell the product at the highest possible price that brings in the greatest amount of profit. However, this is not the case when add-on sales are so important that it is permissible to forego some short-term profits for greater long-term gain.

It must also be noted that it is always much easier to lower the price in the future than raise the price, and also that the price you initially set will have an impact on the consumer's perception of the product's value.

There is a story that illustrates this point. Two Indians were sitting by the side of the road behind seemingly identical piles of blankets. One was holding a sign that said, "Blankets For Sale

£2.95." The other held a sign stating, "Blankets For Sale £4.95." After carefully examining both sets of wares, a curious tourist asked the second Indian, "Your blankets are the same as the £2.95 blankets. Why do you charge more?" "That's easy," he said. "Some people would rather pay £4.95."

NEW PRODUCT MARKETING IDEAS

Follow these additional tips to get the most out of your new product introduction:

- Analyze your market by segments, not as one amorphous mass. Then tailor your marketing strategy to these identifiable segments. The words you should live by: "Target Marketing." The words you should forget: "Mass Marketing."
- Don't introduce more than one product at a time, unless they are very closely related. It confuses the marketplace and dilutes your marketing focus.
- A new product doesn't have to be revolutionary. In fact, very few new products can be described this way. Your task as a marketer is to make the ordinary seem extraordinary.
- Positioning is critical for a new product. Re-read the earlier chapter on positioning before you announce the product. Establish your positioning statement and make sure that all your marketing activities support this statement.
- Make sure you thoroughly understand who the real customer is and concentrate your efforts accordingly. Often, it will be the end user, but sometimes the dealer or retailer will be much more important to your success.
- Existing products can often be revitalized and marketed as new. For years, packaged goods manufacturers gave sales a boost simply by adding the words, "New

and Improved" to the outside of the package. Yet, not one consumer in a dozen could accurately describe what was "new and improved" about the product.

■ Think "different" and think "unique." You must create the illusion of difference even if none exists.

■ Don't forget the emotional side of marketing. As I stated earlier, people often buy for emotional reasons and justify their purchase with logical reasons. Never forget this.

26

FUND-RAISING

How To Bring in the Fund-raising Dollars

Fund-raising is big business. In 1992, voluntary donations to the top 400 UK charities topped £1.4 billion. Children's charities and Third World top the list of recipients in the UK, but donations are also vital to the following:

- Education
- Human services
- Hospitals and health care
- Humanities and the arts
- Political causes and lobbying groups
- Wildlife and the environment.

People who donate come from all walks of life. However, depending on the cause, fund-raising experts have found that certain groups are much more likely to give. For example in the US:

- Women give more than men.
- The middle-aged and elderly give more than younger Americans.
- Democrats are more likely to give to non-political and social action causes than Republicans.
- Liberals give more than moderates and conservatives.
- Giving increases as income rises until donors reach upper middle class status, then it falls.
- Professionals and executives give the most, followed by retirees and white collar workers. Only a small percentage of blue collar workers donate.

SETTING UP A FUND-RAISING PROGRAMME

Establishing an ongoing programme to raise funds for a non-profit entity has much in common with commercial marketing. But you must recognize the differences as well. Ask yourself these seven questions to get your programme off to a good start. Periodically review your answers to these questions, even if you have a mature programme.

1. What is your reason for being? Consider your answer to this question as the mission statement that will guide all your fund-raising activities. To be effective, the mission statement should be unique, particularly if there are other groups now providing the same types of programmes and services. It should also be compelling since you will be competing for the same funds as many other organizations.

For instance, an international children's organization could either define its mission as saving children from the ravages of hunger and poverty or it could focus on educating third-world children to enter the industrialized world. A medical school has the alternative of defining its mission as educating the finest doctors or providing a first-class education to low-income students.
One of these missions is not necessarily more important than another but it is important to keep the focus on one overriding priority.

2. Where is the need? Your mission must not be created in a vacuum; it has to answer true human needs. You must be able to precisely identify those individuals who will be served by your programs and services. And the more you can humanize the need at the individual level, the more effective you will be.

3. What is your answer to the need? According to Roland Kuniholm, author of <u>Maximum Gifts by Return Mail</u> (an excellent book on fund-raising), people respond to real emergencies. But if the need is stated too strongly, you may imply that no solution is possible. Kuniholm suggests balancing the emergency need with some convincing promise of success, as well as proof of past achievements. Remember, anytime you outline a problem you must also supply the solution.

4. Who will give to support your cause? Sometimes a worthy group fails only because it lacks a sufficient number of potential donors to fund it adequately. Techniques of finding prospect lists are covered later in this chapter and also in the chapter on mailing lists. As with commercial marketing, choosing the target audience will

be your most important marketing activity.

5. How will we communicate with our marketplace? A key component of any programme is the choice of media that you will use to communicate your message and generate contributions. Media choice will be influenced by: where potential donors live; demographics such as age, income, and sex; what they read, watch and listen to; and their values and attitudes. Types of communication tools to consider:

- Direct mail
- Telemarketing
- Direct response television
- Radio
- Public service announcements
- Door-to-door campaigns
- Workplace promotions
- Special events

6. What are our objectives for the programme? The more specific and measurable the objectives, the more likely you are to achieve those objectives. Categories to include:
   A. Total revenue to be generated
   B. Revenue breakdown by media and campaign source
   C. Number of new donors to be added
   D. Average contribution size
   E. Percentage of funds received that go to fundraising

This last objective is very important. As a new group, you will probably find it necessary to pour a large percentage (maybe all) of the funds you generate on your initial prospecting efforts back into fund-raising.

Once you have a large base of donors, the proportion of funds going into programmes and services can increase dramatically. The best managed national groups devote 75 to 90 percent of all funds to programmes and services. Because of the many fund-raising scams publicized in the late 1980s and early 1990s, donors are becoming increasingly educated and will demand greater efficiency and accountability from groups which ask for money.

7. How will we track contributions and maintain contact with our donors? Donors are the most valuable resource of any non-profit group. Failure to accurately track and acknowledge individual contributions and communicate with donors on an ongoing basis will be viewed as a lack of appreciation. And donors who feel unappreciated stop giving.

WHAT MAKES A GOOD FUND-RAISER

I believe that five personal qualities are important for an individual to succeed in fund-raising:

- **Ability to sell intangibles**. Certain marketers are great at promoting products that they can see and touch. But fund-raisers must be able to sell that which can't be seen and touched.
- **Commitment**. The best fund-raisers believe deeply in the causes they promote. They are the type of people who would give to the organization even if they were not paid to promote it.
- **Passion**. Good fund-raisers take their jobs very seriously. Sometimes this passion manifests itself in the tendency to exaggerate the attributes of their organiza-

tions. But they are not individuals who do things half-way. The combination of commitment and passion is necessary to write the type of copy that motivates people to reach for their cheque books.

■ **Education**. Two types of knowledge are important to the fund-raiser. First, an in-depth understanding of what is going on in the world. Second, a solid grounding in the techniques of successful fund-raising. Without this background, it is very easy to make costly mistakes.

■ **Creativity**. After receiving a grounding in the fundamentals, what really separates the successful from the average fund-raiser is the ability to develop highly creative programmes. Competition for funds is so fierce that you must find ways to stand out from the crowd to get your message heard and responded to.

NINE MASTER MARKETER
FUND-RAISING STRATEGIES

Follow these nine strategies to guarantee success in achieving your funding objectives:

Strategy One - Practice Consistent Positioning. Establish a position statement for the organization. This statement should identify the major purpose of the group (its "reason for being") and it should be carried through every communication with donors or prospects. Never allow anything to be published or distributed under your name which violates this position statement.

Strategy Two - Build Donor Relationships. Direct mail has traditionally been a "personal" medium. We remember (and keep) letters from friends and family long after phone calls are forgotten. If you are using direct mail to solicit funds, take advantage of its personal nature by adopting a one-to-one, individual-to-individual style when you write to donors. Your purpose is to be thought of as a friend by the donor, not as an impersonal organization.

Strategy Three - Thank Your Donors. The best way to turn small-dollar, infrequent donors, into large-dollar, frequent donors, is to implement a formal programme to acknowledge all contributions. The purpose of a thank-you programme is to build the relationship between the donor and your group, and to continue the pleasant feelings the donor had when he first sent the contribution. Two keys to an effective acknowledgement programme are to reply promptly (within days) and to continue the one-to-one writing style of the original communication.

Strategy Four - Ask Often. The most successful organizations have discovered an important fact; the more often they mail, the more money they raise. It's no secret why churches and religious organizations raise the most money. They ask most often (as much as 52 times a year in the case of local churches). Many groups which raise funds by mail should be mailing between eight and 14 times each year.

If your organization relies on small-pound donors there is another reason to mail more often. People with low- or fixed-incomes do not have the cash-flow to make large lump-sum donations but can often be encouraged to give a lesser amount more frequently.

Strategy Five - Upgrade Your Donors. You should always be thinking about ways to increase the average dollar contribution amount from each segment of your file. Fifteen pound donors should be turned into £25 donors, and £25 donors should be converted into £50 donors. The best way to do this is to specifically ask for an amount larger than the largest previous gift; but not much larger since you don't want to ask a £15 donor for £50. High-value givers can also be sent different appeals than low-value givers.

Strategy Six - Treat Donors with Respect. There will be times when your donor file isn't producing the amount of revenue that you think it should. You may even feel that donors are acting "disloyal" by not giving more. But never give into these feelings by taking any actions that damage the long-term relationship with your donors, even if these actions raise more money in the short-term. Some of the things you should never do:

- Lie to your donors.
- Threaten to shut down the group unless you receive a certain amount (unless you really mean it).
- Threaten to fire the organization's employees (even if you do mean it).
- Imply that the donor is disloyal for not responding.
- Wildly exaggerate the issue of your appeal.
- Send a new appeal right on top of an unsuccessful appeal.
- Change your position statement to reflect current conditions.

Strategy Seven – Ask Companies. Companies provide less than 10 percent of all donations. They also have different motivations for giving than individuals and should be approached in a different manner. But if you feel your organization's mission has relevance to companies, by all means, start a corporate fund-raising program. Consider these types of appeals: employee matching gifts, donations of products and services, corporate sponsorship of events and locally-based affinity programs.

Strategy Eight - Prospect Aggressively. Much of this chapter focuses on methods of raising funds from existing donors. But equally important is an aggressive programme of prospecting for new donors. This is so because 15 to 40 percent of your donor file will be lost each year due to death, moves, loss of interest, financial difficulty, etc. You need to replace these donors lost to attrition in order to remain even, let alone grow.

Response rates to prospect lists are much lower than to existing donor lists and many prospecting programmes break-even or lose money. But this is acceptable because new donors are highly profitable when lifetime value is calculated.

Conversion ratios can be used to determine your level of prospecting activity. In a simplified example: if your goal is to replace 1,000 donors lost to attrition each year, and your average rate of response to prospecting mailings is 1.0%, you will need to mail 100,000 packages each year to replace the 1,000 donors (100,000 x 1.0% = 1,000).

Strategy Nine - Continually Monitor Results. Results analysis can have a big impact on both existing donor and prospecting programmes. The most important step is to capture all relevant response data including: list source, mail date, package mailed, appeal, average donation, response rate (by list and package), marketing cost, total revenue, cost per response and quantity mailed. This information can then be used to improve the cost-effectiveness and results achieved on subsequent promotions.

DIRECT MAIL FUND-RAISING

Virtually all national interest groups use direct mail as part of their fund-raising media mix. Direct mail works because it is a personalized medium, allowing you to use the information you have on each prospect and donor.

Almost all direct mail fund-raising is structured as a one-step process. In other words, you send the prospect one package which asks him to send money or make a pledge. Two-step offers are usually not effective in fund-raising, unless you are asking for a great deal of money.

Many self-mailer package formats have been tried in fund-raising, but few have proven successful. So, when in doubt, use an envelope package. And the most necessary component in the package is the letter, which is always the heart of a fund-raising package. Nothing is as effective in causing a prospect to reach for her cheque book as a well-written letter.

Some secrets of writing a great fund-raising letter:

- Use a lot of emotion. Remember, you are selling an intangible. Fund-raising letters must be written for the heart, not the brain (sell with emotion and justify with logic).
- Use case histories, particularly individual histories. Don't focus on 100,000 starving Africans but talk about how a specific African mother must slowly watch her two year old daughter die because she can't feed her. Believe it or not, people will more readily respond to the one than the 100,000.
- Get personal. A fund-raising letter must always be written as if from one individual to another. If the budget allows, address the individual by name. This is particularly important if you are writing to previous donors. And if you are mailing to a number of different prospect segments, consider using a unique letter for each segment.
- Tell a story. Everyone loves to hear a story. A good story will capture a prospect's attention and present your message better than self-serving statements. What makes a good story? The same elements that make a good fairy tale. A great plot, a hero, a villain, a seemingly insurmountable problem, and in the end, a solution (the "happily ever after").

- Tie your appeal into a hot current issue. When your appeal is related to a topic which is in the news, it magnifies the strength of the letter.
- Be specific about what the contribution will be used for. People must feel their gift will be used for a real need and not for general administrative purposes or for raising more funds.
- Tell the donor exactly what you want him to do (e.g. "Fill out your survey form and send it in with your £25 contribution"). Quantify the amount of the donation you want and also give the person a range of choices.
- Create a sense of urgency. Make the prospect feel that you need a donation today. Your goal is to get the person to immediately respond and not to put the letter down for future consideration.
- Write long letters. People often tell me that they don't read long letters. I think what they mean to say is that they don't read long letters on topics that don't interest them. The fact is, all other things being equal, the long letter almost always pulls greater response than the shorter letter.

FUND-RAISING APPEALS

The appeal is an important part of the direct mail package. By appeal, I am referring to a combination of the underlying theme of the mailing along with the specific offer - what you are giving the prospect in return for her contribution. This can range from a sense of satisfaction to a premium of some type. Appeal strategies which have worked well include:

- Membership. The prospect's contribution buys him a membership in your organization. Being a member conveys more status than being just another donor.

- Temporary membership. The prospect is sent a membership card which automatically makes her a "temporary member" in your organization. A contribution must be sent to make the membership permanent.
- Premiums. If the premium is unique and valuable to the prospect, it can greatly enhance revenue. You can often increase results with something as simple as a free membership card.
- Involvement devices. An involvement device is anything that requires the prospect to do something other than write a cheque. Involvement devices include surveys, petitions and peel-off, stick-on labels.
- Gifts. Gifts differ from premiums because they are sent with the initial package (front-end) instead of being given only in return for a donation. Although no contribution is required from the prospect, many people feel obligated to send something to "buy" the gift. Gift items range from return-address labels to Christmas cards and books.
- Special recognition. In return for making a donation of a certain amount, the prospect gets his name added to an "Honour Roll" or to a plaque on the new hospital wing. The special recognition strategy is useful for inspiring existing donors to give larger contributions.
- Certificates. Another form of recognition. The new donor gets a handsome certificate (suitable for framing) attesting to her value to your organization.
- The test. This type of package asks the reader to "take a test" to find out how much he knows about a certain issue or how his knowledge compares to others. Tests are irresistible to many people, especially if they appeal to the prospect's curiosity.

RAISING FUNDS BY TELEPHONE

In the US, approximately 20 percent of total charitable contributions are generated by telephone, either as the sole means of solicitation, or as a follow-up to a direct mail, television or print advertisement.

I believe that telemarketing is most effective in a two-part campaign. In a two-part campaign, the prospect first receives a direct mail package, which is followed-up with a telephone call. The telephone rep references the direct mail package and asks the prospect to make a pledge. Letters with reply forms and return envelopes are then immediately sent to those people who pledge.

Using a combination mail/telephone programme, results can be achieved which are double or triple what each of these mediums achieve individually, with a larger average contribution.

DIRECT MARKETING IDEAS FOR FUND-RAISING SUCCESS

- Always test your programmes before committing a lot of money. Consider testing lists, appeals, offers, package formats, contribution levels and copy.
- Use public relations to magnify the power of your direct marketing programmes.
- Spend plenty of time working on your reply device. Use it as a selling tool. Restate the offer and make sure all necessary details are covered. Leave plenty of room for everyone to write in their names and addresses.
- Use either a powerful teaser on the outer envelope or make the package look like personalized correspondence.
- Use a lift note (see chapter on direct mail for explanation). It should help you "lift" response.
- Except in rare circumstances, you will be better off dropping the brochure from your package, since the brochure will often decrease response.

- Respond quickly to new donors with a thank-you note. And while you're at it, tactfully ask for a second contribution.
- Use response lists when available, particularly lists of donors to similar causes. They should pull a greater number of responses than compiled lists.

27

INTERNATIONAL MARKETING:
HAVE IDEA - WILL IT TRAVEL?

by Drayton Bird

Two famous fashion designers were recently asked how they felt about global marketing. "There's no question about it. Global marketing is absolutely the thing," said Calvin Klein. "It's a small world," agreed Ralph Lauren.

International marketing is hardly new: the ancient Phoenicians used to come to Cornwall to barter their goods for tin; the Chinese exported silk to the Roman Empire. One of the main sources of knowledge about early times is archaeological discoveries of traded goods.

What is relatively new is the idea that you can take the same product and market it in much the same way with the same advertising all over the world. The proponent of this thesis was Professor Theodore Levitt, whose idea that you can gain enormous economies through mass producing what you make in just a few huge plants carefully sited around the globe, is very seductive. If you can add further economies by having one advertising campaign everywhere, merely translated into the appropriate local language with a few small changes, so much the better. There is no doubt that this has proved possible for many.

But what kinds of products and services are likely to succeed internationally? What sort of problems should you look out for? And how should you prepare yourself to succeed? In this chapter I shall try to answer these three critical questions, with a number of examples to make the subject come alive.

Much of my career has been in direct marketing so many of my own experiences relate to that, but I see no great difference between the essential principles you must apply whatever your chain of distribution. Equally, although some of my examples date back quite some time, I have seen no real difference in what matters.

I first encountered the realities of international marketing as a young creative director with an advertising agency nearly 30 years ago. We had certain clients whose products and services were advertised and promoted in many countries. The following examples give you an insight into some of the factors governing success. It is useful to see what made an identical approach impractical in many cases.

TWO COUNTRIES SELLING THE SAME THING – DIFFERENTLY

Two of my clients were countries: Britain and Greece, each selling its tourist attractions. In the first case, all we had to do was offer a free brochure in advertisements all over Europe touting the attractions of my native land. This did very well: Britain was a famous country; potential tourists all wanted a free brochure.

The Greeks had a very different problem. Although everybody

knew – vaguely – about Homer, Ulysses and the Parthenon, modern Greece was a new – vaguely –tourist destination, and few people knew much about it. What were today's Greeks like? Were the hotels good? What about restaurants? In their advertising we concentrated on informing people about such practical things – the thousands of miles of beautiful beaches, the warm weather and the welcoming nature of the people. The slogans we used were: "Greece greets you warmly" and "Summer lasts in Greece from April to October".

For our market – Northern Europeans, starved of the sun – this made perfect sense. Of course, had we been trying to attract people from Spain or Italy, you will realise we would have needed a different approach. They already had sun, beaches and vivacious neighbours.

Had we been conducting really sophisticated marketing, we should have segmented the appeal of our advertising for those two destinations. That's because in some countries in Europe – particularly France and Germany – people are far more interested in historical monuments than in others. So in fact an identical appeal was not perfect for marketing these two countries but it worked pretty well.

Believe it or not, we had a *third* holiday client, a company which created package tours, and sold them directly to the British populace.

What would have happened if this company tried to sell their holidays in other countries? They would have had considerable difficulty, because at that time the concept of the package tour was quite unknown in most countries: Britain pioneered this to a large extent.

Sometimes, there are cultural reasons why a product or approach has a special appeal. My next example – of a cigarette brand, State Express 555 – illustrates this. It will be clear to you that people smoke cigarettes for a number of reasons, none physically beneficial, though some people clearly gain psychological benefits.

In fact, State Express 555 was a declining brand and is no longer available on the UK market. But it was, and still is, very popular in the Far East, partly for the simple reason that the Chinese regard the 555 as a favourable set of figures.

Often other local peculiarities matter. Another client sold washing machines. At that time the British market was quite unique (and strange) in that we had washing machines that were divided in two halves. The left hand side was a tub that washed; on the right hand side was a tub that spin dried; and if you wanted to tumble dry, you had yet another machine. In the rest of the world, they sensibly had normal automatic washing machines with one tub.

Our client was the first person to realize what a great opportunity existed in Britain, and imported a machine from Italy with one tub which fulfilled all functions. In the advertising we had to tell people what the machine did. In no other country would this have been necessary, nor would the mere existence of this machine have occasioned any comment.

WHAT MAKES THE PERFECT PRODUCT?

I discovered my first perfect global product when I left my advertising job and took over the task of marketing the Bullworker, a physical fitness device, guaranteed to make you big and strong.

At that time there was one product in this field which was universally successful: the Charles Atlas course. It was successful quite simply because all over the world there are young men – and sometimes not so young men – who want to be big and strong.

The Bullworker was a more appealing product than the Charles Atlas course – and in international marketing as any- where else, a better product is, naturally, the thing you need. I soon discovered that the advertisements I was writing in Britain were working with no change at all in many countries around the world. Indeed, to illustrate how international marketing is nowadays, in early 1993 I met an Indian gentleman in Hong Kong who had been running my copy to sell the Bullworker very successfully in Nigeria all those years ago.

In a surprising number of instances I have seen exactly the same creative approach work in many countries. American Express, for instance, ran a letter for many years soliciting cardmembers, which began "Quite frankly, the American Express Card is not for everyone." It worked almost everywhere in the world. Money is a universal language and so is status. A form of payment which confers prestige and also makes it easier to pay makes sense everywhere.

I once wrote some advertising copy for a cookery course in England which ran successfully in France, as well as a number of other countries. But the idea that a British product about cookery could sell in France always struck me as astonishing – especially as the copy was pretty much a word for word translation of what I had written.

If you have a successful product in one market, it can do well elsewhere as long as the motivation in that market is the same and no local conditions exist to distort it.

Everybody wants to know what's going on: magazines like Time, The Financial Times, The Economist and The Wall Street Journal do well everywhere. Everybody wants to know about strange parts of the world and exotic animals. So at the upper end of the market, The National Geographic Magazine prospers universally; at the bottom end of the market, mail order traders sell collections of cards which feature animals.

The growth of worldwide media empires, such as that of Rupert Murdoch or Time Warner, reminds us that any area of communication, by its nature, is likely to have an international implication. Names like Hutchison, AT&T and Bertelsmann come to mind immediately.

People like to be clean and attractive, so soap, shampoo, detergent and toothpaste do well. People like to keep their babies clean and attractive, so nappies like Huggies or Pampers also succeed. People like to stay alive and healthy, so pharmaceutical products travel well. People have to eat and drink, so McDonald's and Coca Cola are universally successful. People want to make their businesses run better. IBM was one of the first and most successful international companies. Xerox, Microsoft and Apple are other international brands that have prospered.

Of course, people have to advertise what they sell, so there are large successful international advertising chains operating all the way from Helsinki to Beijing. Finally, the whole world continues its infatuation with the motor car; and the motor industry is one of the most international of all.

It would be boring to recite all the types of business that are likely to have international appeal. However, it will be clear to you that those that cater for *basic* human needs and emotions are likely to do well.

Agricultural products, clothing, electronics, luggage, gourmet products, entertainment. It is a big list, and you can easily think of examples, from Benetton to Tina Turner; from Gucci to Sony.

One man, Joseph Segel, has been involved in the launch of two activities, one of which has worldwide appeal and the other of which I have no doubt will too. The first is the Franklin Mint. Years ago Segel perceived that there existed a market of people who wished to collect desirable objects but didn't know what they ought to collect. He set about creating a business which would produce such objects ready-made for them. The Franklin Mint, as far as I know, does well everywhere in the world.

After selling the Franklin Mint, a few years later Mr Segel leapt into the fray again by launching a home shopping network called QVC. This too made sufficient appeal for him to be able to sell it successfully to Barry Diller in 1992. Once again he hit upon something everybody appreciated, the ability to see something on the screen and buy it then and there.

BUT WHAT ABOUT YOUR PRODUCT?

But the question you will be asking yourself is: how can I be sure that the product I have, which seems to *me* to have international appeal, really will travel? What do I have to look out for? What are the first steps I should take?

I suggest that in the first place you arm yourself with a very simple principle which I wrote down about ten years ago. I observed from experience that – as I put it – "men are more united by their similarities than divided by their differences". This is encouraging. But I also added a warning note, "profit from similarities; allow for differences."

To do this you must learn what those similarities and differences are. You must conduct extensive, careful research. What happens when you don't was told to me by a senior Unilever executive in Thailand – with some pleasure, since it was about one of his US competitors.

It seemed, quite rightly, to his competitors that the Japanese had babies and probably would appreciate the idea of the disposable nappy. So this company went into the Japanese market and lost millions; they neglected to observe a few simple facts. The first was that Japanese babies are smaller than American babies. The second was that Japanese consumers are much more demanding than American consumers and expect products to fit perfectly. The third was that Japanese mothers are more fussy than American mothers, and do not want a nappy which will absorb a lot of moisture and stay on for a long time; they change nappies much more frequently – as much as five times a day.

A general once said that time spent on reconnaissance is never wasted. So let's compare the approach of this large American company with that of Honda when they came into America to sell motorbikes. They opened up a very modest establishment on the West Coast and spent quite a long time studying the market and allowing people to try their motor bikes, to see if they would do well. They immediately noticed precisely the reverse of that which the American company failed to notice: Americans have larger bottoms than the Japanese. These and other things led them to adapt their product appropriately.

It is worth quoting a little bit more from Messrs Klein and Lauren, who both made the same point when talking about international marketing. Lauren remarked: "It's not easy to do . . . it takes organization. It's trial and error". However he certainly enjoys the rewards, because he commented that his number one account was Japan where he even designed the uniforms of the boy scouts. Calvin Klein said: "It is not easy to distribute everything you do throughout the world. It is a complicated procedure about distributors, showrooms and manufacturing. So many things to work out".

SIXTEEN PRACTICAL QUESTIONS

So let's look at the questions to ask and the steps you should take. The first is the most important.

1. **Study the Prospective Market Properly and Visit it.** My associate Gordon Ellis-Brown, former INMAC International Creative Director, now advises companies considering export from the United States to Europe. "Amazingly some people don't even *visit* their prospective markets", he reports. It's not enough to send juniors; you must see the market yourself. Failure to do this can cost you dearly.

   I advise you to read the local trade press. Attend any relevant conferences. Meet suppliers. Talk to trade associations. Find out who the acknowledged experts are. Do all the things you would do if you were starting out at home. Obvious. But often overlooked.

2. **What Cultural Differences Exist?** Here is a quote from the journal of the Euro-Asia Center, a division of INSEAD. "So much has been written about cultural differences that by now it might be expected that greater understanding should exist

416

everywhere. Unfortunately, the same mistakes are still being made. Australians think that because they are casual, more easy going people, Asians like them better. They they slap the Chinese on the back, drink beer in the office in a Moslem country . . . and wonder why there is conflict. Americans want to get in there, negotiate the contract and get out again. It's quick, it's clean and it's easy. But it isn't Asian."

Often, motivations are the same between countries although culture is not. For one company I learned that linking offers to particular holidays in the UK – Christmas, Valentine's Day or Easter – worked very well. I suggested to Chinese colleagues that they link their offers to occasions like the Moon Festival and the Chinese New Year. It worked. Same principle; different culture.

3. **How do Business Practices Differ?** When I was at Ogilvy & Mather my colleagues in Germany ran a very successful advertisement aimed at secretaries. The thing that made it so good was that it was all set in shorthand, so only secretaries could understand it. I was thinking of trying it in England, but before doing so I conducted a little research. I got my secretary to find out how many of her colleagues at Ogilvy & Mather Direct in London could do shorthand. The answer was only one in five. So I decided not to try to transplant that little activity.

For one company we wished to use the service engineer as an important link in the selling task. After all, he has a good stable relationship with the customer and is seen by that customer, not as a salesman, but as a credible source of information. But we couldn't do it in Denmark, because the trade unions will not allow the service engineer to be involved in any sort of task associated with selling.

4. **How are Decisions Made?** Discover how decisions are made within companies. The differences between countries are greater than you might imagine.

I found out recently for my client, INSEAD, that a very

similar effect operates when selling Executive Business Courses. Decision-making in some countries is much more individualistic – the executive has much more power over whether he is allowed to go to a course. In others the boss decides, and certainly the human resource people will have a much bigger say in what happens.

5. **What Values do People Have?** What could be more wholesome, American and lovable than Barbie, who has won hearts all over the world – and, more to the point, is the biggest selling toy of all time? But when first introduced in Spain, Barbie caused quite a few problems. The children loved the product. But the average Spanish parent saw Barbie as something of a wild thing. Her lifestyle and clothing were altogether too funky for the average sheltered Spanish girl – at any rate in their view.

6. **What Stage is the Market At?** This is often critical. For instance, when I was working with American Express in Taiwan, the concept of having a bank account and a cheque book was not universally accepted. This was a cash driven society. A bank account was seen as a sign of prestige. The most effective way of launching the American Express Card was to offer it linked with a bank account that gave you a cheque book.

7. **How is your Product Perceived?** A good example is a famous brand in most countries, the Mercedes motor car. In Britain and America it's seen as a prestige car; in most of Europe and indeed in many countries throughout the world, it is seen as a taxi.

   Or take Tang – just an ordinary soda drink in most countries. But in India it is seen as a luxury and sold at a very high price – in fact eight times as much as you would have to pay in the US. To understand the real significance of this you have to appreciate that the average income in India is around $100 a year.

8. **What's the Media Situation?** You will discover wide varia-

tions from country to country. In some countries you will not find nearly as much TV time available as in the US; in others you will find a much more pervasive national press – both factors which will influence your media planning radically.

One thing you can do in the US but can't so easily elsewhere is to target competitive users through widely available lists and proprietary databases. For instance, Dove is being rolled out all over the world. The original US programme for Dove targeted competitive customers, such as Ivory users. The brand is now being promoted in places as varied as England, New Zealand and even India. In none of these countries is it as easy to target competitive users.

9. **Will Legislation Affect you?** Nearly 30 years ago I ran the marketing for a company which sold a "stop smoking" product. It worked brilliantly in France where the name of the company was the Anti Tobacco Centre. This sounded very official. In the UK we discovered we were not allowed to use that name. We also learned it was illegal to offer a money back guarantee, which was important to the advertising. The business never flourished.

    The way I have sometimes put it to American colleagues is that in the US, generally, they allow you to do something, and then if they think it's illegal, they will prosecute you. Very often in other countries – particularly Northern Europe – you aren't allowed to do it in the first place.

10. **Look Very Carefully to Establish what Competition Already Exists or will Exist.** As you move into new markets, remember that not only are domestic companies already entrenched there; there are also other exporters moving in to compete with you.

    Consider alliances. When you're reviewing, you may come across companies which are doing the same sort of thing as you in a similar way. You may find it worth working *with* them rather than *against* them. I would add, by the way, that if you study the way in which the Japanese have entered many markets – particularly the United States – this is precisely what they have done.

11. **Should your Product be Changed?** Keep your eye open for new opportunities which might enable you to develop new products, or adapt existing products. It may be impossible to transfer existing products and promotions without change. But perhaps some markets are so lucrative that you ought to consider special products and special marketing to enter them. Germany would be a good example.

12. **Where Should you Start?** Decide where it is easiest to conduct your test marketing. In Europe, for instance, some countries are more appealing than others for the would-be exporter. American companies like the UK, because the language is similar yet not identical, as you will undoubtedly discover. The Netherlands is centrally situated, people speak English for the most part and it has a strong international trading tradition.

You would be surprised at the number of companies which see an export opportunity, commit to it – and then proceed to mess things up considerably. Companies which you would otherwise think of as being highly professional, behave in the most amateur fashion.

Many neglect the following *very* basic points.

13. **Make Sure you are Properly Funded.** Do you really have enough money for what you want to do to cope with the competition and opportunities that confront you? It is easy to underestimate this factor.

14. **What about Responsibilities?** Who is going to have responsibility in each country – if you are going into more than one – for marketing? Who is going to have overall responsibility for the international marketing?

15. **Do you have Staff with Multinational and Linguistic Experience?** I can tell you that in most cases the answer is "no", but people with these skills are utterly essential. Imagine

going to a business meeting in your own country and not understanding a word that was said.

16. **Do you Think Internationally or Not Within your Company?** This may seem an obvious question, and possibly even mildly offensive, since you wouldn't be reading this, one would imagine, unless you thought internationally. But in my experience, thinking internationally means a great deal more than saying "Wouldn't it be great to export and make pots of money".

There has to be somebody senior within your company with a burning desire to operate internationally. Probably somebody who themselves has international experience and a very broad cultural frame of reference.

It would take a sizeable book, not just a chapter, to tell you everything you need to know about the wonderful opportunities and the equally great perils and pitfalls international direct marketing offers. However I hope this chapter gives you a good guide in the right direction.

SECTION VI

MASTER MARKETING GRADUATE SCHOOL

HOW TO BE SUPER CREATIVE

"All behavior consists of opposites...Learn to
see things backward, inside out, and upside down."
Lao-tzu, Tao-te Ching

Where does creativity come from? How can I get it? Is creativity an art, a science, a skill which can be developed, or a talent that a privileged few are born with?

These are interesting questions, but where do we find the answers? It's not just that people don't know how to be creative, they aren't even sure just what creativity is. Perhaps we should start by defining this elusive thing called "creativity."

In his excellent book, <u>A Whack On The Side Of The Head</u>, Roger Von Oech defines creativity as "combining two previously unconnected ideas." As an example, Von Oech uses Gutenberg's invention of the printing press which resulted from combining the wine press with a coin punch.

In a similar vein, the Nobel Prize winning physician Albert Szent-Gyorgyi stated, "Discovery consists of looking at the same thing as everyone else and thinking something different." The actor James Earl Jones defines creativity as simply "digging deeper." Let's follow Jones' example and dig a little deeper.

It is apparent that creativity is closely related with the ability to use our imaginations. If you have trained yourself to only see the obvious, you will always view the world through the existing perception of what is and what is not.

For example, the average person may describe water as a cool liquid which is used to quench thirst. To a swimmer or boater, water is something to recreate or exercise in. To a scientist, that same water is billions of tiny atoms of hydrogen and oxygen, which combine to form molecules of the substance we call water. And to a fish, water represents the totality of his living environment. The same substance has very different meanings when viewed from these different perspectives.

Master Marketers know that all of these definitions are correct. In fact there is no such thing as an incorrect way of looking at something. There is only that which works and that which doesn't work for a particular situation.

CHARACTERISTICS OF CREATIVE PEOPLE

Creative thinkers start with no advantages. They are given exactly the same tools to work with as non-creative thinkers - the same facts and figures, the same universe of prospects, the same product features and benefits, the same number of words and graphic images, the same budgets and the same amount of time to complete their projects.

Scratch a creative person and you will find very little on the surface that could have predicted this aptitude. He may be a high school dropout or a Ph.D. He may be brilliant or only of average intelligence. He may be brash and outspoken or quiet and reserved. He in fact, is just as likely to be a she, since creativity shows no gender preference. Creativity is also not reserved for the young, or old, or even the "right brain thinker" or the "left brain thinker."

Contrary to popular belief, you can't even predict creativity by job function. There are some remarkably creative engineers and accountants (especially around tax filing time), and sadly, some copywriters and art directors that demonstrate very little creativity.

In fact, after working with a number of highly creative individuals, I have found only one common characteristic: the creative person is extremely curious. He or she is curious about not only how people think and act, but why they think and act in certain ways. They are students of the demographic and psychographic changes occurring in society and how those changes affect the marketing process.

How do you know if you are dealing with a creative person? Look for these signs:

- They ask a lot of questions.
- They are very open to new ideas, regardless of the source.
- They are well-read and probably own a library card.
- They are quick to challenge their own assumptions and beliefs.
- They are disciplined and willing to put in many hours of hard work. While some people may be naturally creative, without the application of elbow grease, their creativity will rarely be manifested in superior achievement.
- They strongly believe in the power of words and images to shape human behavior.

THE GREATEST BARRIERS TO CREATIVITY

Following is a list of five habits and attitudes that suppress the creativity that is inherent in all of us:

Creativity Barrier One - Over-reliance on statistics. For many, marketing has become a scientific process. Most of what we do has been attempted before, and detailed statistics have been maintained on successes and failures. For instance, we know that personalizing a direct mail package and including a free call-in response option will increase the quantity and speed of responses. And we know that photographs draw more attention than illustrations in print ads. As useful as information such as this is, it can't make a mediocre promotion successful.

Creativity Barrier Two - Always following the rules. The only thing more dangerous than a statistic is a rule. I agree with the philosopher who said, "Rules are for the guidance of wise men and the obedience of fools." If you are wise, you will make selective use of the rules but will not become dependent on them. And if you are foolish, you will stifle your creativity through over-reliance on the rules.

People who are short on creativity but long on blind faith in the rules suffer from a sort of inner censorship that prevents them from thinking outside the confines of what they consider "normal." These self-imposed boundaries become something of an inner prison. While the creative mind desperately wants to find its wings outside the brick and iron bars, the logical mind refuses to allow this, and insists that all thinking take place within the four walls.

Any individual who suffers from this malady has been blinded by the very rules meant to ensure his success. He may have the science of marketing down pat, but the art falls victim. And no matter how many rules you follow, marketing without an added measure of creativity is boring, boring, boring. And boring does not sell.

Creativity Barrier Three - Me-too-Itis. "Me-Too-Itis" is the term I use for those who play follow-the-leader marketing. Pick up a current issue of a national trade publication and notice how similar the advertisements are in tone, graphics, colors and copy. Do the same with a three-year-old issue of the same publication and you will probably notice a boring sameness to the ads that ran at that time.

There is a certain safety in me-too advertising. People say, "if the ad theme is good enough for IBM, it must be good enough for my company." Unfortunately, if IBM or any industry leader has already used the same concept, the marketplace is liable to credit the larger company for your advertising. And there is never a good reason for you to pay your money to reinforce a larger competitor's advertising campaign.

Creativity Barrier Four - Conventional thinking. Conventional thinking is the "if it ain't broke, don't fix it" mentality. What has worked before will work again, and so forth. There are two problems with this approach. One, conventional thinking rarely produces more than average results — and Master Marketers abhor being average. Two, the traditional approach may be producing lousy results, not average results. The good news is, if you've been practicing traditional marketing, it may only take a small dose of "outside the circle" thinking to vastly improve your results.

Creativity Barrier Five - Self judgement. It is extremely difficult to create and evaluate simultaneously, since the two processes are vastly different. While they both have a valuable role, if your "inner critic" insists on rendering an opinion on everything you are doing in the middle of the developmental process, creativity will suffer. The answer (easier said than done) is to separate the judge from the creator. Always remember this: first create, then evaluate. Never the other way around.

HOW TO FIND GOOD IDEAS

One of the fastest ways to gain a creative edge in marketing is to start an "idea file" (some people refer to them as "swipe files"). Save every interesting ad, brochure and direct mail piece you can get your hands on. A large idea file is sure to help inspire you to find a new creative theme when you need one. And since advertising creative approaches tends to run in cycles, an old idea with a new twist can be very effective.

In fact, much of what passes for creativity could be more accurately labeled as artful plagiarism. Marketer A borrows ideas from Marketer B, who got some of his best ideas from Marketer C, etc. Sometimes this is purely unintentional. There is little you can do that will prove to be completely original. Our world is too big for this to be so. Probably the best we can hope for is to bring our own insights and perspectives to what already exists, to rearrange the pieces of the existing puzzle until they form a unique picture. If you can do this much, you have achieved creativity.

Another important key to creativity is to collect a sufficient amount of information going in to a project. When crafting a creative theme, an offer and the copy necessary to support the offer, you must thoroughly understand the benefits of your product, service or cause that will compel your prospects to act. It is easy to miss benefits (even the primary benefit), so there is no such thing as having too much information in marketing.

USING BRAINSTORMING TO GENERATE IDEAS

Brainstorming is a name given to "a gathering of two or more individuals for the purpose of generating ideas." Brainstorming can be an informal process. When Pam and Howard (two people on our staff) meet over lunch to "kick around a few ideas," they are brainstorming. But while acknowledging that this level of casual interaction can be a powerful way to generate ideas, we are going to consider brainstorming as a more formal process.

Brainstorming works best for strategic issues, such as creative themes and offers, and not for tactical matters, such as which media or lists to use to promote the product. Also, since formal brainstorming sessions are costly in personnel time, it is a process better suited to major, not minor, issues.

The most important consideration in setting up a brainstorming session is who to invite. First, you will need a facilitator. The facilitator's job is to start and end the session, and keep it running smoothly and productively. He or she must have the respect of all participants and be able to deal with various types of people.

It is also a good idea for the facilitator to help choose the individuals who will comprise the brainstorming team. You want enough people to provide several viewpoints, but not so many that reserved individuals are intimidated into silence. Also try to get people from different work backgrounds and departments to participate, such as marketing, sales, finance, product development and administration. Not everyone needs to be an art director or copywriter to contribute good ideas. You will not only get a greater variety of opinions, but those departments which participated will be more likely to cooperate fully in the implementation of the project.

Here are some additional guidelines to make your brainstorming sessions effective:

- Brainstorming is strictly an idea-generating exercise. It is not meant to be a forum for critically evaluating ideas. Every participant must feel free to bring up any idea, however unusual, without fear that it will be criticized or denigrated. In fact, it is best to allow no critical comments of any kind.
- Encourage participants to offer suggestions which build upon previously proposed ideas.
- Quantity of ideas, not quality of ideas, should be

stressed. Quality will come about as a result of quantity. Your objective should be to come up with pages of possible ideas, not just one great idea.

■ If not captured, the best ideas have no value. Someone should be designated to write down all ideas and make this list available after the meeting. However, do not identify the source of each idea as this will inhibit people who do not want to be on the record. Alternately, the sessions may be audio or video-taped.

■ Allow adequate time for the brainstorming session. It sometimes takes time for a team to gel and begin producing the best ideas.

■ People produce the best ideas in a lighthearted environment. Keep things relaxed and fun. Provide snacks, a good brainteaser or ice breaker game to stimulate thoughts and get the ball rolling.

■ Give equal weight to suggestions from all participants. If you invite top executives and their ideas are given extra weight, other employees can be intimidated into silence.

How can you tell when you've had a great brainstorming session? Not only will you have a good quantity of potentially useful ideas, but most importantly, you will probably not be able to remember who was the originator because so many people were feeding off each other's ideas. This will show that your group has truly worked together as a team. And teamwork is what brainstorming is all about.

EIGHT CREATIVITY ENHANCING TECHNIQUES

Here are eight techniques that will help you develop your creative potential:

1. Make use of your creative peak-time. Everyone has different body cycles. Some are more alert and creative in the morning, others later in the afternoon or evening. Find your peak time and arrange your schedule to do your creative thinking during these periods. Likewise, don't waste your peak-time on repetitive, non-creative tasks.

2. Start creative projects with a small commitment. When faced with a large task, we all tend to become over-whelmed - a feeling which often deteriorates into inactiv-ity. One way to counteract this tendency is to break the task into smaller segments. Then, make a commitment to complete only one segment of the project. After finishing the small task, you will usually find it much easier to keep going.

   The fact is, some people have to go into the water by first dipping a toe, then walking in knee-deep, etc. These people are making a small commitment: "If the water is too cold, I'll stop right here." Others are able to make a major commitment by diving in head first. No way is right or wrong as long as it gets you to your objective.

3. When things are not working, get away from the project. Have you ever spent time with a person whose name you couldn't remember? The harder you tried, the more elusive the name became. Then, when the person left, you stopped thinking about it and the name popped into your mind.

   The same thing happens during creative projects. A point will come when greater effort is counterproductive. The best way to clear the cobwebs at such a time is to take your mind completely off the project. Go to the beach, take a walk, work on another project or take a nap on the office couch (make sure you have an under-standing boss). Although you consciously refrain from thinking about the task at hand, your subconscious may develop fresh insights that will become clear when you refocus your attention on the issue.

4. Make the most of your flow experiences. "Flow" is a term used by psychologists to describe those moments when a person is totally absorbed in an experience, is producing at his absolute best and is unaware of time and place. If you've ever become so absorbed in a task that you look up in surprise to note that several hours have passed, you have probably been in a state of flow. Flow experiences can happen on the tennis court, at home playing with your children, at the card table with friends or in the office working on a project. When you find yourself in such a peak state of mind, reach for pen and paper and be ready to develop the best creative concepts of your life.

5. Purge your vocabulary of idea-killers. "Idea-killers" are statements or expressions that stop good ideas dead in their tracks. Some examples of idea-killers:
   "It's too radical."
   "We already tried this."
   "We can't afford to take the chance."
   "It will never work."
   "We don't have the budget."
   "They'll never go for this idea."
   "The client won't like it."
   "Why change? We've always done it this way."

6. Always look for a second answer. There are very few situations where only one solution or one answer to a

creative challenge exists. By training yourself to dig a little deeper, you can almost always come up with different and (sometimes) better alternatives.

We see this phenomenon all the time at our agency. Someone will suggest a creative concept that is immediately proclaimed the "perfect campaign theme." But since we've trained ourselves to search for the second (or third, or fourth) right answer, we are often able to come up with one or more additional ideas that are so good we never present the first "perfect idea" to the client.

7. Start at the ending. Instead of viewing a problem from where you are today, start by visualizing the best possible outcome and then work backwards. The clearer you are able to picture all the details of the ideal end result, the more likely you are to find just the right solution. This backward-forward process works especially well when scheduling complex projects.

8. Take advantage of your unique talents. If you have a particular talent or skill, you may dismiss it because "it comes too easy," and place greater value on that which is difficult for you. For instance, if you have a natural flair for design but struggle mightily with your writing, you may discount your own talent in favor of those who can write well. This can be a very large mistake. Just because something comes easily to you, this does not mean it has lesser value. Beethoven was not meant to be a writer nor Hemingway a composer. Each took his given talents and developed them to the fullest. Don't try to be what you are not and make the most of what you are. This is the essence of creativity.

I hope that this chapter has convinced you that no matter what your past experiences, you can develop the creativity which you already possess. It is not a matter of learning a new skill but rather learning to accept and release that which already resides within you.

EUREKA, I THINK WE'VE ISOLATED THE PART OF THE BRAIN THAT CONTROLS THE BUYING REFLEX.

29

A FORMULA FOR MARKETING SUCCESS

How to Practice the Art of Friendly Persistence

I hope that you have followed the earlier advice in <u>The</u> <u>Master Marketer</u>. If so, you have spent a good deal of time identifying your best prospects and have built a database of qualified prospects. But you must not stop here. You should begin to aggressively market to your database of prospects until each person or company on the database either takes some positive action (responds, donates, buys, etc.) or is somehow disqualified as a legitimate prospect for your offer.

Never put all your marketing resources into one or two expensive programmes. Marketers who use their budgets on one major effort to attract leads or sales are not Master Marketers. They are in love with their own products and offers, and believe others will be equally interested in hearing all the juicy details.

Contrast this with the Master Marketer approach. Instead of one-shot high-risk efforts, Master Marketers boost their results (and spread their risk) over several smaller campaigns. They know it is usually better to spend a little less on each promotion but to go out with more frequent promotions.

You can do the same by developing a marketing schedule that allows you to create a lasting, positive image in the minds of your prospects, and equally important, to catch them at the precise moment they are in a buying or consideration cycle. If you doubt this is true, investigate your own advertising response habits, and you will soon see the need to communicate with your prospects more often.

The following "Formula for Marketing Success" illustrates this principle and shows why a prospect will or will not respond to a particular marketing promotion:

$$\underline{F \times I \times P.I.O. = R}$$

FREQUENCY

The "F" in the formula stands for <u>Frequency</u>, and refers to how often we share our message with our customers and prospects. Frequency refers to all contacts: broadcast, print, mail, telephone and in-person. Frequency is the portion of the formula most neglected, and we'll discuss in a moment why lack of frequency is so deadly to marketing success.

IMPACT

The "I" in the formula stands for <u>Impact</u>, which is the part of the marketing campaign that has the greatest effect on the results of any particular promotion. Without impact, marketing and advertising programmes are lifeless, dull and worst of all, they don't generate response. High impact is achieved with penetrating copy and graphics, compelling offers, enthusiastic telemarketing and professional person-to-person selling.

PROSPECT INTEREST QUOTIENT

Part three of the formula is the variable you have the least amount of control over. "P.I.Q." stands for <u>Prospect Interest Quotient</u>, which is that position your prospect finds himself in at the exact moment he views your commercial, reads your mail package, or receives your telephone call. P.I.Q. is a complex blend of several different elements, some measurable and some not. Here are a few of the elements which make up a prospect's P.I.Q.:

- **Physical Presence**. If your prospect is out of town or on vacation, he can't respond to your offer.
- **Work Load.** A prospect with more time to read the mail has more time to consider your offer.
- **Point on the Buying Cycle**. Where is the prospect in relation to the purchase of the product/service you are offering? For instance, if you contact a prospect shortly after she purchased a competing product, your offer will probably fall on deaf ears.
- **Current Attitudes**. What is the prospect's attitude toward your product/service, company and industry, at the moment he is contacted by you. If these attitudes are negative, they can be changed over time, but this will not help you with the current promotion.
- **Mood**. Have you caught your prospect in a positive and optimistic frame of mind? Or perhaps your mailing arrives when the prospect is in a negative mood. Witness your own response habits and you'll be amazed at the impact mood can have on your willingness to buy a product or contribute to a charitable cause.

RESULTS

The final part of the formula, "R," stands for <u>Results</u>. Results in any marketing campaign are dependent on the first three elements of the formula. And the most neglected portion of the formula is frequency. While we have control over the creative impact our efforts convey, unless we advertise, mail, telephone or visit in-person often enough, we won't catch enough of our prospects in the right Prospect Interest Quotient (P.I.Q.) to make the total campaign a success.

THE ART OF FRIENDLY PERSISTENCE

There is a perception among many marketers that frequent communications "offend" prospects and make them less likely to buy. This is because all promotions are lumped together as being unpleasant and unwanted. I believe this attitude is wrong and the antidote is "friendly persistence." Once a prospect is identified by you as qualified (has the money, authority, need and desire), that prospect should hear from you on a regular basis.

The key is the "friendly" half of the friendly persistence formula. It relates to the manner in which you make contact with your prospect base. For instance, you should never practice hard-sell techniques. While such tactics may win occasional short-term increases in business, they will scuttle your primary mission of building long-term customer relationships.

"Informational mailings" can be mixed in with your other mail programs to show your prospects that you are an expert in your industry and enjoy sharing this expertise to help your prospects and customers. Newsletter mailings can also help establish the right climate so that when you do make contact by phone, or with a sales-oriented mailing package, it is received as a friendly communication.

Susan Fenley, president of Prime Time Communications, advocates the use of entertainment to involve the prospect and to allow for more frequent promotions. In a recent article, she stated, "Of course marketing should be entertaining. After all, you are trying to capture audience interest. Entertaining people with information about your organization or product is an excellent way to gain customers."

HOW OFTEN TO COMMUNICATE

People often ask how frequently they should run promotions to their prospects and customers. While the answer depends on the organization, product or service, and offer, most companies can achieve their objectives by communicating every six to eight weeks. Fund-raising groups and nonprofit associations can go out to their members and donors as often as every four weeks with no decrease in results.

Never advertise just for the sake of it, however. Always have something new to say. Those who repeat the same old tired message in every promotion find their expensive efforts wasted because once the prospect catches on, he quickly tunes out the message. Remember the importance of "Impact" in our formula.

So keep your message interesting, breezy and unique, and you can keep up a busy and productive marketing schedule. In other words, practice the "art of friendly persistence" and never forget the Formula for Marketing Success: Frequency x Impact x Prospect Interest Quotient = Results.

30

RELATIONSHIP MARKETING

How to Keep Your Customers for Life

Most marketing managers feel that their most important promotional objectives are to sell products, generate leads and obtain favourable publicity for their organizations. While these are certainly worthy goals for any results-focused Master Marketer, an equally important and often overlooked objective is to create or build the relationship between your organization and its prospects, customers, members or donors.

There are many facets to building the relationship, including:

- Increasing name awareness in the marketplace.
- Creating greater receptivity for future sales opportunities.
- Establishing a positive image where none exists.
- Upgrading a current image.

■ Changing the dynamics of the relationship with your prospects and customers.

At any point in time, everyone in your marketing universe will either have an opinion about you or not. If they do have an opinion, it will be shaped by factors such as:

■ The number of times they have been exposed to your advertising and/or public relations messages.

■ Their prior contacts with your employees.

■ Their previous use of your products or services.

■ The impressions they have received from other users of your products or services.

■ Their subconscious reactions to your marketing message and promotional materials.

Unknown – Indifferent – Knowledgeable – Occasional User – Satisfied User – Lifetime Customer

Always keep your customers moving along the continuum

Plotted on a continuum, your association with each prospect and customer can range from total indifference to a rich and rewarding business relationship, with a hundred possibilities inbetween. Our obligation is to keep everyone in our marketing universe moving up the continuum at all times. We want to make those who are indifferent knowledgeable and turn satisfied users into lifetime customers.

CIRCLE OF MARKETING INFLUENCE

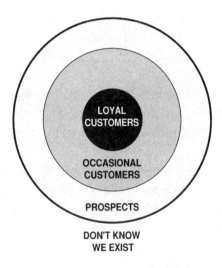

Circle of marketing influence

Another way to illustrate this principle is with a "Circle of Marketing Influence." Starting with your organization at the core, all prospects and customers can be pinpointed somewhere in relation to the center. As those individuals in the outer reaches of our marketing influence are brought closer to us, we say that they are becoming "part of our circle." Those nearest to the core are our loyal, lifetime customers. Those farthest away do not know that we exist.

447

Traditional marketing programmes diagram this movement through the marketing sequence by using terminology such as suspects, leads, cold prospects, hot prospects and customers. And whether you manage this process in a formal manner with a lead tracking system, or informally, by seat-of-the-pants methods, any time you bring individuals into your circle, you are engaged in relationship building.

BUILDING THE RELATIONSHIP VS. MAKING THE SALE

Five major advantages will be gained by marketers who broaden their focus from simply making sales to building relationships. They are:

1. Warm, personal feelings between your organization and its clients can help overcome the unavoidable problems that can otherwise cripple business relationships.

2. An environment of trust makes the working atmosphere smoother and more pleasant for everyone. Your customers are much more likely to give you the benefit of the doubt when a dispute arises.

3. Much more referral business is generated from those you have invested in a relationship with. Remember that a "merely satisfied" customer will probably not mention your company to anyone. But an "unhappy" customer will tell ten people about her negative experience and a "happy, lifetime" customer will encourage ten people to patronize your business.

4. Happy customers are much more profitable and are less likely to quibble over financial matters.

5. Loyal customers give you an extremely strong competitive position. An organization which has invested in building relationships can't be easily dislodged by its competitors.

MARKETING STRATEGIES TO BUILD RELATIONSHIPS

Every part of the marketing programme should be evaluated for its contribution to building relationships. We will look briefly at how the offer, media-mix, message, design and back-end can be fine-tuned for maximizing customer relationships.

Offer - By offer, I am referring to what the prospect receives in return for what you are asking from him in time and dollar resources. An effective offer has two primary requirements:

1. It promises good value for what is asked, and
2. It guarantees unconditional satisfaction.

Customers should feel that your offer proves that you are truly interested in their use and enjoyment of the product. This is not easy to convey, given the disappointments all consumers have faced, but you must try.

One type of offer that helps to build relationships is a free information giveaway. Your willingness to share certain information, with no guarantee of receiving anything in return, helps build a bridge to your prospects. The free information giveaway offer works particularly well for high-value items and small, well-defined prospect universes.

Media Selection - Careful print and broadcast media selection will show your prospects that you are knowledgeable about their needs and wants. Media choice should be based on an in-depth analysis of your existing customer and prospect profiles.

For example, in direct mail, sending large numbers of packages to marginal lists is not only expensive, it is damaging to relationships. This type of indiscriminate marketing spawned use of the term "junk mail." While many in the direct marketing industry feel there is no such thing as junk mail, I disagree. In my judgement, junk mail is any mail that is sent to uninterested, poorly targeted prospects.

For example, I happen to be a sailor but have no interest in gardening. I will willingly read any mail related to sailing, subscribe to several sailing publications, and would rarely refer to mail on this subject as junk mail. But send me a subscription offer for a gardening magazine and I am liable to get on my high-horse about junk mail.

Your prospects feel exactly the same way. They like the mail you send them and the advertisements you run related to their own needs and interests. But to them, everything else is wasted. So every extra minute you spend on prospect identification is time well spent on building relationships.

Message - Each part of your selling copy should convey the theme that your emphasis is on the prospect, not on your product or service. Prospects are more interested in benefits than product features. They want to be spoken to as unique individuals, not as "one of many satisfied users." Your words must indicate that you are interested in establishing long-term relationships, not in reaping short-term profits.

Design - Print advertising and direct mail graphics and package format should reflect your target audience. Designs should be friendly, easy-to-read, and easy to respond to. Use warm colors and pay attention to details such as personalization.

Back-end - Many relationships are spoiled (and sales lost) after the prospect has agreed to try a new product or send away for more information. It never ceases to amaze me how certain organizations can spend so much money to bring in a new customer and then allow that customer to be lost due to stupidity or rudeness. Following are some of the most common relationship killers:

- ■ Failure to respond in a timely manner to a prospect's request for information.
- ■ Failure to fulfill a customer's order on time.
- ■ Rudeness, curtness or hostility toward prospects and customers.
- ■ Lack of concern or lack of empathy for prospects' needs.
- ■ Failure to keep a promise made to a customer.
- ■ Failure to honor the terms of a warranty.

RYAN'S RULES FOR BUILDING RELATIONSHIPS

Follow these four rules to establish and maintain a good relationship with your customers, members or donors:

1. Find out what your customers want. Don't assume you know the answers - ask.

2. Collect as much information as you can about the individuals who buy your products, join your organization or contribute to your cause. Maintain this information on a database so that it can be used to segment and target market the file.

3. Give your customers incentives to become closer to you. Incentives can come in the form of discounts, special offers, premiums, free information and anything else that the customer perceives as having value.

4. Recognize your customers, members or donors often.

Recognition reinforces the message that you care.
Never let your customers think you are taking them for
granted.

VALUE-ADDED MARKETING

Consumers have become irritated by the amount of commer-cial-clutter. With prime-time TV ads up 25% in quantity over the past five years, over-stuffed mailboxes, and promotional messages everywhere (from airplanes flying advertising banners over crowded beaches to ads on rest room walls), it has become almost impossible to escape the deluge of advertising.

To give you an example of the degree of annoyance, in a recent US study, 90% of respondents said that they did not want commercials shown in cinemas. I wonder – who are the 10% who don't mind such commercials?

While commercial-clutter has made traditional advertising more difficult, it does represent opportunities for marketers who practice value-added marketing. "Value-added marketing" re-wards prospects from the first moment they see your promotion, whether or not they decide to become customers.

Try these techniques to add value to your marketing:

Enlighten - People are always hungry for information that makes their personal or professional lives easier and more productive. They will think highly of you if you give them this type of information.

Entertain - Much advertising today is shrill and harsh. Con-sider taking the opposite tack with a lighthearted or humorous approach.

Touch - Advertising that affects the emotions of your audience can be very powerful.

Improve - This type of message shows what your organization is doing to make your community, country or planet a better place. It can range from a retailer sponsoring the local football team, to an international conglomerate changing its business policies to protect the environment.

THREE EXAMPLES OF RELATIONSHIP BUILDERS

Nightingale Conant, Save the Children and U.S. English are organizations that take relationship building seriously and offer valuable lessons in how to stay close to customers, members and donors.

NIGHTINGALE CONANT

Nightingale Conant is a large publisher of audiotapes, videos, books and software on self-improvement, sales training and management skills. Vic Conant, president of the company, places a high value on using research to spot trends. According to Conant, "If we spot a hot new topic on the horizon, we can develop a programme to fill a need almost before the need exists."

When you purchase a Nightingale Conant programme you are not just a customer, you are a "preferred customer." You're not assigned an account number, but rather a "preferred customer number." Orders are taken by a pleasant, knowledgeable customer service person, not a boiler room operator. I have also learned through experience that if you are unhappy with a product for any reason, Nightingale Conant will cheerfully refund your purchase price and even arrange for shipping the product back at their expense.

While in Chicago on business several years ago I happened to drive by the company's headquarters. Stopping in, I introduced myself as a customer and was given a tour of the building. The seriousness that every department places on serving the customer was evident. It's no secret why this 30 year old company is the largest and most successful in its field.

SAVE THE CHILDREN

Save the Children is an international organization with its headquarters in Connecticut. Save the Children's mission is to rescue children from poverty, hunger, ignorance and lack of opportunity. Rather than using traditional fund-raising methods to raise funds, Save the Children asks contributors to become sponsors of a specific child and to make a monthly sponsorship contribution of around £15.

I know something about this organization because eight years ago I began sponsoring a child named Zacharias Santana who lives in a small village in the Dominican Republic. With regular up-dates on Zacharias and a picture and personal letter from him at least once a year, I have been able to follow this young man's development from a small boy to a tall adolescent (and star base-ball player). All Save the Children sponsors can report similar success stories.

In addition to its monthly sponsorship program, the organization generates revenue with special appeals. Before every Christmas, the sponsor receives a holiday card which is to be signed and returned to the sponsored child (along with an extra donation of course). The first paragraph from last year's holiday appeal should give you the flavor of the letter:

"Dear Mr. Ryan,
Just imagine how Zacharias Santana's face will light up with joy this holiday season when your card arrives in Las Matas/Pan De Azucar, bringing with it a very special message for the holidays: "I'm thinking of you, I care about you, and I believe in your future."

This appeal and Save the Children's entire programme, proves that this worthy organization has been successful because it not only knows how to build the relationship between itself and its donors, it also knows how to build relationships between its individual donors and the children they sponsor.

U.S. ENGLISH

U.S. ENGLISH is a non-profit organization founded in 1983 with the goal of getting English designated as the official language of the United States. Debra MacLean, U.S. ENGLISH's former director of development, strongly believes that donor recognition pays off. Two campaigns she developed prove this point.

U.S. ENGLISH decided to print the names of its thousands of members in a full page ad to be run in USA Today. The ad was timed for Thanksgiving Eve, the busiest travel day of the year in the US, to give the organization greater public awareness. A draft copy of the ad, printed on newsprint, was included in the direct mail package. Members were solicited for their opinions on how to improve the ad and were also given the option of excluding their names from the ad (few did).

While a few people reacted negatively to the ad, most loved it. Most important, it created a great deal of excitement among the members and achieved an increase in results of 28 percent over the average special appeal mailing. When the USA Today ad finally appeared, so many members had signed up that U.S. English had to extend the ad to a page and one-half, with ten regional splits.

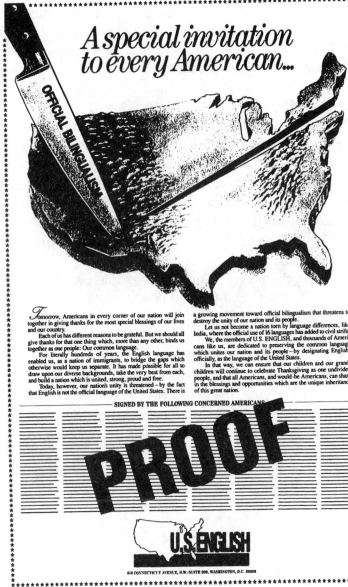

Debra MacLean's second relationship building campaign involved a paperback book. A highly personalized package was sent to major donors. The package, which had seven components, also contained a full draft outline of the book. Donors were asked to sponsor the book project by making a contribution at one of four levels. With a contribution of £100, the donors name would be printed in the book as a recognition of support.

Again, donor involvement and recognition paid off. In fact, the book sponsorship project produced even higher response rates than the <u>USA Today</u> ad campaign. The promotion was also attractive to U.S. ENGLISH's foundation givers, producing grants in the range of £10,000 to £20,000. Another benefit was the tremendous publicity this programme gained for the organization.

These three examples of organizations that practice relationship building show that consistency and commitment are the keys to long-term success.

HOW TO KEEP YOUR CUSTOMERS FOR LIFE

Every Master Marketer knows that generating new customers is only half the battle. It will do little good to create a first-class marketing effort that is successful in bringing in business, if the customers are then lost because of stupidity or carelessness.

Few of us have so much business that we can afford to lose any customers. But losing customers is more costly than most people realize. As I noted earlier, the average unhappy customer will tell ten of his friends and associates about the negative experience. Thus, you not only lose current revenue but future revenue as well; revenue that no amount of advertising can salvage.

The good news is that the word-of-mouth process can work just as easily to your benefit as to your detriment. Super-satisfied consumers will willingly tell everyone within earshot of their pleasant experiences with your firm. This is true because people love to talk about their shopping and purchasing experiences. Your most satisfied customers can become your best source of new business.

Richard Thalheimer, president of Sharper Image, put this sentiment well: "People expect a certain reaction from a business, and when you pleasantly exceed those expectations, you've somehow passed an important psychological threshold." A personal example will illustrate Mr. Thalheimer's point.

In late 1991, I purchased a cross-country ski exerciser from NordicTrack, an exercise equipment manufacturer located in Chaska, Minnesota. Six months later the electronic measuring device malfunctioned. I had no idea whether the component was under warranty and expected the usual bureaucratic runaround from the folks at NordicTrack.

To my surprise, when I called the company's friendly customer service agent, she immediately ordered another electronic device for me, and asked me to send the offending unit back at my convenience. I got the new unit within days. This was a good example of how a company can exceed customer expectations. Have I told others about my experience? You bet, not to mention every reader of this book.

Perhaps the best way to maintain happy customers is to practice the age old Golden Rule, "Do unto others as you would have them do unto you." Author Kenneth Goode put it a different way when he said, "Find out what people like, and do more of it. Find out what people don't like, and do less of it."

This issue of customer relations may be more important than you might think. Experts such as Hugh Aaron believe that the rift between companies and customers is one of the biggest problems facing American industry. In an article in Business Marketing, Aaron stated, "What's wrong with American business is our blind 'Hooray for me, screw you' syndrome. This demonic attitude is invading the dependability of our products, our capacity to innovate, our effectiveness to produce and the very quality of our lives."

Although many Americans feel that the difference in product quality is the only reason for the ascendancy of Japanese industries, there may be more to it. In Japan, a company's character and reputation are considered to be more important than differences in products. Japanese are renowned for service and will do anything for a valued customer.

Japanese companies and their customers often formalize the working association by forming groups called "Keiretsus," where each party is deeply concerned with the success of the other. Contrast this with the typical adversarial relationship between American customers and vendors, and you begin to see why we have a competitive problem.

NINE WAYS TO KEEP CUSTOMERS FOR LIFE

Follow these nine rules and you will truly be a Master Marketer at keeping customers:

1. **Practice Relationship Marketing**. Read and re-read the beginning of this chapter on relationship marketing until every part of your marketing effort is geared toward building lifetime relationships.

2. **Calculate the Economics**. The best reason to care about satisfying customers isn't because you'll feel better inside, but because you can generate greater levels of revenue and profit. Selling more products and services to existing customers costs as little as one-tenth as much as to new customers. When you share the numbers with others in your organization, they will see that it makes little sense to focus so much attention on attracting new customers and so little on keeping the customers you already have.

3. **Be Nice**. You may find this a little simplistic and self-evident. However, there is a certain hardness about doing business today. Many otherwise efficient companies fail miserably when it comes to practicing good old-fashioned courtesy. People want to do business with other friendly people. Niceness stands out and is rewarded. To be effective, this friendly attitude must permeate your organization. Whether dealing with the telephone receptionist or the MD, the customer must feel that she is wanted and appreciated.

    One way to show that you are nice is to stop the telephone interrogations. It seems to be a "badge of honor" in some companies for its employees to prove that their time is more valuable than that of the person who is calling. They prove this by forcing callers to pass through a screening process. This practice is by no means limited to senior executives. Scores of middle managers and administrative staff also play this game.

Probably the worst question from the caller's vantage point is "Will Mr. Smith know what your call is about?" I never quite know how to answer this question. First, if Mr. Smith already knew what the call was about, why would I have to call him in the first place? Second, the reason I called Mr. Smith was that I wanted to impart information to him, not his secretary.

Third, my business with Mr. Smith may be too complex to reduce to a 20 second summation for the call-screener. And, fourth, it is possible that I am more important to Mr. Smith than Mr. Smith is to me (I may even be a customer!). So why begin the relationship with a hostile attitude?

4. **Be Available**. While technology has helped us as a society in many ways, if mismanaged, it can distance us from our customers. To me, the biggest culprit is voice mail. While voice mail was created to make us always available to our customers, in truth it is often used to separate us from them. For instance, I know of several people who use voice mail and answering machines as call-screening devices. Since these individuals almost never answer their phones, you find yourself wondering if they are really absent, or if they are just ducking your call.

Being available means that you will sometimes have talk to someone you would rather not (heaven forbid, a salesperson may get through!), but the goodwill you generate will more than make up for this minor inconvenience.

5. **Be Flexible**. Nothing aggravates a customer more than being subject to petty rules and procedures. You know you have a problem if you hear your employees saying, "Sorry madam, that's our policy," or "Sorry sir, that's just the way we do things here." As I said elsewhere, "Rules are for the guidance of wise men and the obedience of fools." And from the way the rulebook is thrown around, there are plenty of fools in business.

   I am not saying that all rules and procedures are wrong. But I am saying that it is the way they are applied that is wrong. Rules must be used to serve the customer and protect the company (not the other way around). At our agency, we delegate the authority to bend the rules to <u>everyone</u> who deals with clients. Of course, major issues are brought to the attention of senior management, but we still try to resolve the matter as fast as possible, and more often than not, we resolve it in the client's favor. Do clients take advantage of our generosity? Very rarely.

   So don't rip up your company's rulebook. But do make sure that your first and most important rule is, "Always make the customer happy."

6. **Communicate with Your Customers When You're Not Trying to Sell Them Something**. One of the best ways to do this is to call or write your customers a week or two after they have done business with you. Although most companies acknowledge this as a good idea, they are afraid that customers will use the communication to express dissatisfaction. While this is true, you should welcome any chance you have at this point to rectify a problem before you lose the customer

permanently.

Periodic customer surveys are a good way to gauge ongoing satisfaction. However, they should not be conducted as an excuse to pat yourself on the back. The real purpose is to find out where the small problems are before they have a chance to turn into large problems. As a bonus, customers will be delighted that you want their opinions on the relationship.

7. **Get to Know Your Customers.** By "getting to know them" I mean that you should find out all you can about your customers as human beings, including their lifestyles, hobbies, likes, dislikes and so forth. This will allow you to relate better to the customer and target your marketing more effectively.

8. **Deliver More than You Promise**. If you really want to shine with your customers, make it a point to always deliver more than you promise. Some examples:

- The drycleaner that sews a missing button on your shirt, for free, without being asked.
- The mail order company that sends out an unexpected small gift to thank you for your first order.
- The solicitor that completes the contract draft hours before it was due, giving you extra time for review.
- The bank that calls to tell you how to earn a little more interest on your deposits.
- The computer company that gives you a free loan machine while yours is being repaired, even though it is not their normal policy.
- The car dealer that informs you that the service you requested is not necessary.

9. Be Easy to do Business With. This is really the sum of all eight previous points. Everything that your organization does must be geared toward making it easier and more pleasant for the customer to buy and use your products and services. Anything that makes this more difficult must be ruthlessly omitted or refined. When your customers say to you, "We find it easy to do business with you," you will truly have customers for life.

31

HOW TO PROMOTE YOURSELF

The Art of Personal Marketing

Master Marketers are aware that their organizations can sometimes flourish to the extent that they are able to successfully promotes themselves. In the cases of two well-known self-promoters, Lee Iaccoca of Chrysler and Victor Kiam of Remington Shaver, the ability to present a successful personal image to the public was critical to the very survival of the unhealthy companies for which they were responsible.

Although each has seen his image tarnished in recent years, few could argue with Iaccoca and Kiam's initial decision to craft their promotional strategy around the "cult" of their business personas.

Every day, throughout the business world, there are thousands of similar success stories being created, albeit on a smaller scale.

The good news is that you do not have to be the head of a large organization to gain benefits from self-promotional activities. Any individual who is wise enough to implement these ideas early in his career will find the journey to the top much smoother and faster.

BENEFITS AND PITFALLS OF
A SELF-PROMOTION PLAN

Here are a few of the benefits you can achieve with a solid self-promotion programme:

- If conducted properly, it will have a positive impact on your organization.
- You will achieve a greater degree of credibility in your industry, which can lead to greater sales and larger profits.
- You will gain marketplace notice. This is important because people buy from those they know, or those they have heard of. If you make enough positive impressions on a prospect, you have a good chance of being contacted when he has a need for your product or service.
- You will have a higher financial worth in the market, both to your current and potential future employers.
- You will have a greater likelihood of being promoted.
- Your ideas will have greater perceived value and will be more likely to gain acceptance.

Obviously, with all these benefits, a self-promotion effort is worthwhile. But you should be aware of these pitfalls:

- Many of the activities involved in self-promotion are the same as those of public relations. The self-promotion programme should either be carried out under the umbrella of the overall PT plan, or at the least, it should never conflict with it.

■ You must be careful to avoid stepping on the toes of senior people in your organization. Your ambition must not be perceived as a threat to senior managers of your company.

■ Don't bite off more than you can chew. Building credibility takes time and attempts to circumvent the process can damage your reputation beyond repair.

■ Keep your humility. Always remember that today's hero can be tomorrow's goat. No matter how successful you become, treat everyone with respect. Remember the expression, "Be careful how you treat people on your way up because you may need these same people on the way down."

YOUR PERSONAL SPHERE OF INFLUENCE

Self-promotion is the art of increasing your personal influence among those who are important to you and your organization. Groups and individuals that you will want to bring into your sphere of influence include:

Your employer - It can be difficult, if not impossible, to be successful at self-promotion if your employer does not agree with your goals. You must convince him that your activities will have benefit to the organization and that, when they conflict, you will always put the company's interests before your own.

Employees - Subordinates can support you or hurt you in many ways. If they do not believe in what you are doing, you should spend whatever time is necessary to improve the internal situation.

Customers - If you maintain positive relations with your customers and keep them up-to-date on your activities, they will be proud of your efforts and reward you with more business. However, they must never feel that you are ignoring their needs in order to promote yourself. This can be a tricky balancing act but it can be accomplished.

Prospective customers - Self-promotion can have a large payoff with prospects. If your expertise is noted by outside sources, sales can be easier and more profitable.

Shareholders and investors – This group will judge your promotional program by one yardstick — does what you do increase the value of their investments or cause an increase in the stock price? If the answer is no, you have a big problem.

Industry leaders - Renowned marketing experts such as Regis McKenna (author of <u>The Regis Touch</u> and <u>Relationship Marketing</u>) have long maintained that marketers could reap large dividends by focusing more attention on influencing the key leaders in an industry.

Business and trade press - Wrongly or rightly, people believe what they read in the press. The third-party endorsement implied by positive press mentions can influence the marketplace far more than paid advertising.

Consider every group listed above to be one of your constituencies. And just as a political candidate must consider how his actions will affect every constituency group, you must make sure that your personal promotion plan takes each of these groups into account.

THE IMPORTANCE OF PERSONAL STYLE

Although we each like to think that we have special knowledge or have something to offer that is different from everyone else in our industry, the fact is, it is often difficult to differentiate one company from another, one product from another, or even one Harvard MBA from another.

In a world of individuals and organizations crying out to be noticed, what separates the superstars from the obscure? The answer in one word is "style." And while style is a word with broad meanings, when it comes to self-promotion, your style should have four characteristics:

1. **It is unique**. What you do, what you say, and who you are must be seen as being different from all others in your industry group. You must find a way to stand out from the crowd. One business leader I know always wears a carnation on his lapel. For this man, the carnation is both a personal trademark and a conversation starter. Is he noticed? You bet. Is he remembered? Of course.

2. **It is dramatic**. Being unique is not enough. What you say and do must not only be different from the crowd, it must be better, bigger or more spectacular.

3. **It is relevant**. Politicians often say, "I don't care what they write about me in the press as long as they spell my name right." I would amend this to say, "I don't care what they write about me as long as it doesn't hurt my image and is related to my professional goals."

4. **It is congruent**. By "congruent" I mean that your style should not conflict with your basic personality. Don't

make the mistake of copying someone else's style, no matter how much you admire that individual. A style must be based on a careful assessment of your unique values, weaknesses and talents. Anything less than complete honesty will hurt you.

The well-balanced personal promotion plan contains four categories of activities: publishing, speaking, networking and media relations. Although these categories will be discussed individually, remember that it is the way in which they are orchestrated that determines the success of the overall program.

PUBLISHING STRATEGIES

PUBLISH A BOOK

There is something about the written word that adds to an individual's credibility and reputation. And the greatest credibility builder of all is to publish a book. To determine whether you should take on a book project, ask yourself these questions:

- Do you have special knowledge in your field of expertise?
- Would others benefit from your knowledge?
- Do you have a hook - a unique way of presenting your information?
- Do you have the discipline for such a large undertaking?
- Can you set aside the necessary time?
- Can you write reasonably well and do you have access to a good editor?
- Do you have a burning desire to see your work published?

If you answer yes to every one of these seven questions, then you are ready to write your first book.

Like every author, I learned valuable lessons writing and publishing my first book, <u>The Direct Marketing Challenge</u>. The following pointers can help make the road a little easier for any first-time author:

A. Remember that writing a book is similar to pushing a loaded wheelbarrow. It's very hard to get started, but once you begin, momentum will make the task much easier.

B. If you doubt your ability to come up with enough material for the book, give yourself the benefit of the doubt. You probably know more about the subject matter than you originally suspected and what you don't know can be learned through research.

C. Break your book project into manageable chunks. Start with the easier chapters and defer difficult sections until later. You will also minimize pressure if you set interim goals (such as finishing the next chapter), instead of always focusing on the goal of finishing the entire book.

D. Overcome your perfectionist tendencies, especially when writing the first draft. Your goal is to get as much information down on paper as you can. There will be plenty of time for editing later.

E. Utilize outside resources. Since there are few truly original thoughts, don't try to pretend everything in your book is a divine revelation. It's not the ideas themselves that are most valuable; it is your unique expression of those ideas. Every author has had his own teachers along the path so don't be afraid to admit this yourself. But you must be sure to give full credit when you do use outside sources or editorial contributors.

F. Make full use of technology. Notwithstanding the romantic appeal of hacking away at a manual typewriter complete with broken keys, things will go much smoother if you use a word processor. Plus, I've never seen a manual typewriter with spell-checker, God's greatest gift to us novice spellers.

G. Write even when you don't feel like writing. The fact is, you may go for weeks without having the "feeling." Even on those days you can't stomach the thought of facing your computer keyboard (or typewriter, if you weren't paying attention to the previous pointer), give it a try for a few minutes.

If the ideas still won't come, don't torture yourself. Try doing something else for a few minutes. For me, taking a 20-minute break from writing to toss a ball or play a video game with my sons, Michael and Colin, has always been a great way to clear the cobwebs and recharge my creative batteries.

The toughest part of the process is getting published. While the art of publishing is outside the scope of this book, don't despair because there are library shelves filled with information on this subject. If, after repeated attempts, you can't interest a publisher in your work, do not hesitate to publish it yourself. Dozens of best-selling authors got started in this fashion and you could be the next success story.

WRITE ARTICLES

Trade and business press editors are always interested in articles of interest to their readers. If the information you have to share fits in well with the editorial focus of the publication (or the focus of a particular issue), there is a good chance you will be published.

An important key to getting your article published is persistence. You have to be aggressive (pleasantly so) with the very busy editor who will determine the fate of your masterpiece. If national trade and business publications are not interested in your submission, try the local business and consumer press. They are always willing to consider a story with a local slant.

As difficult as it may seem, once you get your first article published, the rest should be relatively easy. If you are lucky, you might even get a call from an editor who stumbled across your article and wants you to do one for his publication. A different version of this story happened to me when an editor representing Prentice Hall (a large publisher) contacted me to ask whether I would be interested in producing a book based on the concept of an article I wrote for a national trade publication.

You will always have a better chance of getting published if you build your article around a concept or "hook." For example, the following are titles of four recent articles published under my byline:

"How to Sell the $12 Potato"

"What to Do When the Fish Won't Bite"

"How to Use Personal Selling Techniques in Direct Marketing"

"How to Market in the Era of the Consumer"

Each of these articles concerns a different aspect of marketing and each was picked up by the first publication to which it was submitted. I could have given each one a watered-down, generic title such as "How to Get More Out of Your Marketing Program" but chose to go with the more interesting titles. I have no doubt that the interesting titles of the articles contributed to their quick acceptance.

Hopefully, you will have a greater purpose for writing articles than just seeing your name in print. The article should be related to your professional expertise because it can help bring you business, but only if readers of the article know what you do and how to contact you. This information is usually printed at the end of the article and can be as sparse as your company name, or as detailed as a complete description of the services or products you provide along with your phone number.

Rarely will an editor solicit a more complete description from you since he does not want to appear to be giving an editorial plug to your business. So it is up to you to push for the extra publicity. Always include the longer description at the end of the copy that you send to the editor. But only do this after the editor has agreed to run the article, not in the query stage. It is then up to the editor to delete or reduce the copy.

Should you ask for payment for your article? It depends. By all means ask for payment if you believe you have a good chance of getting paid, without jeopardizing the assignment. But the truth is, until you achieve a reputation as a credible industry resource, it will probably be difficult to get paid more than an occasional token for your articles. Plus, the income you will receive from writing will be very low compared to the income that can be earned from potential customers who read your article.

After your article has been published, ask the editor for permission to reproduce it. Then you can copy the article and send it to prospects, customers and industry contacts. Enclose a note to the effect that "Here is some information that I thought you might find useful." Include a reply card to allow the recipient to contact you for more information about the subject of the article and to learn more about your products or services.

PRODUCE A NEWSLETTER

The subject of newsletters is covered in some detail in the chapter on public relations. And while newsletters are usually published by organizations and not individuals, there are many ways you can use a newsletter to promote yourself.

First, if your organization is not using newsletters as part of its promotional strategy, consider initiating one yourself. This way, you can probably serve as the editor. If a newsletter already exists, see if there is a place for you as a contributing writer. Believe me, the editor will be very pleased to have your assistance.

Newsletters take a tremendous amount of work and you may

rue the day you took my advice by starting one. Fresh ideas are difficult to come by and it seems you're always on deadline. But there are definite benefits. A newsletter forces you to stay on top of your industry since your words are in print for the world to read. Publishing a newsletter is also a highly visible undertaking which could have a major impact on your future.

How do I know this? It happened to me. Early in my career I started a newsletter on marketing called The Strategic Marketing Report. One of the people on my distribution list was Ron Friedman, then Vice President of Sales and Marketing of Group 1 Software (Ron has been Group 1's President for the past seven years). Ron had been thinking about starting a newsletter for Group 1, and when he received The Strategic Marketing Report he gave me a call. The result, a fantastic new position for me as head of public relations and a newsletter for Group 1 (The Group 1 Report).

Follow these tips to get the greatest self-promotional value out of your newsletter:

- Always include a prominently-featured letter from the editor on the front page (especially if you're the editor).
- Distribute the newsletter to all those who are in, or who you want to be in, your personal sphere of influence. Especially important are senior managers in your own organization, the press and valuable industry contacts.
- Don't neglect internal politics. Use the newsletter to make friends by mentioning those important to your career in your articles. Offer to write feature stories under these people's bylines.
- Produce a quality product. Quality can be measured in two ways. First, in terms of the timeliness and importance of the information contained in the newsletter. Second, in terms of the newsletter's physical appearance. It must look professional in layout and typestyle,

and you should avoid sloppy grammar and typos at all costs.

PRODUCE AN AUDIO PROGRAMME

Spoken words can have an impact as great as the written word. If you have a pleasant speaking voice and 20 to 30 minutes worth of useful information, take advantage of this and produce an audio cassette programme.

The type of information to put in an audio programme is the same as you would use for articles and newsletters. This is good news because you may be able to use your previous writings to give you the necessary information to fill up your programme. The only real difference is that you must revise the text so that it is suitable for the ear, not for the eye. Depending on your writing style, the two may be very similar, or it may take substantial rewriting to produce the cassette script.

The costs involved in producing an audio cassette are not as high as you might think. If your budget permits, I suggest that you use a recording studio. A home-made tape production will not help your credibility and as long as you do your preparation before the recording session, you can produce a professional sounding 30-minute programme in two to four hours of studio time.

There are four primary uses of an audio cassette program:

1. If the information content is good, you will be able to sell the tapes.

2. You can send free cassettes to potential clients and important industry contacts.

3. You can send the tapes to those who book speakers for seminars and conferences to give them an example of your expertise and speaking style.

4. You can send your tape to the press with the suggestion that it be excerpted for an article or series of articles.

PUBLIC SPEAKING METHODS OF SELF-PROMOTION

There is nothing you can do to promote yourself as quickly or as powerfully as public speaking. Rightly or wrongly, a perception exists that anyone who is invited to speak on a subject must have special knowledge of his or her subject matter. Also, unlike writing, speaking allows you to make personal contact with your audience. Instead of just seeing your words on paper, the audience gets to see you and hear you.

Almost all organized groups need speakers on a regular or occasional basis. Speakers are not only needed for industry conferences and seminars, but for breakfast, lunch and dinner meetings as well. These opportunities can range from an informal 20 minute talk at the local Rotary club, to a one hour keynote address at a major industry conference.

Naturally, it is much easier to get booked at the former type of event than the latter. Speaking before local civic groups gives you the opportunity to fine-tune your message and practice the art of speaking in public.

This is exactly what I did. Before I started speaking in front of industry groups (and potential clients) where the stakes were high, I gave dozens of talks to local business and civic groups. Each one of these speeches increased my confidence level and, by the time I started speaking to larger audiences, I felt thoroughly at ease on the podium.

If you follow the earlier advice on publishing articles and newsletters, you will pick up speaking opportunities. Networking is another good way to get noticed. But in many instances, the direct approach is the best. Either call or write the programme directors (or presidents) of groups you would like to speak to, and provide a brief outline of one or more talks you could do for the group. Make sure you convey the benefits that the audience would receive by hearing your message.

Since speakers often cancel, let the group know that you are available to speak on short notice. I have accepted invitations as little as 24 hours before the event. This flexibility will make you a lifelong friend of the program planner.

Here are some of the types of groups you might want to contact to get started as a speaker:

- Civic clubs such as Round Table or Rotary, etc.
- Service organizations
- Chambers of Commerce
- Networking groups
- County or regional organizations
- Public libraries (they often sponsor lecture series)
- Political groups
- Trade associations
- Professional associations
- College or continuous education programmes

While early on it is probably advisable to accept any speaking invitation (I have spoken to as few as six people), there will come a time when you need to establish more stringent criteria. When I started, my criteria was "any group of two or more people who are breathing and will sit through my talk." I now use the following checklist to evaluate whether or not to accept a speaking engagement:

1. Is it a paid assignment? Even though many of the fees paid are very small, it is hard to beat the feeling of getting paid for something that is so enjoyable (it may not sound enjoyable now but trust me, this will come with time).

2. Can the speech lead to other business opportunities? Will there be any potential clients in the audience?

3. Will the speech increase my stature in the industry?

4. How easy will it be to prepare for the speech? After you have done several talks, or published several writings on various topics, it is sometimes possible to pull together an effective program with only minimal effort, by tailoring your material to the specific audience.

5. How many people can be expected to attend the programme? Watch out for exaggerations here. Programme planners often inflate the size of the audience to entice you to accept the assignment (they are optimists by nature). If the programme planner tells me 100 people are expected, I figure I am doing well if 65 are in the audience.

6. Will the organization promote my participation in their programme?

7. Will there be an opportunity to meet the audience? Is there an occasion set up for the speaker(s) to circulate among the group members? I prefer to meet the audience after my talk, not before.

8. Will the group help to sell my books and tapes to the audience members?

SEMINARS

The primary difference between seminars and speaking assignments is that in your own seminar, you will have greater control over the programme's format. Seminars are very popular because they solve the dual challenge that organizations face: the continuing educational needs of their employees and the desire of individuals who are interested in continuing their own personal development.

One way to get involved is to offer to speak at existing seminars. These can be seminars put on by trade and professional associations such as the Institute of Management or by seminar companies such as Hawkesmere of IIR.

To give you the greatest degree of control and personal exposure, however, consider starting your own seminar programme. You can create exactly the type of seminar that best showcases your talents and has the most likelihood of attracting potential clients.

I know of one group of individuals who have done this in the software industry. Their seminar is on the subject of how to market computer software through direct mail. Not only does the seminar make money in its own right, enough clients are generated in the two months the seminars are held to keep the speakers busy and prosperous throughout the rest of the year.

TEACHING

Colleges, universities and Training and Education Council (TEC) regional centres offer industry-specific courses for adults, both through their regular curriculum and continuing education instruction. Often, these courses are taught by business people and practitioners, not full-time academic staff. If you have expertise in your field of endeavour that is worth sharing, I would encourage you to explore the teaching option.

The best way to find these opportunities is to write query letters to the department heads of your local schools. But first, gather the prospectuses of these institutions so that you are familiar with what is currently being offered. You may find that there are many courses now scheduled that you would feel comfortable teaching. If so, let the institution know that you would be happy to serve as a substitute or replacement teacher.

An even better way to get a teaching assignment is to propose a new course. Most often, this will not be something entirely out on a limb, but rather, an extension of their existing programmes. Make sure that you illustrate where the unmet need for such a programme lies. The question asked by every programme planner when he evaluates your course will be, "Will this programme attract enough people to make it profitable?"

Teaching will definitely increase your stature in your industry. After I started teaching a college course, my industry friends jokingly referred to me as "Professor Ryan." But behind this good natured kidding was a tinge of respect.

Whether you are speaking, running seminars or teaching at your local college, follow these rules to receive the greatest benefit:

- Prepare for every speaking opportunity thoroughly. I adopted this habit after reading that Winston Churchill wrote down every word of his speeches. Churchill admitted that he often spoke without reference to this written text, but felt that the intense preparation always paid off.

  You should also prepare well out of respect for your audience. You have an obligation to these people to do your best because they are taking their valuable time to listen to you. I recently heard a speaker say the following: "I really didn't have time to prepare for today's programme so I'll just talk to you about my experiences with the subject." I, and everyone else in the audience, was insulted by her cavalier attitude, especially since we had paid a princely sum to attend the seminar.

- Get as much mileage as possible out of your speaking assignment. Excerpt your speeches into articles or record them and send them to potential clients on audio cassette.

- Be yourself. Every one of us has a unique style that is

far more effective than any we could copy. Don't sell yourself short. Learn to let the real you shine through.
- ■ Focus on the audience, not on yourself. This is something that comes to all speakers with practice. You will find that the more time you spend thinking about serving the audience, the less time you have for negative emotions such as anxiety and worry.
- ■ Be unique, but don't reinvent the wheel. Many speakers feel that they must come up with totally new information, or risk disappointing the audience. This is simply not true. What you should strive for is to take the existing information you have (some of which the audience already knows) and rearrange it in a new way, using your own personal style.

NETWORKING FOR SELF-PROMOTION

You've no doubt heard the expression, "It's not what you know, it's who you know." While this does contain a certain ring of truth, the Master Marketer understands that it is both what you know and who you know that count. All the knowledge in the world won't help if you can't share your knowledge with the individuals who can positively influence your career. And all the best contacts won't make you successful if you have no substance to back you up.

Unless you are born into the right family, you will have to undertake some networking activities to meet influential people. If you are like me, you find the forced camaraderie of networking uncomfortable at best. But I am still willing to network because it has proven to be an essential part of building my business.

Remember that the real purpose of networking is not to meet large numbers of people, but rather to meet the right people. And the right people are those who you want to be part of your personal sphere of influence. You are much more likely to find these "right people" receptive to your business ideas if you have first established personal relationships with them through networking.

Sometimes it is next to impossible to meet the precise individuals who can be most helpful to you. But don't give up. There is an old saying that "anyone can reach anyone else with only three or four levels of contacts."

For instance, let us assume you need to contact the Prime Minister but he refuses to accept your phone calls. Using the "three to four levels" theory, you would call someone you know, who would call someone he knows, who would call someone she knows, who would call the Prime Minister on your behalf. While I think this example oversimplifies the art of networking, it does point out that many of the best opportunities are those that come from referrals, not directly from people you know.

Where do you go to network? The answer is that you should go where the best contacts are. Most often these people are found at professional lunches, seminars and meetings. But they can also be found at charity, community and political meetings.

Try these ideas for more productive networking experiences:

- Networking is a subtle game. Don't come on too strong. Your initial objective should be to meet people, not to sell them anything.
- People will remember you more favorably if you get them to talk about themselves. Even the most important people enjoy favourable attention from others.
- Ask open-ended, and not direct-answer questions. A question such as "What are some of the things you like about being a member of this group?", will keep the conversation going much longer than "How long have you been a member of this group?"
- Bring plenty of business cards and distribute them liberally. But it's even more important to gather cards from others. If you have a contacts database, enter all

the information about your new contacts immediately upon returning to the office, while it is still fresh in your mind.

- Send new contacts a short note. For example, "Bill, it was great to meet you at the Advertising Association luncheon. Let's look for an opportunity to do business together." Not only will such a note make a favourable impression on your new contact, but your chances of being remembered will quadruple.

- Industry groups are always looking for volunteers who are willing to get involved with committees of various types. This is an excellent way to gain visibility. However, I would caution you against becoming known as a "worker bee." Many people get labeled this way and their image can suffer as a result. Remember that it can be just as easy, and a lot more prestigious, to run the committee as it is to work for the committee.

  I have found that many industry groups have become paper-bound bureaucracies, with a large amount of waste and duplicate effort. I made the decision several years ago not to add to the problem by agreeing to serve only on groups where I have the potential to make a significant contribution. Anything less is not fair to me or to the organization. The same is true for you. Time is your most precious asset, so resolve to use it only for valuable purposes.

- The best way to be invited to participate in something is to ask. People almost always make a spot for someone who does what he says he will do. As soon as you gain such a reputation, you can have your pick of committees and activities.

MEDIA RELATIONS FOR SELF-PROMOTION

Individuals can be promoted through the non-paid media, just like organizations. Many of the techniques for getting press for your organization (see the chapter on public relations) are exactly the same as those you should use to gain favorable publicity for yourself. But there are a few subtle differences.

First, remember that it is perfectly appropriate to send out press releases on your own accomplishments. Subjects for personal press releases include: receiving an industry award, receiving a community service award, appointment to a board, sale of a large account, publishing a book or audio programme, receiving a job promotion, making a speech or setting an industry or job-performance record.

Second, you will improve your relationship with editors and reporters to the degree that you are seen as a valuable industry resource. You should contact all important editors and reporters (preferably by letter) to let them know what your field of expertise is, and that you are always available to act as an expert source, either by providing written information about a particular topic or by being interviewed for an article.

It is particularly important to let the press know that they can always depend on you, both for the accuracy of the information you provide, and for your willingness to cooperate when they need you. Then you will build a base of trust with the press; trust that will certainly be rewarded in favorable publicity for you and your organization.

THE PRINCIPLE OF LEVERAGE

Leverage can be a powerful force in self-promotion. Anytime you undertake any promotional activity, whether it is speaking, writing or media relations, you should look for other ways to make use of your efforts.

The article that follows: THE GREAT POTATO CAPER, provides a good example of how leverage works. As the article indicates, it all started with an audio cassette programme, which

487

was then used in a three-part mailing campaign. This innovative audio-cassette and mailing campaign led to a great deal of business for our agency.

What the article doesn't say is that the tape and mailing series also served as the basis for two published articles and three speeches. And some of the information on the tape programme can also be found in <u>The Master Marketer</u>. From a relatively small investment, we were able to reap large rewards. This is the whole idea behind the principle of leverage: gaining a very large benefit from a small investment in time and dollars.

THE GREAT POTATO CAPER

Half-Baked Idea or Mashing Success?

by *Christopher Ryan*
President
Ryan King Renninger, Inc.

My agency recently completed a rather unusual and attention-generating promotional campaign that we affectionately refer to as "The Great Potato Caper." The campaign sparked significant reactions, offered valuable lessons and provided an excellent case study of integrated marketing.

It all began at a brainstorming meeting including yours truly, Liz Breitsameter, our VP of agency operations, and two of our creative staff, Veronica Delaney and Howard Schwartz. The purpose of the meeting was to discuss methods of promoting an audio-cassette program I authored which had the working title, <u>16 Key Strategies to Help You Gain the Critical Marketing Edge</u>.

We then began to discuss the principle of visuals being used to enhance the image. One of the 16 strategies on the tape was that style can be more important than substance in marketing. To illustrate my point, I used the analogy of a potato. One potato can be sliced-up, deep fried and sold for 79 cents at a fast food restaurant, or, carefully garnished and served on china at a French restaurant and sold for 12 dollars. Thus, we decided to title the program, <u>How to Sell the $12 Potato</u>.

Veronica suggested sending the cassette program to our clients and prospects as a way to showcase our agency's expertise. Someone else recommended sending everyone a Mr. Potato Head (this idea was quickly rejected). After mulling over other ideas, the team finally agreed on the following promotional schedule.

Mailing One

The first mailing package in the series featured a genuine Idaho potato, resting on a bed of straw, inside a plain brown box with no return address. Inside the package was a note, containing only the words, KEEP YOUR EYES PEELED... These packages were sent Priority Mail to control delivery time. After all, who wants to be on the receiving end of a stale idea?

Mailing Two

Two days after package one dropped we mailed a copy of the cassette program, How <u>to Sell the $12 Potato</u>. Enclosed was a note from me which began: "Received any good potatoes lately? This should clear up the mystery." The note went on to say that the tape was a gift from Ryan King Renninger, and closed with the words, "I hope you enjoy the tape...and the potato!"

The Results

After the second package dropped we held our collective breaths waiting for the first response. We expected the mailing to generate at least a trickle of attention. What we received was an avalanche!

Our first call came from a noticeably upset gentleman who told me he spent two sleepless nights wondering who was out to get him. He claimed that he viewed the potato as a "warning" that something sinister was going to happen. At first I thought he was joking but he later admitted he had good reason to be apprehensive at this time in his life. He closed the conversation by predicting we would receive many calls from others who had felt threatened by the potato.

Self-promotion article

PREPARING FOR THE FUTURE

Marketing Opportunities,
Obstacles and Ethics

*M*arketing techniques and technologies have progressed so far in a short time that it can be hard to figure out where you stand today, let alone properly prepare for the future. But prepare we must. Future opportunities will belong to those who anticipate and embrace the inevitable changes.

One of the primary reasons for the accelerated pace is that marketing is undergoing a metamorphosis. From creative-driven to technology-driven, from mass-appeal to targeted-appeal. And the tool that made this possible is the computer.

While nothing is so important to today's marketer as information, without the technical means to compile and manipulate data, information is useless. Computers help by performing two tasks that are necessary to allow us to properly make use of information. First, computers allow large amounts of data to be collected, updated and output efficiently (such as names, mailing addresses, and purchasing history). Second, computers give us the ability to segment customer and prospect files in a wide variety of ways.

TECHNOLOGY'S IMPACT ON MARKETING

Technology will have an impact on the future of marketing in five important ways:

1. The decline in viewership of network television will continue from 65% of the total audience in 1990 to approximately 50% in the year 2000. Technologies such as satellite transmission (so-called "wireless cable") mean that the number of channels available to each household will more than double. While this makes it more difficult to reach a mass audience, it will increase the opportunities for reaching narrow audience segments.

2. Interactive marketing methods, such as videotext and audiotext, will allow the consumer greater freedom of choice. Individuals will be able to view full-colour product demonstrations on their television screens, receive a print-out of the product specifications, and order the product of choice, without leaving their easy chairs. This means that consumers will be much more informed about performance, pricing and warranty issues.

   Video marketing will also affect certain other marketing channels, such as catalogue and retail distribution. Home-shopping programmes are now commonplace on cable networks, and the technical qualities and demonstration capabilities of television make this a medium that can only continue to grow.

3. Marketing databases will grow larger and more sophisticated. The number of mailing lists will decrease when
many existing files are combined. This consolidation
means that much more information will be maintained
on each individual, as data from these various lists are
combined. However, it must be noted, as you will see in
a moment, that this move toward increased amounts of
data does have a negative side, and may be countered
by government restrictions.

Response lists and compiled lists will be maintained
in the same databases, giving direct marketers the
ability to combine information about known responders
with the extensive demographic and psychographic data
available on compiled lists. Marketers will have access
to these databases on-line, and be able to select and
manipulate data without involving the list owners. This
also may not be entirely good news as you read my
later thoughts on the threat to consumer privacy.

4. Telephone companies are developing the capability to
link-up all homes to a central computer bank through the
use of optical fibres. These fibres can carry television
signals, video-telephones and interactive input devices.
Using such a network, a consumer could call up a 30
minute video presentation on an auto he was considering purchasing - have an audio/video conference with a
sales representative, and enter his order through a
computer keypad or touch screen.

Credit approval would be almost instantaneous, as
the system would be connected to a national credit
database, and the consumer could review the terms of
several credit offers on-line. His down-payment would

be transferred electronically from his bank account. The consumer would also have the ability to transfer funds between accounts and make other investment transactions (such as stock purchases) through the network.

5. Electronics is replacing typography (print) as a communications tool. People are reading less, watching more, and have much shorter attention spans, at least when it comes to advertising receptivity. For these reasons, it will no longer be enough to inform prospects and then persuade them. We must make entertainment value a part of all of our promotional vehicles.

CHANGING DEMOGRAPHICS AND LIFESTYLES

Evolving lifestyles of consumers and changing demographics will continue to favor the use of target-marketing over mass-marketing. One such change is the growth in the number of two-income households. Women who used to have more time to shop now have careers and time commitments as demanding as those of men. The increasing numbers of the elderly also bode well for direct marketing, since people aged over 50 control an increasing proportion of the nation's buying power. For house-bound people, direct marketing may be the only way they have to purchase consumer goods.

In addition to the elderly, growing markets include ethnic minorities, the youth market, and the gay population. Other profitable niche markets include the affluent, family groups such as single-parent households, and married couples with no children. Each of these market segments will require special attention and cannot be successfully penetrated using mass-marketing approaches.

THE GLOBAL ECONOMY

Perhaps the greatest change faced by marketers is the globalization of the world's economy. Technology has given people everywhere the opportunity to share data and ideas with those around the corner or across the planet. We are also entering the age of the international home market, where someone in Asia can place an order for an item from a European company (or vice versa), and have that item delivered within days.

PERSONALIZED ADVERTISING

The same large databases that make interactive purchasing possible will lead to the growth of powerful personalized advertising techniques. Many catalogues are already using a technique known as "selective-binding" which customizes certain pages of the catalogue based on information known about the prospect's interests and past purchases.

For example, a 16-page catalogue featuring outdoor clothing may contain four pages of descriptions of fishing garb for the known fisherman and, alternately, four pages of hunting clothing for the known hunter. All other pages in the publication would remain the same. This technique also allows magazines and catalogues to insert personalized advertisements and messages inside the publication, again based on a consumer's known interests and purchasing patterns.

THE PRIVACY ISSUE

The technology and demographic changes mentioned above, while confusing to many, will bring new opportunities to the Master Marketer, but only if he understands how to overcome obstacles such as the threat to consumer privacy.

Larger databases mean a greater amount of data will be maintained on each individual. To identify potential purchasers, list compilers will match characteristics from multiple lists to develop buyer profiles. This new data is then added to the database.

For instance, how secure are vehicle licensing and drivers license records? Are medical records properly protected? Credit bureaus sell the names of those with good and bad credit records. In the US, voter registration bureaus sell lists of registered Democrats and Republicans, including those who voted in previous elections.

Have you had occasion to fill out a warranty registration card for a new product recently? These cards usually ask for a few details on the purchaser, such as income range, age and number of children in the household. The card often states that this information is to be used to "better identify and serve our market," or something equally harmless. An unspoken threat comes with these cards; fill it out or your warranty will be invalid.

The truth is, while the manufacturer does indeed use the data to better identify the market, he may also be selling the information to other mailers and list compilers. And you better believe the company sells all the information, not just your name and address.

If the above isn't sobering enough, consider that the compiler may have access to information on the magazines you subscribe to, the health club you belong to, and the religious, political and charitable organizations to which you donate. To give you an example of how much data a compiler may have about you, in August 1992, Polk Direct, a division of R.L. Polk & Co., ran an ad for its new "Kidsbase" database of information on children and their parents. The ad brags that the database contains up to "294 items of data on families and their members." The ad visual features a young boy with surrounding copy listing the type of information that Polk Direct knows about the boy and his family:

> Has two older sisters
> VCR owners
> Plays video games

Has home computer
Family owns a motorcycle
Camps in a recreational vehicle
TV sports viewers
Family owns a boat
Parents both work (their names are Kathleen
and Matthew)
Mail-responsive household
Moved from Chicago to Milwaukee last year
Lives in an upwardly mobile household
Parents own their own home.

The ad doesn't mention anything about knowing the child's blood type, but I think you get the picture. While it is unlikely that a compiler would knowingly misuse this data, the potential for abuse exists. Remember George Orwell's <u>1984</u> and the way it portrayed a "big brother" who knew everything you said and did. <u>1984 </u>was supposed to be science fiction and the culprit was supposed to be big government, not list compilers.

In case you think this is an isolated example, consider American Express. According to the May 18, 1992 issue of <u>DM News</u>, American Express has shared the names of its cardmembers with firms that accept the card for years. Included with the name and address information are modeling capabilities to help a firm zero in on people with a propensity to purchase specific types of goods. American Express believes it can predict potential purchasers by analyzing past and current use of the American Express card. I have heard an American Express official brag about his company's ability to predict who is likely to move, who is likely to tip higher and who is likely to take up the sport of skiing.

Although this executive stated that the company would never allow such data to be misused, I got the chilling feeling that the Inland Revenue Service would love to have AmEx's database so that they could predict "who is likely to cheat on his taxes." Not that I would ever cheat on my taxes, but I canceled my card that day and now feel better "leaving home without it."

INFORMATION GLUT AND PROMOTIONAL CLUTTER

For some time we have been in a transformation from a "machine age" to an "information age." According to futurist Marvin Cetron, the amount of raw data available to us will double in the next ten years and continue doubling every decade into the foreseeable future. Much of this data will be contained in large public domain "infobases." The challenge will not be to search out new sources of information, but rather to absorb, assimilate and use the information that already exists.

Marketers face a problem even more serious than information glut: promotional clutter. Consumers at businesses and homes can be exposed to as many as 2,000 promotional messages a week, making it harder to break through this confusion and convince a skeptical prospect to try your product or service.

This is especially true for fund-raisers, since the pool of potential donors to charitable causes is shrinking. Every known donor is besieged by requests from worthy charities. In the US, the Heart Fund rents its list to Cancer Research and Cancer Research rents its list to the Kidney Fund, and so forth. If a prospect is generous enough to donate to one worthy cause, many other groups will also ask him for money. Although the donor may give more in total, each competing group is less likely to receive a contribution.

The same holds true for business marketers. Anytime there is a relatively stable number of known prospects for a product or service, there is a danger of over-saturation. For example, in the mainframe computer software marketplace, data processing managers are besieged with mail from software vendors - in some cases receiving as many as 80 pieces of advertising mail each week.

George Wiedemann, president of the worldwide direct response agency, Grey Direct, believes that people are becoming increasingly irritated over the lack of control over the amount of catalogues and other direct mail they receive. Wiedemann believes that the answer lies in using mass-marketing media to get consumers to "self-select" their interests, and thereby, what types of direct marketing promotions they will receive. I agree completely.

TELEMARKETING ABUSES

Telemarketing abuses capture the ire of the public like no other issue. Even those of us who earn our livelihoods in marketing get annoyed by telephone sales calls that arrive at inopportune times. Somehow the telephone sales reps know exactly when the Ryan household sits down to dinner because that's when they always seem to call.

Worse than the annoyance factor are the scams and semi-legal schemes perpetuated by dishonest telemarketing operators. Of course, these practices make every consumer more careful and less likely to transact business by phone. One voice crying out for reform is Bruce Murray of Murray Marketing in Rockport, Massachusetts. Bruce reported on two abusive telemarketing practices in a recent column for DIRECT magazine:

"It has taken 25 years to build an understanding with consumers that an 0800 number telephone call is toll free . . . Some marketers are abusing that trust by asking 0800 number callers to punch codes into their phones that convert the calls to a billable number – and the callers aren't aware of the change. Other sweepstakes marketers are promoting calls for prizes worth far less than the cost of the call."

Bruce and I agree that these scam artists give the entire industry a sordid reputation, and are the reason many states are considering legislation to regulate telemarketing. There is no doubt that the telemarketing industry will either have to police itself on this issue and help to drive the con-artists out of business, or learn to live with whatever regulations ensue.

MAILING LIST THEFT

Hundreds of thousands of mailing records can be maintained on a nine-track magnetic tape approximately the same size in diameter as a record album. Computer service bureaus handle thousands of such tapes every year. Given these circumstances, and the fact that nothing in the direct marketing industry is as important as mailing list information, there is little wonder that list theft is a growing problem.

The depth of the problem ranges from mailers who use rented lists two or more times, while only paying for one-time use, to outright theft and resale of the data. While most readers will never have such problems, I would suggest that, if you ever send your list for outside processing, make sure you "seed" the list. Seeding your list (also known as "salting") means that you enter your own and others' names and mailing addresses into the list database. This way you are certain to receive any unauthorized mail sent to the list.

One key point when seeding a list is to either use a phony first-name or misspell something in the name or address. For instance, I may enter the name "Charles T. Ryan" on a particular list (instead of Christopher Ryan), so that I can be absolutely sure of any unauthorized mailings to that list.

Another benefit to having seed names on your list is to verify that legitimate mailings were processed correctly and reached their destinations. If you are using seed names for this purpose, try to include names from several geographic areas.

MARKETING ETHICS

As mentioned previously, governments around the world have become increasingly active in the areas of privacy and consumer protection. Great Britain is following the lead of the European

Community in this regard, and as European marketers will tell you, such regulations make it very difficult for all marketers, especially direct marketers.

Professional organizations such as the Direct Marketing Association, Institute of Sales Promotion and the Institute of Practitioners in Advertising have long urged members and non-members alike to practise a code of ethical conduct, and to regulate themselves before the government does the job for them. The Advertising Associations "legal, honest and truthful" campaign has reminded both advertisers and consumers of the need to exercise caution and there are specific guidelines on activities such as mail-order advertising or special offers to protect consumers and honest advertisers.

I believe that ethics in marketing would take a quantum leap forward if all business, consumer and fund-raising advertisers followed Article One of the DMA Guidelines:

"All offers should be clear, honest, and complete so that the consumer may know the exact nature of what is being offered, the price, the terms of payment (including all extra charges), and the commitment involved in the placing of an offer...."

We should all resolve to conduct every marketing activity by the letter and spirit of these words.

33

MARKETING WAR STORIES

*T*he Master Marketer knows that there are many valuable lessons to be learned from the successes and failures of others. Using short case histories, this chapter highlights some challenges faced by organizations in several different industries and outlines how these clever Master Marketers were able to turn their lemons into lemonade.

THE PIZZA OVEN MAILING

THE SITUATION: A fund-raising organization was mailing out an appeal using first class postage. The group made certain that the package weighed under one ounce, because the extra postage on a two ounce package would cost a small fortune.

Despite the precautions taken, everyone was in for a surprise when the mailing was brought to the post office. When the packages were weighed by postal employees, they averaged slightly over one ounce.

What was the cause of the sudden weight gain? Surprisingly, the mailing components had absorbed humidity from the rainy weather and had "gained weight" as a result. The group was in a panic; almost all the profits expected from the mailing could be eaten up by the postage costs.

Just when the fund-raisers had resigned themselves to paying thousands of dollars in extra postage, the mailhouse manager came up with an unusual idea. The entire mailing was taken to a local pizza restaurant where the company arranged to rent the ovens for several hours. All the extra weight soon evaporated in the dry heat of the giant pizza ovens. The entire mailing was then delivered back to the post office and mailed at the original weight of under one ounce.

THE LESSON: It is a good idea to leave yourself a little breathing room. If not, make sure there is a nearby pizza restaurant.

Contributed by: Catherine Lincoln, *Database America*

THE TYPO TEACHERS DIDN'T CATCH

THE SITUATION: A client called an agency that handled the account of a national teachers' organization, desperate to run an advocacy ad in <u>Newsweek</u>. Because the closing date for ad materials was that same day, the agency was rushing to get it out by deadline.

Since the client had insisted on supplying its own copy, the agency faxed the ad directly to <u>Newsweek</u> for typesetting. It was then returned to the client for approval. The day the magazine issue was delivered, the client called the agency, furious. Unfortunately, the ad was riddled with misspelled words, not at all what you would expect from a group of teachers.

Even though the words were misspelled in the client's original copy, the agency felt very badly. Everyone held their breath expecting an onslaught of angry letters from teachers. But strangely, not one reader responded to <u>Newsweek</u> or the client about the errors.

THE LESSON: Never send anything out without first checking for errors. It was just a fluke that no one noticed the mistakes.

Contributed by Julie White, *Sallie Mae*

HOW A MINIATURE LIGHT BULB GOT BIG PUBLICITY

THE SITUATION: A company whose major product was a miniature light bulb the size of a grain of wheat wanted to gain visibility for itself and its products. Instead of a full-scale media blitz, the marketing consultant wrote a news release and distributed it electronically to approximately 1,000 media sources at a cost of only $500.

This very simple task required little effort but achieved great results. The "no-brains" release ended up in ten trade magazines and ran on two television networks, one of which was a PBS series shown nationally to colleges and universities. As a result, the company was inundated with calls from large corporations like Ford, Chrysler, Delco-Remy and many others.

THE LESSON: Public relations can achieve a large impact on a very small budget. By preparing a good news release for the media, you can do their work for them. Editors are always looking for compelling stories, so if you write a good one, it will probably be used.

Contributed by: Robert Strock, *The Corporate Network*

A NEW WAY OF PROMOTING BANK SERVICES

THE SITUATION: A group of bank employees came up with the idea of using video segments to distract customers while they waited in line for the cashiers. They figured it would be an easy way to inform customers of all the products and services the bank offered and keep them from noticing how long they were waiting in line.

However, the bank's marketing department initially rejected the idea, claiming that video was useful only as a training tool and not for selling services. But finally, after months of persistence, they reluctantly agreed to test the idea.

Six commercials were taped and run at three branch offices. Between the ads, a seven-second spot offered a free stuffed animal to anyone who mentioned they saw the video. Each branch was provided with 500 stuffed animals for the four weeks that the spots were to be run. The videos were so successful that supplies of the stuffed animals were depleted by the end of the first week and employees were having trouble getting customers away from the monitors and up to the cashiers' windows.

Despite these amazing results, the marketing department hesitated to adopt the video program. Six months went by until they gave branch offices new video segments; a series of poorly designed ATM usage ads. The marketing department then used this as proof that "video doesn't work."

THE LESSON: A good idea is a good idea, regardless of its source. The bank's marketing department was practicing the "not invented here" syndrome, causing it to discard an idea which could have proven extremely successful.

Contributed by: Norman Hecht

THE VALUE OF TESTIMONIALS

THE SITUATION: A company starting up a proprietary school system experimented with a variety of marketing strategies to help build enrollment. After testing everything from direct mail to door-to-door canvassing, they found that direct response television accounted for over 80% of the school's attendance.

The company employed expensive, award-winning agencies to create glitzy ads. But following his intuition, John McCullough also produced a few less expensive, simpler spots featuring testimonials from satisfied students. Testing proved that the simple testimonial ads had a stronger impact on the audience than the much fancier commercials. They decided to use only the testimonials and enrollment increased almost 350%.

THE LESSON: This campaign points out two valuable lessons. First, the costlier solution is not always the best solution because all the expensive advertising in the world can't buy credibility. Second, testimonials can be a very powerful and effective advertising format.

Contributed by: John M. McCullough,
Roy Jorgensen Associates, Inc.

IT'S NEVER TOO LATE

THE SITUATION: When I was a production manager for a small agency, one of our clients was a medium-sized software company. Each year, this company hosted a user's conference and our mission was to promote the event with direct marketing.

We designed a direct mail package and our client provided the brochure copy which included the conference agenda and speaker biographies. As always, we followed standard approval procedure with camera ready artwork and ozalids.

A few days after the mailing dropped, I received a phone call

507

from my panicky client. One of her company's executives had received his package in the mail at home and had discovered that his title had been left off the brochure. He insisted that the entire mailing be redone immediately and threatened her job if it wasn't taken care of.

We made the type change right away and rushed it over to the printer, who delivered the new brochures to my house on Sunday. I spent my Sunday evening stuffing and sealing the packages, and dropped them off at the post office Monday morning on the way to work.

To my horror, when I checked the brochures in the sample packages, they contained the same error. The printer must have used the old plates. I knew that my client would lose her job if her boss discovered the repeat mistake. A co-worker suggested (jokingly, I think) that we break into the postbox and get the letters back. But even a client isn't worth going to jail for. Plus, everyone knows that you can't get a letter back once it is dropped into a postbox. Right?

After tearfully pleading my case to five or six people at the post office, I was put through to the postmaster. Not only was he sympathetic, after a great deal of begging, he agreed to have someone check the box for my mail. I described the package to him and quickly left for the post office.

The postmaster greeted me with great news. He had recovered about 80% of my mailing, including the package going to the executive's home. The day was saved!

THE LESSON: The brochures should have been checked as soon as they arrived from the printer. But once the mistake is made, the lesson is that there is always a solution if you look hard enough.

Contributed by Elizabeth Breitsameter,
Ryan King Renninger

BUILDING A PROSPECT FILE FROM SCRATCH

THE SITUATION: A mainframe software company faced the challenge of marketing new products which were useful only to companies that had both the VM operating system and IBM's SQL database system (a rare combination at that time). Although the company had a very good list of VM sites, there was no list of SQL sites available, except at IBM, and IBM would not release the list.

The solution was to build a database of SQL companies. It was decided that the only way to get a large number of qualified prospects to identify themselves was to offer a free premium that had meaning only to the target audience. A very handy SQL reference tool called the "SQL User's Guide" was developed and offered as a premium in a mailing to all VM sites which also had the SQL database system.

The mailing was so successful that the company identified 80% of all the companies in the U.S. which met its criteria and ended up with a better list of SQL sites than anyone except IBM. Instead of broadside marketing, the company could now use an in-house database of highly qualified prospects.

THE LESSON: You can't sell to prospects until you know who they are. This programme pointed out the importance of creating an in-house prospect file as well as the results-producing power of an information premium.

Contributed by: Christopher Ryan

SECTION VII

MARKETING RESOURCES

34

MARKETING CAMPAIGN WORKSHEETS

$\mathcal{T}$he following series of worksheets are tools that you should incorporate in your day-to-day marketing activities. Each has been designed to complete a specific stage of strategic planning and campaign execution. Before moving on to the next sheet, make sure that the one you are working with has been carefully thought out. When you complete the set, you will have a winning, Master Marketer campaign.

Worksheet #1

CAMPAIGN ELEMENTS CHECKLIST

At the beginning of each campaign fill out the target completion dates for each element. As each element is completed, enter the date of completion in the right-hand column.

Campaign Element	Due Date	Complete
Prepare Situation Analysis	_____	_____
Establish Campaign Objectives	_____	_____
Define Target Audience	_____	_____
Prepare Positioning Statement	_____	_____
Develop the Offer	_____	_____
Develop the Creative Strategy	_____	_____
Select the Media-Mix	_____	_____
Implement the Campaign	_____	_____
Fulfillment and Follow-Up	_____	_____
Analyze Response and Refine Campaign	_____	_____

SITUATION ANALYSIS QUESTIONNAIRE

In 30 words or less, what is the purpose of this campaign? _____

_____

_____

_____

_____

What is our current market share? _____

Who are our primary and secondary competitors? _____

_____

_____

What are the market shares of our competitors? _____

_____

What are the strengths and weaknesses of our products / services? _____

_____

_____

_____

_____

What are the strengths and weaknesses of competitors' products / services? ____

_____

_____

_____

What marketplace forces favour the success of our products/services? _____

_____

_____

What marketplace forces are working against our success? _____

_____

_____

SITUATION ANALYSIS QUESTIONNAIRE – PAGE TWO

Who are the primary and secondary buyers of our product / service (industry and individual)?

_____

_____

_____

_____

What percentage of our target audience is aware of our products/services? _____

In which market segments have we achieved high penetration (and why)? _____

_____

_____

_____

In which market segments have we achieved low penetration (and why)? _____

_____

_____

_____

What past marketing activities have been undertaken for our products / services? _____

_____

_____

_____

_____

What media and creative themes have been used? _____

_____

_____

_____

How successful have these programmes been? _____

_____

What media and creative themes have our competitors used to promote their products / services?

_____

_____

_____

OBJECTIVES QUESTIONNAIRE

What is the primary purpose of this campaign?   Generate leads (two-step programme) ....☐
Sell products (one-step programme)   ....☐
Increase awareness ....☐
Fill seminar seats ....☐
Other_____ ☐

What is the total revenue objective? .... £ _____

Average size of each sale .... £ _____

Number of new sales needed *(divide total revenue by average sale)* .... _____

Deadline for reaching these sales/revenue objectives .... _____

Conversion rate of hot prospects to sales *(how many hot prospects are needed to make one sale?)* ... _____

Number of hot prospects needed *(conversion rate times number of sales needed)* .... _____

Deadline for reaching these hot prospect objectives .... _____

Conversion rate of raw leads to hot prospects .... _____

Number of raw leads needed *(conversion rate times number of hot prospects needed)* .... _____

Deadline for generating these raw leads .... _____

Revenue amount generated per lead (RPL) - *(total revenue divided by the number of raw leads)* £ _____

Acceptable cost-per-lead (CPL) *(note: generally, the CPL should be 30% or less of the RPL)* ..... £ _____

Current estimated market share for our products / services? _____

Target market share after this campaign? _____

How will this market share be measured?_____

Current audience awareness of our products / services? _____
_____

Target audience awareness after this campaign? _____
_____

How will this awareness be measured? _____
_____

Worksheet #4

CUSTOMER/PROSPECT PROFILE

Which industries or individuals use products of this type most frequently? _____

_____

_____

_____

What size companies are the most frequent users of the product? *(size can be measured by revenues, number of*

employees) _____

_____

_____

_____

Is there a geographic component to the marketing universe? _____

_____

_____

_____

_____

What are the functional titles of the individuals who are decision makers, recommenders and

influencers for the product(s)? _____

_____

_____

_____

Note that a "functional title" is a generic title (e.g. Information Technology Director), not the title listed on that person's business card.

What publications do our customers/prospects read? _____

_____

_____

_____

_____

What associations do our customers/prospects belong to? _____

_____

_____

_____

_____

POSITIONING QUESTIONNAIRE

What is the scope of our positioning problem - is it to position the organization or only a product?

_____

_____

In an ideal world, what is the position we would like to hold in the marketplace? _____

_____

_____

What is the position we currently hold? _____

_____

_____

What is the position held by each of our competitors? _____

_____

_____

_____

_____

Is the position statement for this product or service compatible with our mission statement?

_____

Does the product position statement violate the true nature of our company? Does it match the reality of what the customer can expect from us at the point-of-service? _____

_____

_____

Where is the product on its life cycle? Is it a new product where the prospect asks, "What is this product?" Or is it one in a mature market where the prospect asks, "Why should I buy this product instead of the competition's products?" _____

_____

_____

Given the competition, do we have the necessary resources to reach and maintain our desired position in the marketplace? _____

_____

OFFER CHECKLIST AND STATEMENT

Check all of the offers that have potential for this campaign:

Product Information .... ☐   *Special Pricing* .... ☐
Information Premium .... ☐   *Standard Premium* .... ☐
Free Trial .... ☐   *Demonstration Version* .... ☐
Performance Guarantee .... ☐   *Extra Inducement* .... ☐
Sales Rep Follow-up .... ☐   *Qualified Offer* .... ☐
Introductory Offer .... ☐   *Bundled Products* .... ☐
Trade-in Offer .... ☐

Describe the offer type to be used and the rationale: _____

_____

_____

_____

_____

_____

_____

_____

What is the offer statement? _____

_____

_____

_____

_____

_____

_____

_____

CREATIVE STRATEGY

What is the Unique Selling Proposition (USP) of the product, service or seminar we are offering?

_____

_____

_____

Why is this USP a truly BIG IDEA? _____

_____

_____

_____

Check all creative categories that have potential for this campaign:

Benefit Statement .... ☐   Fear/ Uncertainty/Doubt .... ☐

Strong Claim .... ☐   Curiosity Provoker .... ☐

Industry Expert .... ☐   Humor .... ☐

Competitive Challenge .... ☐   Niche Market .... ☐

Slice-of-Life .... ☐   Testimonial .... ☐

Describe the creative strategy to be used and its rationale: _____

_____

_____

_____

_____

_____

_____

Does this creative strategy meet these five criteria?

1. Will it achieve the stated objectives: Yes ☐   No ☐
2. Is it targeted at the right audience: Yes ☐   No ☐
3. Is it unique: Yes ☐   No ☐
4. Is it memorable: Yes ☐   No ☐
5. Does it re-inforce our company position: Yes ☐   No ☐

Worksheet #8

MEDIA SELECTION CHECKLIST

Primary Campaign Objective _____

_____

Target Audience _____

Reach *(percent of total audience to be exposed)* _____

Frequency *(how many times each prospect to be exposed)* _____

Continuity of campaign *(length of time to be run)* _____

Geographic boundaries of campaign _____

Budget for the campaign £ _____

Based on the above criteria, which media are recommended for this campaign:

PRINT ADVERTISING

Percentage of budget .... _____ %

Amount .... £ _____

Time period for ads .... _____

Ad size(s) .... _____

Number of colours .... _____

Publication	No. of Insertions
_____	_____
_____	_____
_____	_____
_____	_____
_____	_____
_____	_____
_____	_____
_____	_____

DIRECT MAIL

Percentage of budget .... _____ %

Amount .... £ _____

No. of mailings .... _____

Drop date(s) .... _____

Size of mailing(s) .... _____

Package format(s) _____

_____

Mailing list(s) to be used _____

_____

_____

OUTBOUND TELEMARKETING

Percentage of budget .... _____ %

Amount .... £_____

No. of calls .... _____

Time period of calls .... _____

Calling list(s) to be used _____

SEMINARS

Percentage of budget .... _____ %

Amount .... £_____

No. of locations .... _____

Date(s) of seminar(s) _____

EXHIBITIONS

Percentage of budget .... _____ %

Amount .... £ _____

Location of shows _____

Date(s) of shows _____

PUBLIC RELATIONS

Percentage of budget .... _____ %

Amount .... £ _____

Time period .... _____

PR activities _____

_____

Worksheet #9

FULFILLMENT AND FOLLOW-UP

Describe process to be used to follow-up telephone leads: _____

_____

_____

_____

Describe process to be used to follow-up write-in leads: _____

_____

_____

_____

Describe process to be used to follow-up "hot" leads: _____

_____

_____

_____

Qualification information to be collected *(check all that apply)*:

Name .... ☐		Title .... ☐	
Company .... ☐		Address .... ☐	
Phone Number .... ☐		Lead Source .... ☐	
Business Need.................... ☐		Competition Involved .... ☐	
Influence Type .... ☐		Other Decision Influencers . ☐	
Decision Process .... ☐		Budget (yes or no) .... ☐	
Budget Amount................. ☐		Timeline of Need .... ☐	
Follow-up Required .... ☐		Other (explain) _____	

Describe fulfillment material to be mailed to qualified leads: _____

_____

_____

Describe fulfillment material (if any) to be mailed to unqualified leads: _____

_____

_____

RESPONSE ANALYSIS

How is response data to be captured? (check all that apply):

By inbound telephone lead qualifier ...... ☐
On direct mail reply cards .... ☐
By sales reps .... ☐
By follow-up questionnaire .... ☐
By outbound telephone operators .... ☐

What response data is to be captured? (check all that apply):

Date response is received .... ☐
Type of lead (*e.g. direct mail, telephone*) . ☐
Source of marketing activity .... ☐
(*e.g. name & date of publication or direct mail package*)
Functional title .... ☐
Industry .... ☐

Compile the response data on the attached Lead Source Analysis Report.

Marketing Activities

LEAD SOURCE ANALYSIS REPORT

Worksheet #10A

	Source Code	Circulation or Quantity	No. of Responses	Response Rate %	Activity Cost $	Cost per Response	No. of Qualified Responses	Qualified Response %	No. of Sales	Cost per Sale
Print Media										
Print Subtotal										
Direct Mail										
Direct Mail Subtotal										
Other										
Other Subtotal										
Total										

MARKETING ACTIVITY CHECKLIST

PRINT ADVERTISING

Activity	Normal Turnaround	Due Date	Complete Date
Concept developed	one week	_____	_____
Concept approved	two days	_____	_____
Copy & artwork	ten days	_____	_____
Copy & artwork revisions	five days	_____	_____
Final copy/artwork approval	two days	_____	_____
Photography/production	six days	_____	_____
Colour separations	two days	_____	_____
Colour proof approval	two days	_____	_____
To publication	one day	_____	_____
Publication date	10-30 days	_____	_____

DIRECT MAIL

Activity	Normal Turnaround	Due Date	Complete Date
Concept developed	one week	_____	_____
Concept approved	two days	_____	_____
Copy & artwork	12 days	_____	_____
Mailing lists research	five days	_____	_____
Copy & artwork revisions	five days	_____	_____
Mailing lists ordered	one day	_____	_____
Final artwork/copy approval	two days	_____	_____
Mechanical artwork produced	six days	_____	_____
Ozalid proofs produced	four days	_____	_____
Ozalid proofs approved	two days	_____	_____
Mailing lists due	2 1/2 weeks	_____	_____
Merge/purge lists	one week	_____	_____
Printing begins	15 days	_____	_____
Components to mailing house	one day	_____	_____
Mailing house	four days	_____	_____
Posting	one-three days	_____	_____

TELEMARKETING (Outbound)

Activity	Normal Turnaround	Due Date	Complete Date
Calling list research	five days	_____	_____
Calling lists ordered	one day	_____	_____
Calling lists due	2 1/2 weeks	_____	_____
Merge/purge lists	one week	_____	_____
Lists printed out	two days	_____	_____
Script written	five days	_____	_____
Script approved	two days	_____	_____
Callers trained	three days	_____	_____
Calling begins	two-three weeks	_____	_____

CAMPAIGN BUDGETING

Is there a pre-set budget for this campaign?:   Yes ☐ No☐

    If yes, what is the budget .... £ _____

A. PERCENTAGE OF SALES METHOD

    Total anticipated sales from this campaign .... £ _____

    Allowable marketing percentage .... X _____ %

    Sales times marketing percentage .... £ _____ = Budget

B. COST-PER-LEAD METHOD

    Number of leads or sales to be generated .... _____

    (from Worksheet Three)

    Acceptable cost per lead or cost per sale .... X £ _____

    Multiply no. of leads/sales times cost per lead/sale .... £ _____ = Budget

C. CONVERSION RATIOS METHOD

    Number of sales required .... _____

    Conversion ratio of hot prospects/sales .... X _____ %

    Number of hot prospects needed .... = _____

    Conversion ratio of leads/hot prospects .... X _____ %

    Number of leads needed .... = _____

    Cost to generate each lead .... X £ _____

    Multiply no. of leads times cost per lead .... £ _____ = Budget

Allocation of Budget by Marketing Activity

	Amount	Percent of Total
Print Advertising	£ _____	_____ %
Direct Mail	_____	_____
Telemarketing	_____	_____
Seminars	_____	_____
Exhibitions	_____	_____
Public Relations	_____	_____
Fulfillment	_____	_____
Other (specify)	_____	_____

<u>Budget Detail</u>	<u>Normal Cost Range</u>	<u>Amount</u>

PRINT ADVERTISING:

Copywriting	£1,500–3,500	£ _____
Design	£1,000–4,000	_____
Color separations/production	£1,000–3,000	_____
Photography/stock photos	£500–2,000	_____
Space: 1/3 page two-color	£4,000	_____
Space: 1/3 page four-color	£4,500	_____
Space: full page, two-color	£9,000	_____
Space: full page, four-color	£9,500	_____
Total Print Budget:		£ _____

Note: Space rates can vary widely by publication

DIRECT MAIL:

Copywriting	£1,000–4,000	£ _____
Graphic design	£1,000–3,000	_____
Typesetting/mechanical	£200–1,000	_____
Mailing list(s)	.09-.13/name	_____
Printing (3-5 components)	.15-.35/pkg.	_____
Data processing	.03-.05/pkg.	_____
Laser personalize letter	.06/each	_____
Auto-type envelope	.06/each	_____
Mailing house	.03-.08/pkg.	_____
Postage second-class	.198/pkg.	_____
Postage-first class (one oz.)	.29/pkg.	_____
Postage-first class (two oz.)	.52/pkg.	_____
Total Direct Mail Budget:		£ _____

Note: Cost ranges based on quantities of 5,000 - 25,000 packages

Budget Detail	Normal Cost Range	Amount

TELEMARKETING:

Script development	£500	£ _____
Programme set-up	£800	_____
Communicator training	£250	_____
Calling time	£33/hour	_____
Fulfillment	£.75–2.00/pkg.	_____

Total Telemarketing Budget: ....£ _____

SEMINARS:

Audio/visuals	varies	£ _____
Promotion	varies	_____
Giveaway materials	varies	_____
Travel expenses	varies	_____
Hotel and food	varies	_____
Follow-up	varies	_____

Total Seminar Budget .... £ _____

EXHIBITIONS:

Booth graphics	£500–2,000	£ _____
Space rental	£1,000–10,000	_____
Promotional material	£500–2,000	_____
Giveaways	£3,000–5,000	_____
Travel	varies	_____
Hotel and food	varies	_____

Total Exhibition Budget: ....£ _____

35

MARKETING AND ADVERTISING RESOURCES

*T*he following lists of industry groups, marketing publications and advertising publications should be a good starting place to help you find further information.

ADVERTISING AND MARKETING BODIES

Advertising Association
Abford House
15 Wilton Road
London
SW1V 1NJ
Tel: 071-828 2771
Fax: 071-931 0376

(UK advertising tripartite)

Advertising Standards Authority
Brook House
2–16 Torrington Place
London
WC1E 7HN
Tel: 071-580 5555
Fax: 071-631 3051

Association of Mail Order Publishers
1 New Burlington Street
London
W1X 1FD
Tel: 071-437 0706

Audit Bureau of Circulation Ltd
Black Prince Yard
207–9 High Street
Berkhamstead
Hertfordshire
HP4 1AD
Tel: 0442 870800
Telex: 94012104 AUD B G
Fax: 0442 877407

British Direct Marketing Association (BDMA)
Grosvenor Gardens House
Grosvenor Gardens
London
SW1W OBS
Tel: 071-630 7322
Fax: 071-836 1122

British List Brokers Association Ltd
16 The Pines
Broad Street
Guildford
Surrey
GU3 3BH
Tel: 0438 301311
Telex: 449601
Fax: 0438 506331

(Central organization for tracing lists for direct marketing)

Cable TV Association
50 Firth Street
London
W1V 5TE
Tel: 071-437 0549
Fax: 071-734 2546

Cable Authority
Gillingham House
38–44 Gillingham Street
London
SW1V 1HU
Tel: 071-821 6161

Cinema Advertising Association
127 Wardour Street
London
W1V 4AD
Tel: 071-439 9531
Fax: 071-439 2395

Direct Mail Producers Association (DMPA)
34 Grand Avenue
London
N10 3BP
Tel: 081-883 9854
Fax: 081-444 6473

Incorporated Society of British Advertisers (ISBA)
44 Hertford Street
London
W1Y 8AE
Tel: 071-499 7502
Fax: 071-629 5355

(Association of major UK advertisers)

Independent Television Commission (ITC)
70 Brompton Road
London
SW3 1EY
Tel: 071-584 7011
Fax: 071-589 5533

Institute of Practitioners in Advertising
44 Belgrave Square
London
SW1X 8QS
Tel: 071-235 7020
Fax: 071-245 9904

Institute of Public Relations
4th Floor
The Old Trading House
15 Northburgh Street
London
EC1V 0PR
Tel: 071-253 5151

Institute of Sales Promotions
Arena House
66–68 Pentonville Road
London
N1 9HS
Tel: 071-833 1121

Joint Industry Committee for National Readership Surveys (JICNARS)
44 Belgrave Square
London
SW1X 8QS
Tel: 071-245 9123

Joint Industry Committee for Poster Advertising Research (JICPAR)
44 Belgrave Square
London
SW1X 8QX
Tel: 071-235 7020

Market Research Society
The Old Trading House
15 Northburgh Street
London
EC1V 0PR
Tel: 071-490 4911

Newspaper Publishers Association (NPA)
34 Southwark Bridge Road
London
SE1
Tel: 071-928 6928
Fax: 071-928 2067

Outdoor Advertising Association of Great Britain (OAA)
Centric House
390–391 Strand
London
WC2R OLT
Tel: 071-240 2181
Fax: 071-497 8977

Periodical Publishers Association (PPA)
Imperial House
15–19 Kingsway
London
WC2B 6UN
Tel: 071-379 6268
Fax: 071-379 5661

(Magazine publishers'
association)

Public Relations Consultants Association
10 Greycoat Place
London
SW1P 1SB
Tel: 071-222 8866
Fax: 071-222 7249

Radio Authority (RA)
70 Brompton Road
London
SW3 1EY
Tel: 071-581 2888
Fax: 071-823 9113

Radio Marketing Bureau
46 Westbourne Grove
London
W2 5SH
Tel: 071-221 2535
Telex: 24543
Fax: 071-229 0352

PUBLICATIONS

Admap
Admap Publications
44 Earlham Street
London
WC2H 9LA
Tel: 071-379 6576
Telex: 265906 HBR G
Fax: 071-836 1310

BRAD Direct Marketing Lists: Rates and Data
Maclean Hunter Ltd
Maclean Hunter House
Chalk Lane
Cockfosters Road
Barnet
Hertfordshire
EN4 0BU
Tel: 081-441 6644
Telex: 299072 MACHUN G
Fax: 081-441 1796

British Rate and Data (BRAD)
MacLean Hunter Ltd
(see BRAD Direct Marketing Lists)

Campaign
Haymarket Marketing Publications Ltd
22 Lancaster Gate
London
W2 3LY
Tel: 071-402 5266
Telex: 8954052
Fax: 071-402 8603

Creative Review
Centaur Publications Ltd
St Giles House
50 Poland Street
London
W1V 4AX
Tel: 071-439 4222
Telex: 216352
Fax: 071-434 0510

Direct Marketing International
Ferrary Publications
91–93 Charterhouse Street
London
EC1M 6HR
Tel: 071-250 0646
Fax: 071-250 0637

Direct Response
Macro Publishing Ltd
416 High Street
Hoddesdon
Herts
EN11 8TA
Tel: 0992 501177
Fax: 0992 500387

Incentive Today
Langfords Publications Ltd
Ridgeland House
165 Dyke Road
Hove
Sussex
BN3 1TL
Tel: 0273 206722
Fax: 0273 736250

Marketing
Haymarket Marketing Publications Ltd
(see Campaign)

Marketing Week
Centaur Publications Ltd
(see Creative Review)

What's New in Marketing
Morgan-Grampian plc
Morgan-Grampian House
Calderwood Street
London
SE18 6QH
Tel: 081 856 7777
Fax: 081 855 2342

Willing's Press Guide
Thomas Skinner Directories
Reed Information Services

(see Business Lists Register)

MARKETING BOOKS PUBLISHED BY KOGAN PAGE

The Business of Image, Nicholas Jenkins, 1991.
Great Advertising Campaigns, Nicholas Ind, 1993.
Commonsense Direct Marketing, Drayton Bird, 1993.
Customer Care, Sarah Cook, 1992.
Effective Industrial Marketing, Norman Hart (ed), 1994.
Effective PR Management, Paul Winner, 1993.
European Sales Promotion, Alan Toop, 1992.
Handbook of European Advertising, Roger Bennett, 1993.
Handbook of International Direct Marketing, Adam Baines (ed), 1992.
Handbook of Telemarketing, Michael Stevens, 1991.
How to Improve your Marketing Copy, Ian Linton, 1993.
How to Organise Effective Conferences and Meetings, David Seekings, 1992.
International Public Relations in Practice, Margaret Nally (ed), 1994.
Institute of Public Relations Handbook, 1994.
The Marketing Person's Guide to Database Marketing and Direct Mail, Robin Fairlie, 1993.
New Directions in Marketing, Aubrey Wilson, 1994.
The New How to Advertise, Kenneth Roman and Jane Maas, 1992.
Sales Promotion, Julian Cummins, 1994.
Targeting Media Relations, David Wragg, 1993.

GLOSSARY OF MARKETING AND ADVERTISING TERMS

Active Buyer – A buyer who recently made a purchase, usually within the last twelve months.

Agency Commission – How advertising agencies earn fees from the placement of print and broadcast advertising. Commissions are paid by the media, not by the agency's client.

Artwork – Also called "mechanical art," the term for camera-ready copy and graphics.

Back End – Everything that happens after the advertising has commenced. Back end includes tallying responses, fulfilling orders, analyzing the effectiveness of individual promotions, and other activities.

Barcode – A series of small vertical bars printed on the lower right corner of a return envelope or Business Reply Card. These codes allow the Postal Service to sort the cards and envelopes by machine so a mailer receives a discount on barcoded return mail.
NB This service is not yet widely available in Europe.

Bingo Card – A response card, usually postage-paid, which is bound into a magazine.

Bleed – Term used by printers to describe ink that runs to the edge of a document.

Body Copy – That part of a direct mail piece or print ad which forms the bulk of the text. The remainder is comprised of headlines, the address block, and other elements.

Break Even – The point at which revenue from a specific marketing programme equals the costs of that programme.

Broadside – A piece of paper which is folded for mailing and opens into an advertisement.

Bulk Mail – A category of direct mail usually involving a large number of identical pieces. Can be mailed at substantial discount over standard postal rates.

Business Reply Service – Cards or envelopes pre-printed with the mailer's return address and the words "Postage Paid." The mailer pays the postage plus extra handling when he receives the returned pieces. Requires a permit from the Post Office.

Camera Ready – Artwork and text which is ready for the printer's make-ready department. Also known as "mechanicals."

Circulation – Refers to the number of people who receive a certain publication.

Closing Date – The day when all ad copy and artwork must be given to the medium if the ad is to appear in a certain issue.

Collateral Materials – Brochures, pamphlets, flyers and other materials used for promotional purposes.

Compiled List – A type of mailing list gathered from multiple sources, as opposed to a single source. Everyone on the list should have something in common, such as a compiled list of executives or homeowners. Generally less expensive than subscriber, donor or purchaser lists.

Computer Labels – Printed one-across to four-across, on standard pin-fed computer paper. Computer labels are affixed to mailing pieces by a labelling machine.

Continuity Programme – A mailing programme comprised of more than one part or series (e.g. Book of the Month Club).

Control Package – A mailing package that has produced carefully documented results (usually successful), by which all other mailing packages are measured.

Controlled Circulation – Individuals or corporations who receive distribution at no charge on the basis of their positions or titles.

Conversion – Turning a prospect into a customer or donor.

Co-op Mailing – More than one offer mailed in the same envelope.

Cost Per Lead (CPL) – The total cost of a mailing divided by the number of leads that mailing produces.

Cost Per Thousand (CPM) – The cost to produce one thousand of anything, such as printed pieces. Also refers to a media's cost to reach one thousand people.

Cost Per Sale (CPS) – Total cost of the mailing and fulfillment divided by the number of sales that mailing produces. Also referred to as Cost Per Order (CPO).

Cropping – Trimming part of the illustration so it fits in a specific space.

Database Marketing – Compiling and maintaining information on prospects and customers and using this information in a proactive way.

Demographics – Information (such as income, sex, age and level of education) associated with names on a customer file.

Direct Response Marketing – Another term for direct marketing.

Display Advertising – Print media advertising that is not in the classified section.

Doubling Day – The number of days after the drop date, at which your mailing will have generated half its responses. A doubling day helps direct mailers project final results without waiting months for all responses to be received.

Drive Time – Those time slots when listeners are driving to and from work. These slots command the highest advertising rates.

Drop Date – Term used to note the date a mailing is accepted into the Post Office's system.

Drop Ship – A term used in mail order to signify that a supplier will accept an order from a third party and ship the product directly to a customer.

Enumeration District – Small geographical area which forms a basis for data collection. Averages about 150 households.

First-Class Mail – Fastest category among the regular classes of mail service.

Fixed Position – A radio spot that is broadcast at a specific time each day.

Flight – An ad campaign that runs for a specified period of time.

Four-Colour – Also referred to as four-colour process printing.

Freelancer – A self-employed writer, designer or consultant who provides services directly to end-mailers and/or acts as a subcontractor to agencies.

Frequency – How often you take a particular marketing action, such as sending out mailing pieces or running print ads.

Front End – What happens at the initial or planning stages of a marketing campaign.

Fulfillment – Part of the back end process. Sending out information or products in response to leads or orders.

Graphic Art – Comprised of all preparation steps before printing, including design, layout, typesetting and mechanical art.

Gross Rating Points – (GRP) – The index which measures the "reach" and "frequency" of a broadcast schedule. A GRP of 100 means that the equivalent of 100% of the target audience will hear or see the message one time.

Guarantee – A pledge to the consumer by the seller.

Imprint – The space where the local dealer "imprints" his name or logo on an advertisement.

In-House List – A mailer's internal file or database. Usually consisting of purchasers, donors and/or known prospects.

Inquiry – Also referred to as a response or lead. Someone who takes action on your offer – whether by sending in a response card or calling a telephone number.

Insert – A loose promotional piece inside a magazine or newspaper.

Insertion Order – Instructions from an advertiser authorizing a publisher to print an ad with size, dates and price specifications.

Involvement Devices – Techniques used to "involve" the consumer and elicit a desired response.

Key Code – A code, comprised of letters and/or digits, printed on a mailing label or response device. Key codes are used to tell the mailer which mailing list a response was generated from.

Layout – A sketch-like drawing showing how an advertisement will look.

Lifetime Value – Denotes the value of a customer, donor or member over the life of his association with your organization.

List Broker – A person or company that acts as a liaison between list owners and list renters. The broker does research for its clients and recommends various combinations of mailing lists.

List Exchange – Exchanging names from your mailing list with another list owner. Check local regulations.

List Manager – An individual or company who maintains and markets a list for its owner.

List Rental – Allowing your list to be used by another mailer, on a one-time basis, or more often. Usually rented on a Cost Per Thousand Names (CPM) basis.

List Test – When a mailer rents a small section of a mailing list (often 5,000 names or more) in order to test the list's pulling power.

Mailing House – The place where mailings are processed before dropping at the Post Office. Services include inserting pieces, labeling envelopes and affixing postage.

Make Good – If a commercial or print ad is not run due to a technical error, the station or publisher will "make good" the ad or spot on a different day in the same timeslot.

Market Segmentation – Process of dividing the universe into smaller subgroups, based on common characteristics.

Mechanical – Assembly of pictures and proofs of type, pasted in a desired arrangement (usually on cardboard), to be copied by a camera and made into a plate.

Media – Term used to describe a category of marketing or advertising vehicle, such as print advertising, broadcast, direct mail, telemarketing and outdoor advertising.

Multi-Buyer or **Multi-Donor** – A person who has bought from a firm or donated to a cause more than once.

Negative – A film with black and white areas reversed, used by printers in preparing plates for offset printing.

Negative Option – Technique in which a customer receives a shipment at regular intervals, unless he asks not to receive that specific shipment. Used with subscription, record, and video offers.

Net-Name List Rental – A method of renting mailing lists where the mailer pays only for those names left over after the merge/purge process has eliminated duplicates.

Offer – The terms under which a specific service or product are offered to the consumer.

Periodical – A newspaper, magazine or newsletter published at regular intervals.

Personalization – Computer insertion of information on a letter, form or response device which refers to an individual in a personal manner.

PMS Color – PMS stands for Pantone Matching System. A printer's standard colors which can be accurately matched and reproduced. These colors can be selected from a PMS Chart or PMS Book.

Point-Of-Sale – (P.O.S.) – Various advertising and promotional materials that are used at the place where the product is sold.

Premium – An item or award given away free – or at less than its normal cost – in order to induce someone to take advantage of an offer.

Press Release – A newsworthy story given to publications or radio and television stations.

Proof – A copy of a print ad, given to the advertiser for final corrections.

Prospect – Potential buyer of a product or service.

Psychographics – A segmentation tool for classifying consumers by values, beliefs, personalities and buying motives.

Rating – Television sets turned to a specific station as a percentage of total households in an area.

Reach – Number of people who hear or see a commercial or advertisement.

Reply Device – The item in a mailing package that the respondent uses to signify acceptance of the offer. Examples of reply devices include reply cards, reply envelopes and bingo cards.

Response Rate – Often the most important number to a marketer, which is computed by dividing the number of responses or leads generated by an advertisement or mailing package by the total number of prospects exposed.

Rollout – The portion of a marketing campaign where the greatest number of prospects is exposed.

Run of Paper – (R.O.P.) – Ad is placed anywhere in a newspaper at the paper's discretion. R.O.P. space is usually the least expensive.

Run of Station – (R.O.S.) – Same as "Run of Paper" for broadcast stations.

Seed Name – Also known as "decoy name." Seed names are names and addresses a list owner enters into a mailing list to catch unauthorized users of the list and also to verify delivery.

Self-Mailer – A self-contained mailing package which does not require an envelope. May include a business reply card (BRC).

Service Bureau – Company that processes mailing lists for outside mailers.

SIC – (Standard Industrial Classification) The classifications of businesses.

Storyboard – Series of drawings used to present a proposed TV commercial. Can be used either to get advertiser approval or as a production guide.

Tag – Dealer identification added to the end of a prerecorded commercial.

Target Audience – A specific group of consumers you are trying to reach, usually defined by demographics.

Teaser – Selling copy on the outside of an envelope. Referred to as teaser because it is supposed to "tease" the prospect into opening the envelope.

Telemarketing – Using the telephone as a marketing tool for selling, lead generation, donor acquisition and other activities.

Test – Changing variables in a marketing campaign to discover which elements lead to an increased response rate.

Testimonial – A message from a customer or other third-party endorsing your product or services.

Timeslot – The time during a broadcast day that a particular programme is heard. These groups of timeslots include: morning, morning drive time, midday, afternoon drive time, evening and late night.

Universe – The total number of individuals who could be considered prospects for your product or service. Also can refer to the number of people who are exposed to a particular promotion.

Visual – The detailed layout for a printed piece.

White Space – Extra space on a page which does not have copy or graphics on it. Advantage is that it makes the ad look "cleaner" so it stands out.

INDEX